I0003950

Azure DevOps Server 2019 Cookbook
Second Edition

Proven recipes to accelerate your DevOps journey with Azure DevOps Server 2019 (formerly TFS)

Tarun Arora
Utkarsh Shigihalli

BIRMINGHAM - MUMBAI

Azure DevOps Server 2019 Cookbook
Second Edition

Commissioning Editor: Vijin Boricha
Acquisition Editor: Meeta Rajani
Content Development Editor: Ronn Kurien
Technical Editor: Mohd Riyan Khan
Copy Editor: Safis Editing
Project Coordinator: Jagdish Prabhu
Proofreader: Safis Editing
Indexer: Tejal Daruwale Soni
Graphics: Tom Scaria
Production Coordinator: Jyoti Chauhan

First published: January 2016
Second edition: May 2019

Production reference: 1020519

Published by Packt Publishing Ltd.
Livery Place
35 Livery Street
Birmingham
B3 2PB, UK.

ISBN 978-1-78883-925-9

www.packtpub.com

`mapt.io`

Mapt is an online digital library that gives you full access to over 5,000 books and videos, as well as industry leading tools to help you plan your personal development and advance your career. For more information, please visit our website.

Why subscribe?

- Spend less time learning and more time coding with practical eBooks and Videos from over 4,000 industry professionals

- Improve your learning with Skill Plans built especially for you

- Get a free eBook or video every month

- Mapt is fully searchable

- Copy and paste, print, and bookmark content

Packt.com

Did you know that Packt offers eBook versions of every book published, with PDF and ePub files available? You can upgrade to the eBook version at `www.packt.com` and as a print book customer, you are entitled to a discount on the eBook copy. Get in touch with us at `customercare@packtpub.com` for more details.

At `www.packt.com`, you can also read a collection of free technical articles, sign up for a range of free newsletters, and receive exclusive discounts and offers on Packt books and eBooks.

Contributors

About the authors

Tarun Arora is obsessed with high-quality working software, continuous delivery, and Agile practices. He has worked on various industry-leading programs for fortune 500 companies in the financial and energy sectors. For many years, Tarun has been a Microsoft Most Valuable Professional in Visual Studio and Development Technologies. His core strengths are designing application architecture for cloud scale and everything DevOps. He was recognized as an MVP by Microsoft in 2014 for going over and above in supporting the product teams and community with his contributions. Tarun is an active open source community contributor, speaker, and Blogger. Follow Tarun on Twitter `@arora_tarun` for the latest and greatest updates in DevOps.

To my 6-month-old son Ryan and my beautiful wife Annu. You both are the best part of my life!

Utkarsh Shigihalli is passionate about technology and has a keen interest in developing tools and extensions. Currently working for Avanade in the United Kingdom, he has experience in the areas of Azure, DevOps, Agile, and Architecture. Over the years he has worked for many top companies as an architect, independent consultant, and as a DevOps coach in India, the United States, Netherlands, and United Kingdom.
He has been awarded as Microsoft Most Valuable Professional five times. He regularly writes at Visual Studio Geeks and you can follow him on Twitter at `@onlyutkarsh`.

I would like to thank my father Dr. Balanna Shigihalli and my mother Mrs. Padmaja Shigihalli for their love, care, and encouragement. I am extremely thankful to my wife Rajeshwari for her patience and continuing support to complete this book. My lovely daughter Kruti for her smiles and hugs. I also like to express my thanks to my sister Kavya, brother-in-law Piyush for all their support and my niece Stuti and nephew Vismay for their love.

About the reviewer

Michael Juřek, after working for Microsoft for many years, is now a freelance consultant specializing in the software development life cycle and DevOps tools and principles. Other areas of his professional interests include software architecture and PaaS technologies in the cloud. In his free time, Michael has various hobbies, such as volleyball, skiing, astronomy, and bee-keeping.

Packt is searching for authors like you

If you're interested in becoming an author for Packt, please visit authors.packtpub.com and apply today. We have worked with thousands of developers and tech professionals, just like you, to help them share their insight with the global tech community. You can make a general application, apply for a specific hot topic that we are recruiting an author for, or submit your own idea.

Table of Contents

Preface

Development teams are judged by the speed at which they can convert an idea into working software. Operations teams are judged on the uptime and stability of the production environment. One wants to deploy changes all the time, the other doesn't want any changes at all. These conflicting goals result in development teams and operation teams working against each other. The introduction of Agile practices has demonstrated that iterative feedback-driven development helps teams cope with changes in business and user requirements. Agile practices help development teams accelerate the creation of ready-to-ship software. Software that's ready to ship but hasn't shipped doesn't provide any value to users.

DevOps has been an emerging trend in the software development world for the past few years. While the term may be relatively new, it is really a convergence of a number of practices that have been evolving for decades. DevOps is a revolutionary way to ship working software quickly and efficiently while maintaining a high level of security. DevOps advocates that everyone and everything that's needed to ship working software to of end users needs to be part of the software development life cycle. Building software is an iterative process; therefore, a high level of automation is needed to make the process of developing, testing, releasing, and monitoring software easily repeatable. The emphasis is on delivering value to end users by collaborating, automating, learning, and constantly improving the software. Simply put, DevOps is the union of people, processes, and products to enable the continuous delivery of value to end users.

While DevOps isn't just a tool you can buy and install, tooling is an integral part of DevOps. Microsoft Azure DevOps Server 2019, formerly known as Team Foundation Server, is a set of collaborative software development tools, hosted on-premises. Azure DevOps Server integrates with your existing IDE or editor, enabling your cross-functional team(s) to work effectively on projects of all sizes. Azure DevOps Server works for any language, and on any platform. Azure DevOps Server has everything you need to turn an idea into a working piece of software. You can plan your project with Agile tools, you can manage your test plans, version your code using Git, and deploy your solution using an incredible cross-platform CI-CD system, all while getting full traceability and visibility across your development activities.

Starting your DevOps journey may seem overwhelming with a product that's so diverse and an ecosystem that's so vibrant. With over 70 hands-on tooling recipes, you'll learn how to accelerate your journey of DevOps by planning, coding, building, testing, and releasing high-quality working software using effective automation techniques with Azure DevOps Server 2019.

Who this book is for

This book is for all software professionals, including developers, operations, testers, architects, managers, and configuration analysts, who are using or planning to use Azure DevOps Server.

What this book covers

Chapter 1, *Planning and Tracking Work,* explains how to create and set up a scrum team project, import requirements as work items from Excel, use work items for collaboration, set up hierarchical backlogs, configure and customize kanban boards, prepare and plan a sprint, use delivery plans to track multiple teams, and use dashboards for planning and tracking work.

Chapter 2, *Source Control Management,* covers the differences between Git and TFVC, why Git is more suited for greenfield projects with distributed teams working on small codebases, how to migrate from TFVC to Git with history, how to access Azure DevOps Git repositories using SSH, and how to import a Git repository from GitHub into Azure DevOps Server. It also explains how to perform Git operations using the command line and Visual Studio Code, how to configure branch policies and use pull requests to review code, how to configure and use Git Hooks, how to manage and store large files in Git, how to use Git branching strategies for CD, and how to search code in Azure DevOps using the code search service.

Chapter 3, *Build and Release Agents,* explains how to set up build and release agents, automate the setup of build and release agents using unattended installation with PowerShell, download agents from GitHub using the GitHub release API, configure deployment groups, run an Azure DevOps agent behind a corporate enterprise proxy, analyze build usage data, automate agent pool maintenance, and configure retention policies for builds and releases. In this chapter, you'll also learn how to use agent capabilities and demands to map build definitions to specific agents in pools, and finally, how to manage and permission agent usage using role-based access control.

`Chapter` 4, *Continuous Integration and Build Automation*, defines continuous integration. It also explains how to configure one build pipeline to build all branches of a code repository, how to reflect the branch quality in the build name by dynamically updating the build name during pipeline execution, how to use web deploy to create a package in an ASP.NET build pipeline, how to organize the output from a build into logical folders, how to use an assembly version to stamp assemblies in a pipeline, how to set up a build pipeline for a .NET Core application, how to set up a build pipeline for a Node.js application, and how to set up a build pipeline for database projects. You'll also learn how to use SonarQube in a build pipeline to manage technical debt.

`Chapter` 5, *Continuous Testing*, shows the direction Microsoft is taking with its testing tools, along with the rationale behind discontinuing some of the testing tools. It also shows how to run NUnit-based unit tests in a pipeline, how to use feature flags to test in production, how to distribute multi-configuration tests on agent pools, how to configure parallel execution of automated tests to speed up overall test execution, how to run functional Specflow tests using Azure pipelines, how to analyze test execution results from the runs view. You'll also learn how to export test artifacts and test results from Test Hub, and finally, how to chart test results on dashboards in Azure DevOps Server team projects.

`Chapter` 6, *Continuous Deployments*, defines continuous deployment. It also explains how to deploy the database to SQL Azure using Azure release pipelines, how to consume secrets in Azure pipelines from the Azure Key Vault, how to deploy a .NET Core app into Azure App Service, how to deploy an Azure Function using Azure Pipelines, and how to publish secrets to Azure Key Vault. In this chapter, you'll also learn how to deploy a static website on Azure Storage, and finally, deploy a VM to Azure DevTest Labs.

`Chapter` 7, *Azure Artifacts and Dependency Management*, explains how to leverage artifacts to break down monolithic applications into microservices, how to publish a NuGet package to artifacts, how to consume a NuGet package feed in Visual Studio, how to publish an NPM package to an artifact feed in Azure DevOps Server, how to test NuGet packages using artifact views, and how to secure your packages by scanning for known vulnerabilities in your dependencies using WhiteSource.

`Chapter` 8, *Azure DevOps Extensions*, explains how to leverage the Azure DevOps Server APIs to extend Azure DevOps Server, how to create a new publisher in Visual Studio Marketplace, how to create a simple task to clean folder, how to create a UI extension, how to create a service connection to connect to GitLab, how to create a pipeline task to consume the custom service connection and download GitLab sources and finally how to publish extensions to Visual Studio Marketplace using Azure Pipelines.

To get the most out of this book

The book assumes you have a working setup of Azure DevOps Server 2019, basic knowledge of DevOps, and some familiarity with Azure DevOps Server. A free trial of the Azure subscription may be needed to try out some of the recipes.

Download the example code files

You can download the example code files for this book from your account at `www.packt.com`. If you purchased this book elsewhere, you can visit `www.packt.com/support` and register to have the files emailed directly to you.

You can download the code files by following these steps:

1. Log in or register at `www.packt.com`.
2. Select the **SUPPORT** tab.
3. Click on **Code Downloads & Errata**.
4. Enter the name of the book in the **Search** box and follow the onscreen instructions.

Once the file is downloaded, please make sure that you unzip or extract the folder using the latest version of:

- WinRAR/7-Zip for Windows
- Zipeg/iZip/UnRarX for Mac
- 7-Zip/PeaZip for Linux

The code bundle for the book is also hosted on GitHub at `https://github.com/PacktPublishing/Azure-DevOps-Server-2019-Cookbook-Second-Edition`. In case there's an update to the code, it will be updated on the existing GitHub repository.

We also have other code bundles from our rich catalog of books and videos available at `https://github.com/PacktPublishing/`. Check them out!

Conventions used

There are a number of text conventions used throughout this book.

`CodeInText`: Indicates code words in text, database table names, folder names, filenames, file extensions, pathnames, dummy URLs, user input, and Twitter handles. Here is an example: "Create a new file called `azure-pipelines.yml`."

A block of code is set as follows:

```
var printaz = require("print-azure-devops")
printaz.printAzureDevOps();
```

When we wish to draw your attention to a particular part of a code block, the relevant lines or items are set in bold:

```
var colors = require("colors")
exports.printAzureDevOps = function () {
    console.log("Azure DevOps Server 2019".blue)
}
```

Any command-line input or output is written as follows:

```
C:\Users\utkarsh>node -v
v10.15.3
```

Bold: Indicates a new term, an important word, or words that you see onscreen. For example, words in menus or dialog boxes appear in the text like this. Here is an example: "To do this, first, head to the **Artifacts** hub and click on the **+ New Feed** button."

Warnings or important notes appear like this.

Tips and tricks appear like this.

Sections

In this book, you will find several headings that appear frequently (*Getting ready, How to do it..., How it works..., There's more...,* and *See also*).

To give clear instructions on how to complete a recipe, use these sections as follows:

Getting ready

This section tells you what to expect in the recipe and describes how to set up any software or any preliminary settings required for the recipe.

How to do it...

This section contains the steps required to follow the recipe.

How it works...

This section usually consists of a detailed explanation of what happened in the previous section.

There's more...

This section consists of additional information about the recipe in order to make you more knowledgeable about the recipe.

See also

This section provides helpful links to other useful information for the recipe.

Get in touch

Feedback from our readers is always welcome.

General feedback: If you have questions about any aspect of this book, mention the book title in the subject of your message and email us at customercare@packtpub.com.

Errata: Although we have taken every care to ensure the accuracy of our content, mistakes do happen. If you have found a mistake in this book, we would be grateful if you would report this to us. Please visit www.packt.com/submit-errata, selecting your book, clicking on the Errata Submission Form link, and entering the details.

Piracy: If you come across any illegal copies of our works in any form on the Internet, we would be grateful if you would provide us with the location address or website name. Please contact us at copyright@packt.com with a link to the material.

If you are interested in becoming an author: If there is a topic that you have expertise in and you are interested in either writing or contributing to a book, please visit authors.packtpub.com.

Reviews

Please leave a review. Once you have read and used this book, why not leave a review on the site that you purchased it from? Potential readers can then see and use your unbiased opinion to make purchase decisions, we at Packt can understand what you think about our products, and our authors can see your feedback on their book. Thank you!

For more information about Packt, please visit `packt.com`.

Planning and Tracking Work

The best software teams ship early and often. In order to successfully plan and track a software project, it is important to understand the types of work involved in software delivery. All work that's undertaken for software delivery can be categorized into one of the following four categories:

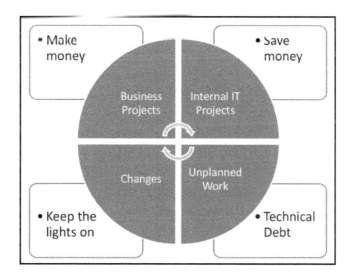

Technical debt is a metaphor for the eventual consequences of poor software or infrastructure within your organization. It is considered debt because it is work that needs to be done before a particular project can be considered complete. If you don't pay down technical debt, then your unplanned work will continue to increase. Left unchecked, technical debt will ensure that the only work that gets done is unplanned work.

Azure DevOps Server allows you to plan and track work using work items. Work items can be used to classify work into different categories. Work items allow you to decompose high-level ideas into smaller, workable units. These can then be prioritized, planned, and scheduled into iterations. Every team has a unique process for shipping software. Regardless of whether you follow Agile or Waterfall, Azure DevOps Server offers a range of out-of-the-box process workflows, along with giving you the option to create your own custom process workflows.

Over the last decade, agile software methodologies such as Scrum and Kanban have mostly displaced traditional Waterfall-driven software delivery for complex systems with evolving system requirements. Agile methodologies feature self-organizing teams that are empowered to achieve specific business objectives. Agile methodologies focus on the rapid and frequent delivery of partial solutions (also known as minimum viable products) that can be evaluated and used to determine the next steps for the business. In this way, solutions are built in an iterative and incremental manner. Agile methodologies have been shown to deliver higher-quality products in less time, resulting in improved customer satisfaction. The annual Agile survey report available here `http://bit.ly/ agileReport` (refer to page 8) shows why organizations are adopting Agile software development over traditional methodologies.

While most organizations are very diligent when tracking planned work, unplanned work doesn't always get tracked. Work is work – whether it's planned or unplanned, it needs to be tracked. Hidden work robs you of focus. The primary goal of any DevOps setup within an organization is to improve the delivery of value for customers and the business; things that aren't tracked aren't measured. In the famous words of Peter Drucker, *"you can't manage what you can't measure."*

We've all been on a project where no data of any kind was tracked, and it was hard to tell whether we were on track for release or getting more efficient as we went along. On the other hand, many of us have had the misfortune of being on projects where stats were used as a weapon, pitting one team against another to justify mandatory weekend work. So, it's no surprise that most teams have a love/hate relationship with metrics. There are as many ways to measure a project as there are to build it. If you only measure one key metric, it is easy to get tunnel vision. Whether the teams are focusing on just making the metric better (often through gaming the system) or management is using the measure to drive all decisions, you can end up with a product or organization that looks good but is really driving off a cliff. To foster a culture of continuous improvement, Agile teams tend to focus on the following metrics:

- Lead time
- Cycle time
- Cumulative flow
- Velocity
- Product burn-down and product burn-up

We'll cover some of these metrics and how they can be tracked using Azure DevOps in detail later on in this chapter. Read on to learn how work items allow you to plan and track work in your software projects.

In this chapter, we will cover the following recipes:

- Creating a team project for an Agile team
- Importing requirements from Excel
- Getting social with work items
- Portfolio backlog hierarchies and decomposing work
- Configuring and customizing backlog boards
- Preparing and planning a sprint
- Visualizing progress in a sprint
- Delivery plans to track multiple teams
- Dashboards for planning and tracking work

Creating a team project for an Agile team

Azure DevOps Server provides a set of integrated tools that allow teams to effectively manage the life cycle of their software project. The team in Azure DevOps Server is encapsulated within the container of a team project. A team project is a logical container that's used to isolate all tools and artifacts associated with a software application in a single namespace.

The conceptual boundary that was introduced through the team project eliminates the problem of having access to unrelated artifacts such as code, work items, or release information that isn't relevant to your application's development. Related team projects can be grouped together into a team project collection. Team project collections can be used to introduce a physical separation between a group of related team projects by hosting them in separate databases.

An instance of Azure DevOps Server is capable of supporting multiple team project collections, and each team project collection can internally host multiple team projects. A team project can house multiple teams. As illustrated in the following diagram, the process template is scoped at the team project level. Multiple team projects in a team project collection can use different process templates; however, multiple teams within a single team project will need to use the same process. Teams, however, have autonomy on the level of the backlogs they choose and the workflows on the Kanban board. The delivery framework of choice is applied through the **Process Template**, which, in turn, applies the delivery framework-specific terminology, artifacts, and workflows to the team project and all teams within the team project:

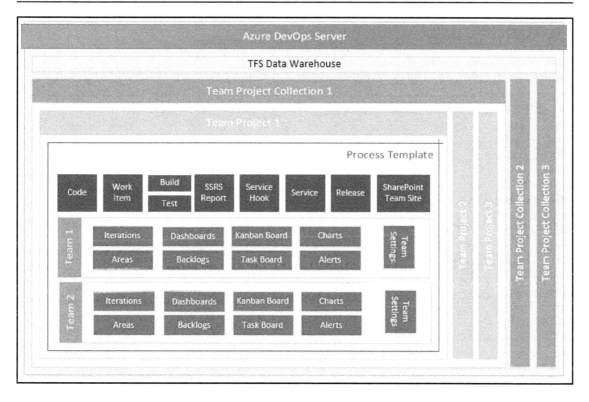

The process template defines the set of work item types, queries, and reports that can be used to plan and track the project. In this recipe, we'll learn how to create a new **Team Project** using the Scrum template.

TFS 2018 and later versions no longer support native integration with SharePoint products. If you're planning to upgrade to Azure DevOps Server 2019, read *About SharePoint integration* (`https://docs.microsoft.com/en-us/azure/devops/report/sharepoint-dashboards/about-sharepoint-integration?view=azure-devops`) to learn about the options available to you.

Getting ready

To create a team project, you need to be a member of the Project Collection Administrators group. If you aren't already part of this group, gain membership by following the steps provided here `https://docs.microsoft.com/en-us/vsts/security/set-project-collection-level-permissions`. Alternatively, follow the steps provided at `https://docs.microsoft.com/en-us/vsts/security/set-project-collection-level-permissions` to be added to one.

How to do it...

To create a new team project from the web, follow these steps:

1. Launch a browser and navigate to the Azure DevOps Server Portal.
2. From the top right side, click the **+Create project** button:

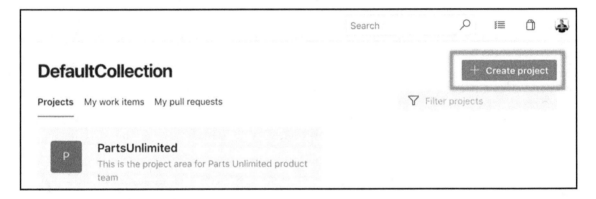

3. Provide a name for your new team project, select its initial source control type, and select a process to create a team project. The work item process is a one time choice and cannot be changed once set. See *Choosing the right version control for your project* (`https://docs.microsoft.com/en-us/azure/devops/repos/tfvc/comparison-git-tfvc?view=azure-devops`) and *Choose a process* (`https://docs.microsoft.com/en-us/azure/devops/boards/work-items/guidance/choose-process?view=azure-devops`) for guidance:

The ability to work from both Git and TFVC repositories from the same team project has been supported since TFS 2015 Update 1. See Git team projects (`https://docs.microsoft.com/en-us/azure/devops/repos/git/team-projects?view=azure-devops`) or TFVC team projects (`https://docs.microsoft.com/en-us/azure/devops/repos/git/team-projects?view=azure-devops`) for more information.

How it works...

The following items are created for you as part of the team project creation process:

- **Dashboards**: A canvas to bring key information radiators to raise visibility within and outside the team
- **Code**: A code repository (Git/TFVC) based on your selection is provisioned
- **Work**: All agile planning and tracking tools are nested under this hub.
    - **Team**: A default team with the same name as the team project is provisioned.
    - **Area Path**: A default Area Path with the same name as the name of the Team is provisioned. The teams' backlog is configured to show work items assigned to this Area Path.
    - **Iteration Path**: The set of iterations is pre-created for the team.
    - **Team Portal**: The Team Portal allows the Team members to connect to TFS to manage source code and work items, and build and test efforts.
- **Build & Release**: Automated pipelines to build and release your application
- **Test**: Plan, track, and execute tests
- **Wiki**: To share knowledge and documentation with the team

These are shown in the following screenshot:

 Azure DevOps server simplifies navigation across the portal, and for those who prefer the keyboard to the mouse, there is a great support for navigation through the keyboard in both global and local hubs. Hold *Shift* + ? in the portal to see the full list of supported keyboard shortcuts.

There's more...

Azure DevOps Server makes the process of setting up a new team project very straightforward—so much so that you may be inclined to create a new team project for every software project. I would generally not recommend this; with support for multiple teams and backlog isolation at the team level, it is possible to have a logical separation, along with the ability to share within a team project. In principle, you should consider a team project for each product, and a team for each work stream. The only time you should consider splitting a product team out into a separate team project is if it needs to follow a unique process, since process templates are scoped at the team project rather than at the team level.

If you find yourself organically needing to grow out into a new team project to use a different process template, you can consider leveraging the *VSTS Migration Toolkit* (`https:/` `/nkdagility.com/vsts-sync-migration-tools/`) to carry out a full fidelity migration.

Importing requirements from Excel

In Scrum, the taskboard is a visual display of the progress of the Scrum team during a sprint. It presents a snapshot of the current sprint backlog, allowing everyone to stay synchronized and focused on the work to be done. Most of the time, smaller teams are distributed across multiple locations, and in these situations, tracking work with a digital tool helps distributed teams synchronize more effectively. Some of us are lucky enough to land on green field projects, which gives us the opportunity to start tracking the requirements of work items from inception. Other times, projects are planned in tools that don't natively support integration with Azure DevOps Server. Luckily, most planning tools allow you to extract the data to Excel. Azure DevOps Server natively supports importing work items through Excel, but the challenge is mostly working out which fields in the spreadsheet should map out to work items in Azure DevOps Server. In this recipe, we'll learn how to import requirements from Excel into work items and refresh updates from work items back into Excel.

Getting ready

If you don't have Office Excel, install it. For Azure DevOps Server 2019, you'll need Office 2013 or a later version. The Excel plugin for Azure DevOps Server is installed by installing one of the latest editions of Visual Studio or the Azure DevOps Server Standalone Office Integration installer. Azure DevOps Server Standalone Office Integration supports connecting to Azure DevOps Server from Excel, Microsoft Project, and the PowerPoint-based storyboard tool.

If you don't intend to install Visual Studio but need Office integration, download and install Azure DevOps Server Standalone Office Integration (free) from `https://www.visualstudio.com/downloads/`. Once the installation is complete, the Excel Plugin will show up under the **Team** ribbon in Excel, as shown in the following screenshot:

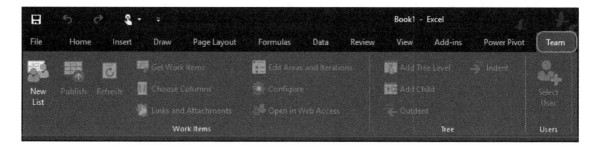

If you don't see the Team ribbon, perform the following steps to enable it:

1. Click the **File** tab in Excel and choose **Options**.
2. In the **Categories** pane, click **Add-ins**, and verify that **Team Foundation Add-in** shows up in the **Disabled Application Add-ins** section.
3. In the manage box, select disabled items and click **Go**.
4. Select the **Azure DevOps Server Add-in** and click **Enable**. Finally, exit the dialog by clicking **Close.**

 If you are continuing to run into issues with **Add-in** not showing up in Excel, you may be able to resolve the issue with the procedures provided at the following link: `https://docs.microsoft.com/en-us/vsts/work/backlogs/office/tfs-office-integration-issues`.

How to do it...

Now that we have the Azure DevOps Sever excel plugin installed, in this section we'll learn how to use it.

Start by performing the following steps:

1. Launch Excel and start with a blank sheet. Navigate to the **Team** ribbon.
2. Click on **New List** to connect to your project in TFS.

3. If you are connecting to Azure DevOps Server from Excel for the first time, you will have to add your server details to the list of recognized servers. The steps for this are shown in the following screenshot:

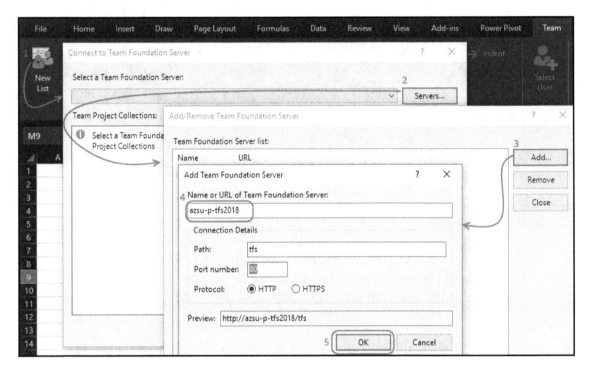

4. Select the **PartsUnlimited** team project and click **Connect**:

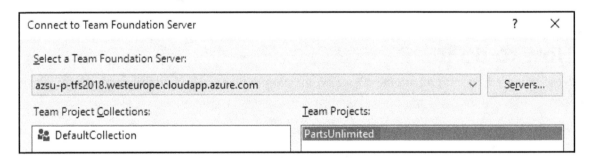

5. When asked which type of work item list you want to create, choose **Input list**. An Input list gives you a blank template that is linked to your team project:

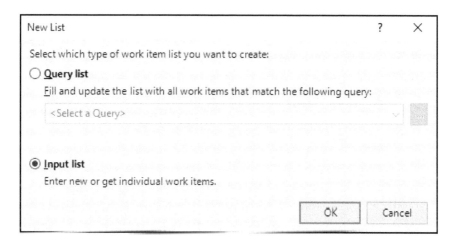

6. Your worksheet will now be bound to your team project as a flat list. What this means is that you can add work items to the team project from the worksheet or add work items to the worksheet from the team project. Fill out the details of the work items you want to add and their work item type. The Excel plugin defaults the list type to flat, but you can change it to a tree list if you wish. A tree list allows you to create and view hierarchically linked work items, like so:

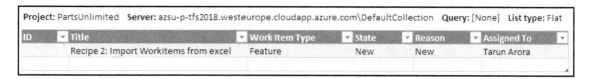

7. Publish the changes by clicking the **Publish** button from the Team ribbon.

You can add more work item fields as columns to this template. Right-click within the table mapped to Azure DevOps Server, and then from the context menu, select **Team | Choose columns**.

How it works...

To validate whether the changes have been synchronized to Azure DevOps Server, launch the web portal in a browser, and navigate to the work hub in the PartsUnlimited team project. The newly added work item should show up under the features backlog, as shown in the following screenshot:

Follow these tips to keep your work in sync:

- When you first open a saved worksheet, use the **Refresh** button in Excel on the Team ribbon to download the latest data from the data store
- Enter data for additional fields by adding columns to the worksheet using the **Choose Column** icon in Excel on the **Team** ribbon
- To avoid data conflicts, publish your additions and modifications often
- To prevent loss of data before you publish or refresh, save your workbook periodically

The Azure DevOps Server Excel plugin uses the Azure DevOps Server REST APIs, which are wrapped into an SDK. This allows for safe and secure bulk editing of work items. The plugin supports two-way updates, and changes that are made to work items in Azure DevOps Server web portal can be refreshed back into Excel by clicking the **Refresh** button. Refreshing the data does not overwrite any calculations or formatting that you may have applied to the worksheet. If you spend a lot of time using Microsoft Project, you'll be excited to know that the Azure DevOps Server plugin can also be used from Microsoft Project.

There's more...

The marketplace features the Azure DevOps Open in Excel extension (`https://marketplace.visualstudio.com/items?itemName=blueprint.vsts-open-work-items-in-excel`). This is a free extension that was created by Microsoft DevLabs, and adds the option of opening work items in Excel from various access points, such as work item queries, backlogs, and selective work items:

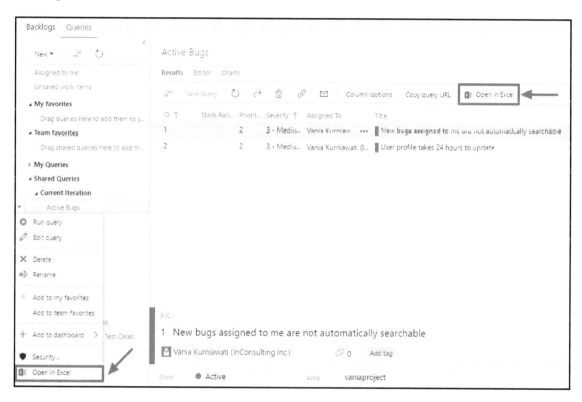

Another noticeable extension in the marketplace is the **Requirements Integrator** (`https://marketplace.visualstudio.com/items?itemName=jgarverick.RequirementsIntegrator`). This is an open source extension that was created by Microsoft MVP Josh Garverick, which introduces the capability of mapping external requirements into Azure DevOps Server to create a traceability matrix with work items. This extension introduces a new sub-tab called **Requirements** in the work hub, which allows you to import external requirements into TFS using a predefined Excel template:

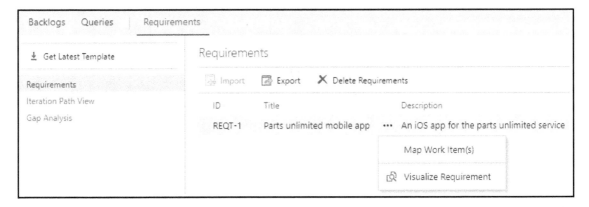

The extension allows you to do the following:

- Manage requirements to work item mapping
- Display a sprint view that shows the requirements covered by a sprint
- Display a traceability matrix, including gaps, for requirements that are imported and mapped to WIs
- Restrict import usage to non-CMMI process templates
- Requirement visualization (visual traceability)
- Export requirement information to Excel

I encourage you to look at the marketplace (`https://marketplace.visualstudio.com/`) as it has a range of extensions that enhance the experience of planning, tracking, and managing work items. While this extension isn't necessarily a replacement for the Excel add-in, you'll find that it enhances the work planning, tracking, and management experience.

Getting social with work items

To provide a fresher, more modern experience in tracking work, the old and clunky work item form has been given a makeover. Along with the noticeable responsive form layout, the new form introduces a lot of new features. In this recipe, we'll see how to put the newly added work item discussion control to work. The following screenshot shows the new work item form:

It's fair to say that projects are tracked using work items, while discussions are tracked using email. Often, decisions aren't reflected back into work items, which results in work needing to be done later. The new work item form makes it really easy to stay on track by letting you have conversations within a work item. The discussions control provides a rich editor, giving you the ability to associate images, mention people, and link work items. The power of work item search and the social features of alerts and notification follow work items, and my work items make it really easy to stay involved and informed.

Getting ready

Before we dig into work item discussions, let's see how easy it is to populate your team project with sample data. The sample data widget, which can be found at `https://marketplace.visualstudio.com/items?itemName=ms-devlabs.SampleDataWidget`, is a free extension that was developed by Microsoft DevLabs, and it makes it really easy to generate demo work items in bulk. This extension also provides an option to generate and set up work item data inline with the **Scaled Agile Framework** (**SAFe**), giving you a great jump-start into implementing SAFe with TFS.

Once you've installed the extension, navigate to the dashboard in the PartsUnlimited project web portal. Add the sample data widget to the dashboard, select **Getting started** in the dropdown, and click **Create**. Once this awesome extension has completed its magic, you'll see your team project become populated with new features, user stories, and active iterations—all ready for you to start playing with everything they offer.

How to do it...

Let's perform the following steps:

1. Launch the PartsUnlimited web portal and select the **Search work items** control:

2. In the work item search box, type add. The keyword add is searched across all work items in the team project. The search results are summarized in the left-hand side panel. The search results are ordered by relevance, and can be reordered using a different field:

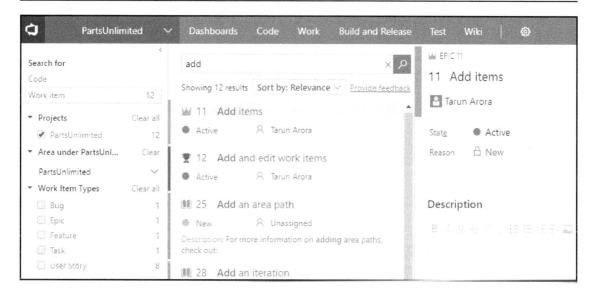

3. The work item search understands the work item schema, which allows it to support complex work item search queries. For example, by changing the search query to `add and s:active and t:feature`, we can filter the results down to the work item type `feature` and set the work item status to **Active**:

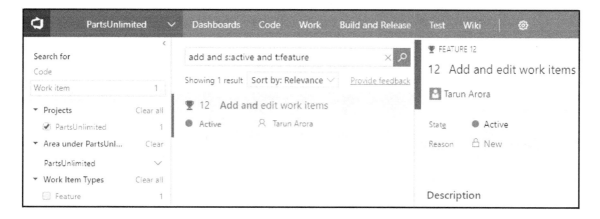

4. To search for work items that need review, change the search query to a new tag: `needs review`. The new follow functionality allows you to subscribe to work items and be notified when changes are made to them. Click on the **Follow** button to follow one or more work items:

5. Double-click the first work item in the search result and navigate to the **Discussion** section in the work item form. Here, you can add a comment, use # to link a work item, or use @ to mention a person:

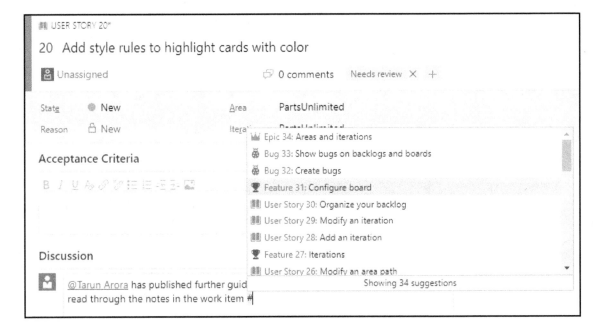

6. Click **Save** to persist the changes. The linked work item is automatically linked to the work item as a related work item. This mention triggers a notification workflow, and an email is sent out to the mentioned individual, in addition to others who are following this work item. You can click **Maximize Discussion** to enter an expanded discussion view:

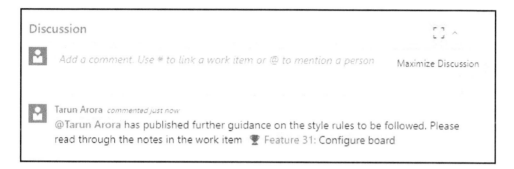

7. My favorite feature is being able to paste images into the work item form without having to save them and attach them manually. In your discussions, you can use rich formatting, links, images, and more:

How it works...

It is super easy for you to access artifacts that are most important for you. The redesigned account page has a personalized experience that shows the **Projects**, **Favorites**, **Work**, and **Pull Requests** you care about. You can go to one place and quickly find everything you need to do and care about.

Start your day with the **My work items** page to be able to easily access all the work items that have been assigned to you across all projects. It also lets you check and access the status of all the work items that you are following, those you have been mentioned in, or those that you have recently viewed:

Work item search allows you to search across all projects. You can scope the search and drill down into an area path of choice. You can easily search across all work item fields, including custom fields, which enables more natural searches. The snippet view indicates where matches were found. Quick inline search filters let you refine work items in seconds. The dropdown list of suggestions helps you complete your search faster. For example, a search such as `AssignedTo: Tarun WorkItemType: Bug State: Active` finds all active bugs assigned to a user named Tarun.

One of the design principles of the work item search team has been to keep the search actionable. The work item search interface integrates with familiar controls in the **Work** hub, giving you the ability to view, edit, comment, share, and much more, right from the search results.

Notifications help you and your teams stay informed about activity in your team projects. TFS 2018 introduced a new experience that makes it easier to manage what notifications you and your teams receive. Users have their own account-level experience for managing notification settings (available via the **Profile** menu).

This view lets you manage personal subscriptions and also view subscriptions that have been created by team administrators for all the projects in your account:

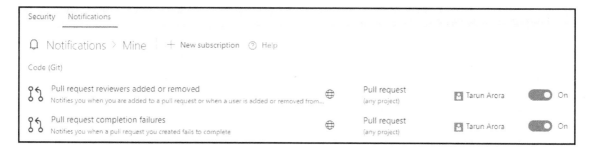

You can set up new notifications by clicking on the **New subscription** link. This new notification experience gives you access to WIQL so that you can create filter criteria for specific conditions. In addition to this, you can set up notifications to be delivered to other email addresses and soap endpoints:

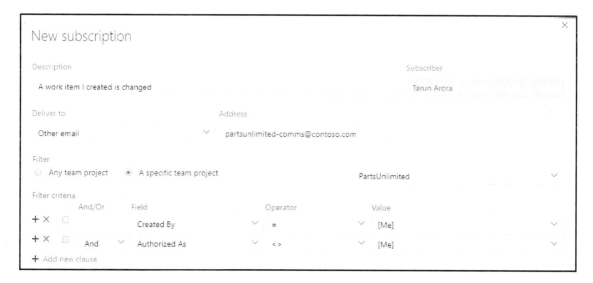

You, as an individual, also have the option of unsubscribing and opting out of a team or OOB notification subscription. Whether you are an administrator or not, toggling a shared team subscription from your notification settings only impacts you and not other team members.

You must configure an SMTP sever in order for team members to see the **Notifications** option from their account menu and to receive notifications. This can be done by following the steps provided at `https://docs.` `microsoft.com/en-gb/vsts/tfs-server/admin/setup-customize-` `alerts`.

There's more...

The TFS marketplace features the *Activity Feed* extension, available at `https://marketplace.visualstudio.com/items?itemName=davesmits.VSTSActivityFeed`. This free extension, created by Dave Smits, brings in the capability of viewing what's happening in your team project at a glance in one place. The extension is available as a dashboard widget, as well as a subpage in the work hub. *Activity Feed* gives a summary of all recent changes in work items, commits, pull requests, and builds. It tells who changed a task, who logged a bug, and who committed code. The extension supports configuration, so you can decide to filter out what's not relevant or simply configure which backlogs the work updates should be published from:

Activity Feed Work

Dave Smits updated **Product Backlog Item 2146** 'Make a circle of the icon of people', Changed state to Committed, Moved to iteration VSTS ActivityFeed\Sprint 7, 10 minutes ago

Dave Smits updated **Product Backlog Item 2136** 'Remove JQuery as dependency', Moved to iteration VSTS ActivityFeed\Sprint 8, 31 minutes ago

Dave Smits updated **Product Backlog Item 2137** 'Stop using types/moment', Moved to iteration VSTS ActivityFeed\Sprint 8, 31 minutes ago

Dave Smits updated **Product Backlog Item 2130** 'Use react and office fabric to get better UI ', Moved to iteration VSTS ActivityFeed\Sprint 8, 31 minutes ago

Dave Smits updated **Product Backlog Item 2145** 'Move from home hub to work hub', Changed state to Done, Added a new comment, a day ago

Dave Smits completed **pullrequest 72** 'Merge feature/move-to-workhub to develop', a day ago

Dave Smits updated **Product Backlog Item 2140** 'Add a license', 13 days ago

Dave Smits updated **Product Backlog Item 2135** 'Minify js again', 13 days ago

Dave Smits completed **pullrequest 71** 'Merge feature/license to develop', 13 days ago

Dave Smits updated **Bug 2139** 'When too much git repositories are in team project not all should be checked by default in the configuration', a month ago

Dave Smits updated **Product Backlog Item 2104** 'Support for multiple area path's', a month ago

Dave Smits updated **Impediment 2109** 'Retrieving user photo's is very inefficient', Assigned to Dave Smits , 2 months ago

Dave Smits updated **Impediment 2108** 'No paging options in the wiql query', Assigned to Dave Smits , 2 months ago

Dave Smits updated **Impediment 2107** 'Can't retrieve the Continuation token when using the getBuilds function', Assigned to Dave Smits , 2 months ago

See more updates...

The team rooms functionality has been completely removed in TFS 2018 `https://blogs.` `msdn.microsoft.com/devops/2017/01/04/deprecation-of-the-team-rooms-in-team-` `services-and-tfs/`. However, the introduction of social experiences built around you, including the search, follow, and comment features in work items and the activity feed extension, provides a far more engaging solution.

Portfolio backlog hierarchies and decomposing work

Requirements come in all shapes and sizes! While many teams can work with a flat list of items, sometimes, it helps to group related items into a hierarchical structure. Perhaps you would like to start with a big picture and break it down into smaller deliverables. Or, perhaps you've got an existing backlog and now need to organize it. No matter your starting point, TFS offers you hierarchical backlogs so that you can bring more order to your backlog. Two backlog levels are enabled in each team project by default—in the Agile process template, it's features and stories. An additional backlog level—**Epic**—can be enabled optionally. The user story backlog level is used for sprint planning; the feature backlog level and the epic backlog level, also known as the **Portfolio backlog**, can have multiple uses. This is shown in the following diagram for ease of understanding:

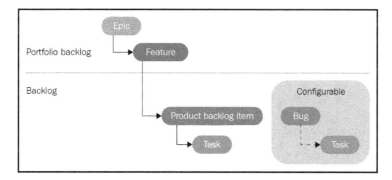

Use your backlogs in conjunction with portfolio backlogs to plan your project and do the following:

- Manage a portfolio of features that are supported by different development and management teams
- Group items into a release train
- Minimize size variability of your deliverables by breaking down a large feature into smaller backlog items

With portfolio backlogs, you can quickly add and group items into a hierarchy, drill up or down within the hierarchy, reorder and reparent items, and filter hierarchical views.

Getting ready

TFS 2018 allows you to add one-level child links to work items with ease. However, when you are in a planning discussion, you sometimes want to rapidly create sub items at different levels of work item hierarchies. The TFS marketplace features the decompose extension (`https://marketplace.visualstudio.com/items?itemName=cschleiden.decompose`), a free extension that was created by *Christopher Schleiden*, which allows you to quickly break down work items into sub-hierarchies. Appropriately named, this extension makes decomposing work items into sub-items very easy, and very useful during team discussion and planning sessions. Once you've installed this extension, you'll see the **Decompose work item** option in the work item context menu and the backlog and boards work item context menu:

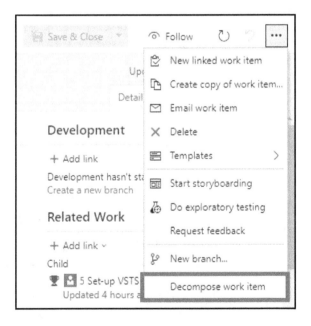

How to do it...

Let's perform the following steps:

1. Launch the PartsUnlimited team portal and navigate to the work hub.
2. To configure the team settings, click the gear icon under the velocity chart in the backlog view. The team settings window has several options to configure and style backlogs and boards, which we'll cover in later recipes:

3. In the **Settings** window, under the **General** section, click **Backlogs**. This presents the backlog levels that are available to your team. This setting is configurable per team. Adding or removing a backlog level will only affect the team for which it's being done to, and not every team in a team project. To add the Epics backlog level for the PartsUnlimited team, simply check the Epics backlog level and click **Save**:

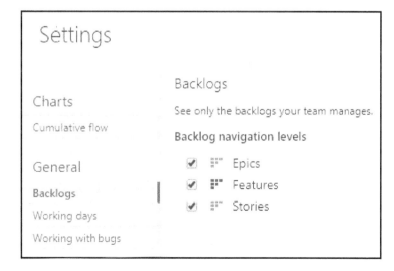

4. Open an epic from the Epics backlog and choose **Decompose** from the context menu. Hit *Enter* to add a feature and indent to create the user story; indent again to create the task. Once you have decomposed the work item, click **Create** to save your changes:

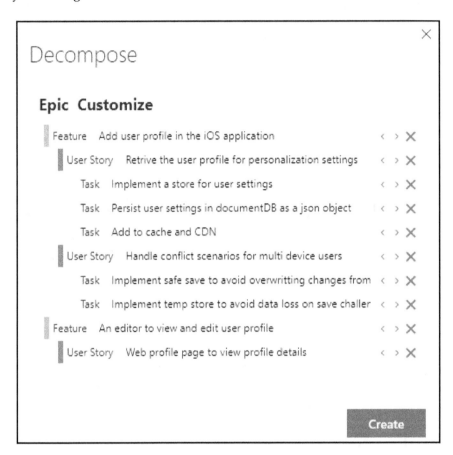

How it works...

The newly created work items are linked to each other. You can see this linking by expanding the linked work items in the Epics backlog:

Epic	⌄ 👑 Customize	••• ● New	Business
Feature	⌄ 🏆 Add user profile in the iOS application	● New	Business
User Story	⌄ 📖 Retrive the user profile for personalization settings	● New	Business
Task	☑ Implement a store for user settings	● New	
Task	☑ Persist user settings in documentDB as a json object	● New	
Task	☑ Add to cache and CDN	● New	
User Story	⌄ 📖 Handle conflict scenarios for multi device users	● New	Business
Task	☑ Implement safe save to avoid overwritting changes from one device	● New	
Task	☑ Implement temp store to avoid data loss on save challenge	● New	

With the growth in work item usage, there will be growth in the work item dependency tree. I usually find a list of dependencies meaningful until the depth of 3, after which I hope I could just visualize the dependency through a graph. Luckily, the TFS marketplace features the *Work Item Visualization* extension (`https://marketplace.visualstudio.com/items?itemName=ms-devlabs.WorkItemVisualization`), which is a free extension that was developed by Microsoft DevLabs. It allows you to visualize work item dependencies from within the work item form. The unique selling point of this extension is that it allows you to see how work items relate to each other, as well as code, tests, test results, builds, and external artifacts. You can even drill into your commits to explore the changeset details. Among other things, the extension also allows you to annotate and export visualizations, an example of which is provided by the following screenshot:

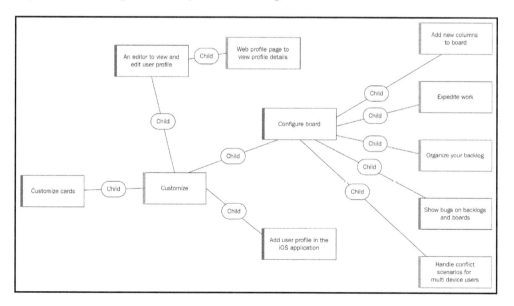

There's more...

Story mapping is a popular way of visualizing the product backlog with Agile teams. Story mapping is a top-down approach of requirement gathering. Story mapping starts from an overarching vision. A vision is achieved via goals. Goals are reached by completing activities. To complete an activity, users needs to perform tasks. And these tasks can be transformed into user stories for software development. Story maps are traditionally created using sticky notes on walls or whiteboards, and have proven to be popular among Agile development teams. However, these traditional storyboards are not without their disadvantages: walls are not transportable and the physical nature of these maps means they are only temporary.

The TFS marketplace features the *SpecMap* extension (`https://marketplace.visualstudio.com/items?itemName=techtalk.specmap`), which was created by TechTalk software, and gives you the ability to create digital storyboards. This extension allows you to use existing work items in the system, which means that SpecMap goes further than just depicting story maps: creating a story map in SpecMap helps you plan iterations in TFS and structure your backlog items in the process. The following screenshot depicts a story map of the PartsUnlimited iOS feature team, who are identifying the user journey for the new iOS application that they are creating for both free and paid users:

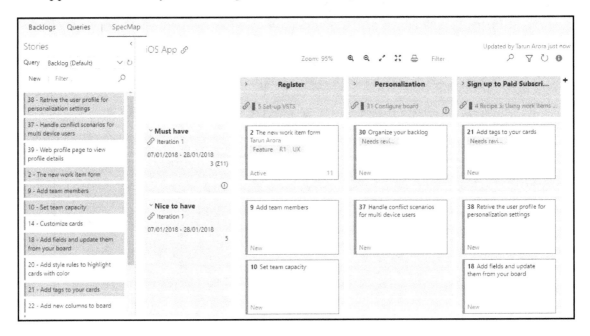

Configuring and customizing backlog boards

Backlogs display work items as a list, while boards display them as cards. In TFS, each backlog comes with its own board. The backlog board is also known as a Kanban board. To maximize a team's ability to consistently deliver high-quality software, Kanban emphasizes two main practices. The first, *visualize the flow of work*, requires that you map your team's workflow stages and configure your Kanban board to reflect this. The second, *constrain the amount of work in progress*, requires you to set **work-in-progress** (**WIP**) limits. You're then ready to track progress on your Kanban board and monitor key metrics to reduce lead or cycle time.

Your Kanban board turns your backlog into an interactive signboard, providing a visual flow of work. As work progresses from idea to completion, you update the items on the board. Each column represents a work stage, and each card represents a user story or a bug at that stage of work. The Kanban board has come a long way from when it was first introduced in TFS 2012. In TFS 2018, boards offer great flexibility to adapt to the processes, workflows, and customizations that work best for you and your teams.

Getting ready

Kanban literally translates as signboard or billboard. Accordingly, your number-one task is to visualize your team's workflow. You do this by identifying the types of work and handoffs that occur regularly as your team moves items off the backlog and into a shippable state. The main workflow stages performed by our PartsUnlimited team are captured here as **Analyze**, **Develop**, **Test**, **Deploy**, and **Feedback**. Each column corresponds to a work stage the team performs on each item before it can be considered done:

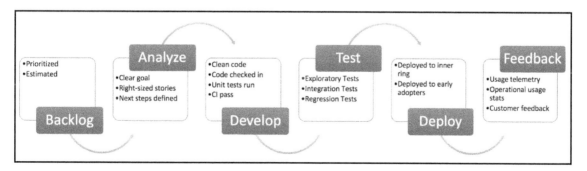

The work item does not have all of these states, but the beauty of the Kanban board is that it allows you to map multiple workflow stages to a work item state. So, in our example, the develop, test, and deploy stages can be mapped to the work item state *active*. This can be done right from within the **Configure team settings** dialog in the board view, without having to modify the process template. Columns allow you to visualize the workflow that's used to deliver requirements to production. Swim lanes, on the other hand, help visualize the different streams of work. Let's see how we can set up columns and swim lanes.

How to do it...

Let's perform the following steps:

1. Launch the PartsUnlimited team portal and navigate to the work hub. Open the **Stories** board and click on the gear icon to configure the team settings.
2. The **Columns** section in the Settings dialogue allows you to configure board columns. Rename the **Active** column to **Analyze** and update the **Definition of done** section:

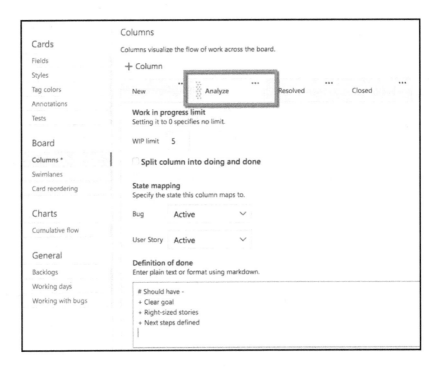

3. Add a new column for **Develop**, **Test**, **Deploy**, and **Feedback**, and map this to the work item state Active. The WIP limit should be set to *limit overloading a specific team will more work than they can deliver at one time*, which would only end up creating a bottleneck in your delivery workflow. You can also track bugs on the board, since you have the option of mapping a different workflow for bugs:

4. Navigate to the **Swimlanes** section in the team settings dialogue. Add a new swimlane and name it Emergency. While urgent issues will follow the same workflow for delivery, the swimlane allows you to give them better visibility:

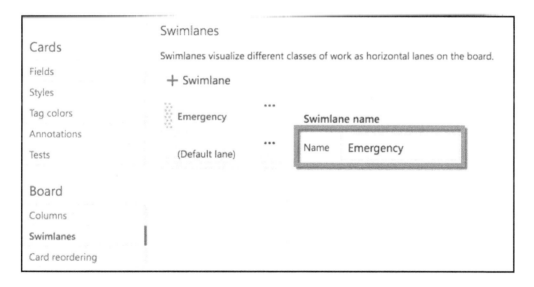

5. Next up, use the fields section to add the fields you would like to see on the cards in the Kanban board. A good idea might be to include the field for **Value Area**. With this change, the cards on the backlog will display the value area the work item delivery is contributing to.

6. Use the styles and tag colors section to define styling rules using a combination of fields and values. It might be a good idea to create a styling rule to show the card background as red if there is a tag that's *blocked*, for example. This can be done by using the following styling rule:

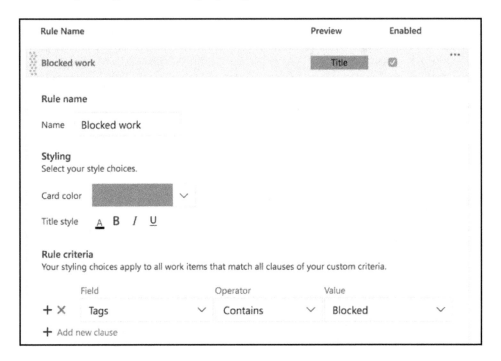

How it works...

Setting up a workflow using columns and streams of work with swim-lanes, in addition to styling rules, makes visualizing requirements a lot easier. As you can see in the following screenshot, the columns have an information icon, which reflects the **Definition of done** setup through the team configuration dialog:

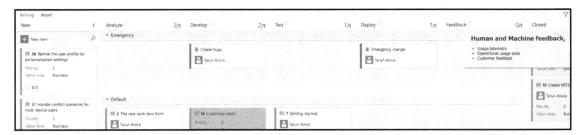

I've briefly touched on WIP limits in the implementation steps. To optimize the flow of value, you want to identify and eliminate bottlenecks. Bottlenecks indicate that waste exists in the overall workflow process. By monitoring your Kanban board over time, you can learn where bottlenecks occur. When several items sit in a column that hasn't worked for several days, a bottleneck has occurred. Bottlenecks typically occur when WIP limits are too high. On the other hand, no bottlenecks could indicate that WIP limits are too low. There is no right answer to what the correct WIP limit is for a column; this is something that can be discovered using empirical data by using the process and tools over time.

There's more...

The TFS marketplace features the free *Query based boards* extension (`https://marketplace.visualstudio.com/items?itemName=realdolmen.querybasedboards`), which was created by RealDolmen, and allows you to visualize the result of work item queries on a board. After installing the extension, navigate to the **Work** hub and select **Queries**. When opening a query, a new tab called **Board** will be available to visualize the results on a board:

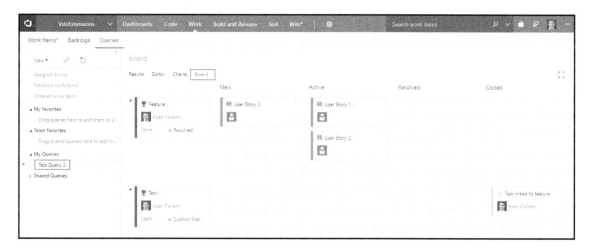

The extension is available as a dashboard widget, as well as a subpage in the work hub. The **Activity Feed** gives a summary of all the recent changes that have been made to work items, commits, pull requests, and builds. It tells you who changed a task, who logged a bug, and who committed code. The extension supports configuration, so you can decide to filter out what's not relevant or simply configure which backlogs work updates should be published from. Some people would agree that the more boards, the merrier!

Preparing and planning a sprint

The product backlog shows the list of work that has been planned by the team, and the items at the top are usually more valuable. A product team constantly reviews the backlog and pre-prioritizes the backlog based on user feedback and changing business priorities. Agile planning tools in TFS support defining and managing work within sprints.

This process is started off by defining a time box, referred to as a sprint, that corresponds to the cadence your team delivers. Many teams choose a two or three-week cadence. However, you can specify a shorter or longer sprint cycle. TFS also allows you to wrap multiple sprints into a release schedule. The sprint backlog represents a subset of the backlog; the team builds the sprint backlog during the sprint planning meeting. Planning meetings typically consist of two parts. In the first part, the team and product owner identify the backlog items that the team feels it can commit to competing in the sprint. These items get added to the sprint backlog. In the second part, your team determines how it will develop and test each item. They then define and estimate the tasks that are required to complete each item. Finally, your team commits to implementing some or all of the items based on these estimates.

Getting ready

Let's start off by prioritizing the product backlog. To do this, navigate to the **Backlog** view for the PartsUnlimited example team. Frequently reviewing and prioritizing your backlog can help your team know what's most important to deliver next. Reorder your backlog by simply dragging work items. Alternatively, if you prefer the keyboard route, hold the *Alt* key and use the up and down arrows:

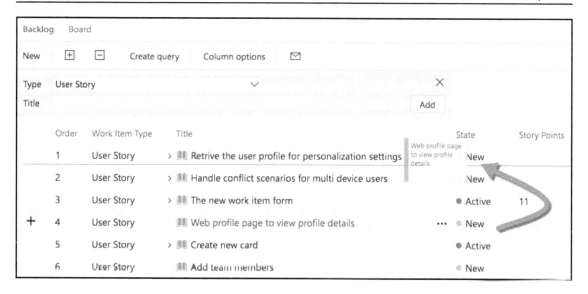

A prioritized backlog without an estimate of how big the work is only half as good. It is suggested that software development teams review and resize the backlog multiple times in a sprint, as this keeps the backlog in a ready state for future sprint planning sessions. While there are many sizing techniques, Fibonacci numbers are a good way to size the work into logical buckets. Once the work items have an estimate, you can use the Forecast tool to get an idea of how many items you can complete within a sprint. By plugging in velocity, you can see which items are within scope for the set of sprints the team has activated. Teams use the forecast tool to help their sprint planning efforts. By plugging in a value for the team velocity, the Forecast tool will show which items in the backlog can be completed within future sprints. Both tools are team-specific tools that rely on the team's ability to estimate backlog items:

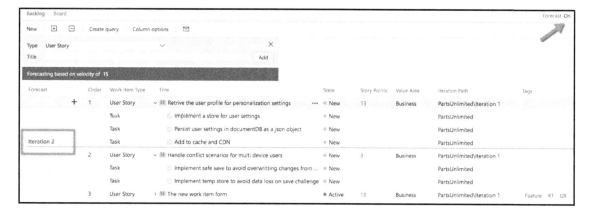

With a sized and prioritized backlog in place, there is just one more thing left to do before you start to plan the sprint. To quickly get started, you can use the default sprints, also referred to as iterations, that were added when your team project was created. Note that you must be a member of the Project Administrators group in order to add sprints and schedule sprint dates. Choose **Iteration** under the **Backlog** tab and then click the dates to edit them. With the dates configured, you are now ready for sprint planning:

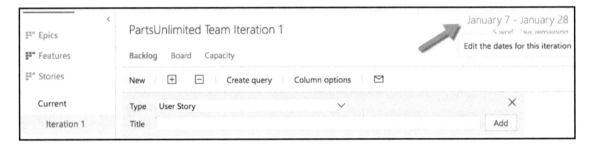

How to do it...

Sprint planning is a real team effort and a great way to get everybody aligned. The planning is kicked off by discussing the sprint goal. The Product Owner then shares the vision of the sprint goal with the team. The appropriate PBIs (which should be on top of the backlog by now) are selected to meet this sprint goal. Follow these steps to get started:

1. Begin your planning efforts by moving prioritized items from your backlog to your current sprint, one item at a time.

2. Simply drag each item from the product backlog into the sprint, as shown in the following screenshot:

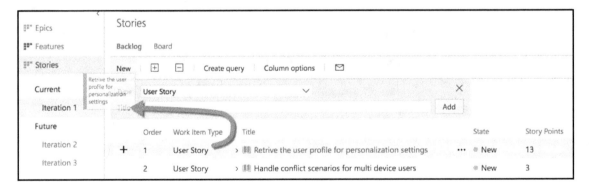

The Product Owner then starts reading the stories out and going through the acceptance criteria. This is a great opportunity to briefly discuss and clarify any requirements or acceptance criteria. Team velocity is a good measure of how many story points of backlog items the team takes into the sprint. The TFS marketplace features the quick calc extension (`https://marketplace.visualstudio.com/items?itemName=duffy.vsts-quick-calcs`), a free extension that was developed by Mike Duffy and allows you to quickly see total effort, % complete, and other metrics for a selection of work items. This is especially useful during a sprint planning meeting when you want quick answers on the total count of story points for the selected work items. This extension is shown in the following screenshot:

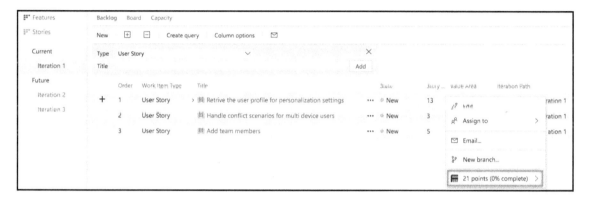

Next, the team needs to know the total available capacity within the sprint. The availability of each individual and their role can be tracked using the capacity tools in TFS. Whereas velocity correlates your team estimate requirements, capacity correlates to actual task time. Capacity takes into account variations in work hours of team members, as well as holidays, vacation days, and non-working days. Most teams specify the capacity in terms of hours, but you can also specify it in days if you so wish:

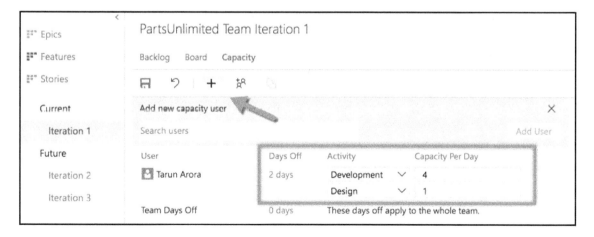

Now, you have a clear view of how much work your team can commit to. In the next part of the sprint planning meeting, the team creates a plan of work by breaking the requirements into tasks and then estimating them. Tasks capture the plan of action and add as many tasks as needed to capture the work required to complete each item. Tasks can represent different work that needs to be done, such as design, code, test, content, and sign off. TFS makes the process of adding tasks friction free, giving you the ability to access and add task functionality from multiple entry points without any overhead. Tasks can be added right from the sprint backlog, the sprint board, and the product backlog board:

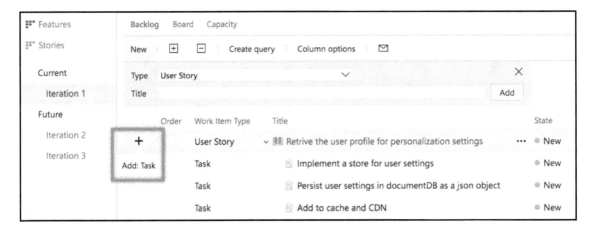

You can capture as much detail as you need in the task, including the effort estimate to complete the work. The effort estimate is netted against the actual capacity to provide a view of whether the work has been overscheduled:

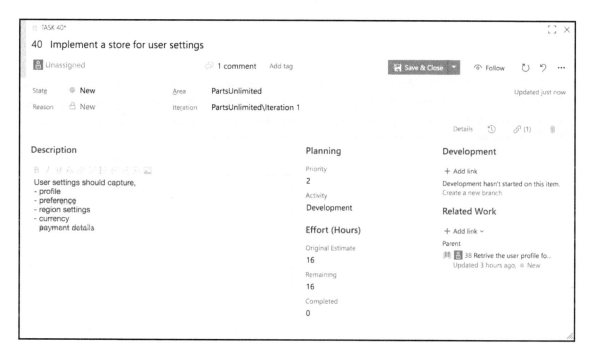

How it works...

With the team capacity set up, the product backlog decomposed, and the tasks estimated, the sprint plan is ready. The team members can now allocate work to themselves by dragging the tasks to their names:

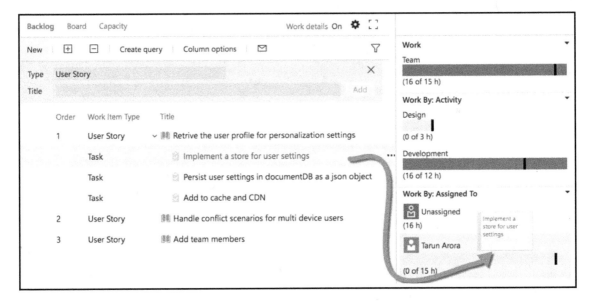

After you've defined all the tasks for all the items, check whether your team is at or over capacity. If your team is under capacity, you can consider adding more items to the sprint. If your team is over capacity, you'll want to remove items out of the backlog. Next, check whether any team member is under, at, or over capacity, or if someone hasn't even been assigned any work. Use the capacity bars to determine this. Once you have done this, the sprint backlog provides a view that should allow you to start delivering your sprint with confidence:

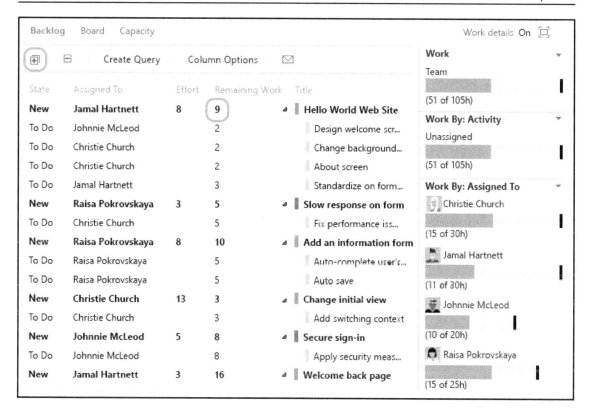

There's more...

The TFS marketplace features the *Sprint Goal* extension (`https://marketplace.visualstudio.com/items?itemName=keesschollaart.sprint-goal`), a free extension that was created by Kees Schollaart allows you to record the sprint goal in sprint planning tools. Once you've installed the extension, you'll see a new tab called **Sprint goal** in the sprint planning tools. This is a great way to make the sprint goal visible to the entire team.

Sometimes, people with unique skills are shared across multiple teams, which makes it hard to track their available capacity. The TFS marketplace features the team capacity management extension (`https://marketplace.visualstudio.com/items?itemName=tfc.team-capacity`), which was created by TFS consulting and provides an overview of the assigned capacity of individual team members across multiple teams within a team project. This gives you a bird's-eye view of capacity across all the teams in the team project. It provides a single *pane of glass* so that you can see where the team members are active and how much of their time has been allocated:

	Backlogs	Queries	Team Capacity			

User	PartsUnlimited Team ...	Team 1 ...	Team 2 ...	Team 3 ...	Total Capacity Per Day
TA Tarun Arora	5	0	0	0	5

Visualizing progress in a sprint

During a sprint, the team can use the taskboard and the sprint burndown chart to track progress. The sprint burndown chart provides you with an at-a-glance visual so that you can determine whether your team is on track to meet their sprint plan. Your taskboard provides a visualization of the flow and status of each sprint task. With this, you can focus on the status of backlog items, as well as work that has been assigned to each team member. It also summaries the total amount of remaining work to complete for a task or within a column. The taskboard supports pivoting the work by stories and people, and further filtering on individuals. The taskboard supports customization of the cards, which helps you surface more information during standup or generally out to stakeholders. The taskboard can be customized using the team settings dialogue (which we looked at earlier for backlog board customization). The field setting gives you the option to track bugs on the taskboard, as shown in the following screenshot:

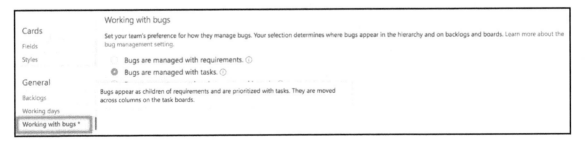

The **Fields** settings allow you to display more work item fields on the taskboard for product backlog items, tasks, and bugs. For example, you may be interested in seeing the priority of the bugs and which area of the application they belong to versus the board column for the product backlog item. Additionally, you can create styling rules to configure the style for the cards. For example, by rendering impeded work as red, you can base the style on work items tagged as blocked:

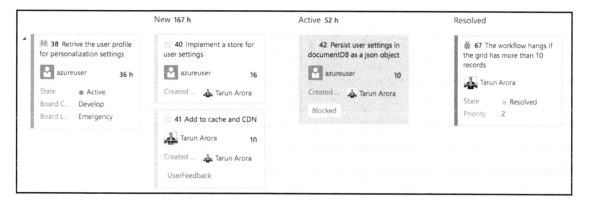

When a lot of work is being done, it is sometimes hard to visualize the dependencies between multiple tasks that could result in key deliverables being delayed. In this recipe, you'll learn how you can organize tasks in a sprint on a calendar view and identify dependencies between them.

Getting ready

The sprint burndown chart is a great indicator of whether the team will be able to complete all remaining work within the sprint time box, and the taskboard helps you visualize the remaining work on each task. The *Sprint Drop Plan* extension (`https://marketplace.visualstudio.com/items?itemName=yanivsegev.Drop-plan-extension`), which was created by *Yaniv Segev,* is an organizational tool that helps team members sync their tasks by visualizing their work status and dependencies on a sprint-based calendar.

Once you've installed the extension from the marketplace, you'll see a new tab called **Drop Plan** in the sprint tools:

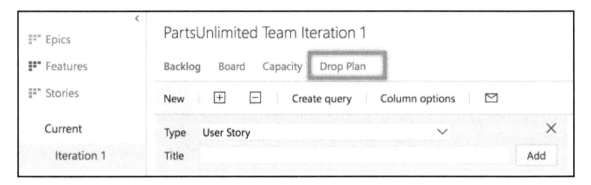

How to do it...

1. Once you're in the **Drop Plan** view, you'll notice that there is a swimlane pivoted against a calendar view for each individual, and a lane for all unassigned work. Tasks assigned to the individual show up in their respective lane on the sprint end date:

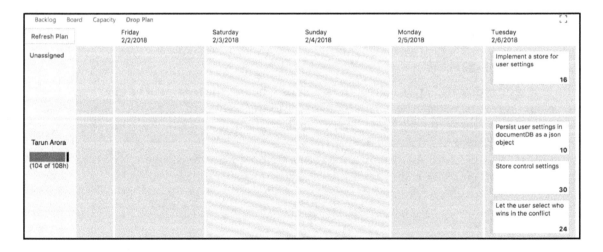

2.   Next, start to schedule the tasks by dragging them to the date you forecast they'll be completed by:

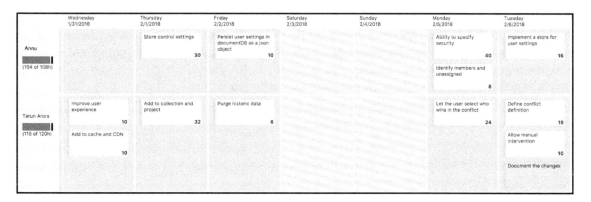

How it works...

When you hover over a task of interest, the drop plan will render dependency links out to tasks that are related to the task you have selected, in addition to the product backlog item all the tasks are linked to. In this case, you now know that the product backlog item has three key tasks in flight, one of which is only likely to complete on the last day of the sprint. This gives you an opportunity to discuss the order in which the tasks are scheduled. For example, in this case, if you think the task scheduled for the last day of the sprint has more value, it should be brought forward in place of something else. In addition to this, the extension allows you to visualize an individual's and team's days off, as well as blocked tasks:

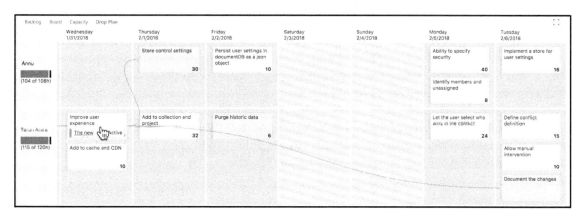

There's more...

The team foundation marketplace features the *Team Calendar* extension (`https://marketplace.visualstudio.com/items?itemName=ms-devlabs.team-calendar`), which was created by the Microsoft DevLabs team and helps busy teams stay on track and informed about important deadlines, sprint schedules, and upcoming milestones. Team Calendar is the one place where you can view and manage the dates that are important to your teams, including sprint schedule, days off (for individuals or the team), and custom events:

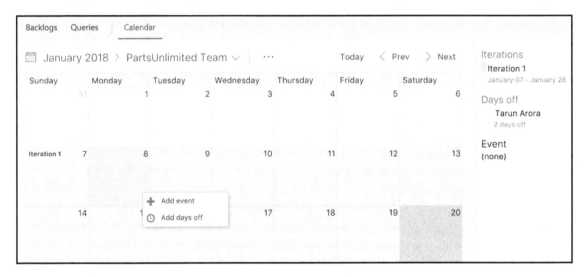

Delivery plans to track multiple teams

There was a certain revolution a few years back that was instigated by one single team project that was tracking and managing work for all teams and projects. This stemmed from the lack of tooling to track and manage work across multiple teams and projects. When you're planning and tracking work, it's often necessary to view work across teams and projects. While there were natural benefits from this approach, it also cluttered a single team project with code and artifacts from multiple unrelated initiatives. With TFS 2017, Microsoft released the delivery plans extension to address this gap. With delivery plans in the mix, I don't really advocate one large team project. Instead, you should have a team project for every software product in your organization.

A delivery plan is a view of the work from multiple teams (and multiple projects) laid out on a calendar with each team's iterations. Each row in the view represents the work from a team's backlog, with each card corresponding to a work item – user story, feature, or epic. As you horizontally scroll through the calendar, work in future (or past) iterations comes into view. Like the Kanban board, a delivery plan is an interactive work board, although one was designed for multiple teams. You can add teams from across all the projects in your collection. If the plan needs updating, you can simply drag cards to update the iteration path. Like the Kanban board, you can customize card fields so that you can see relevant information for your work.

Getting ready

Install the delivery plans extension (`https://marketplace.visualstudio.com/items?itemName=ms.vss-plans`) from the marketplace. Developed and maintained by Microsoft, this extension is free for all TFS users except stakeholders. With the extension installed, you'll see the **Plans** page in the work hub:

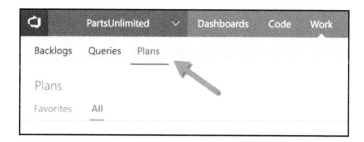

To see all the features of the **Plans** extension, you need multiple teams and projects. Use the sample data widget we discussed in the *Getting social with work items* recipe to create multiple projects. Since delivery plans are based on creating a portfolio of work in flight, it relies on a sprint's schedules for the teams.

How to do it...

Let's perform the following steps:

1. Click on the **New plan** button to create a new plan. Call the plan `myDeliveryPlan`:

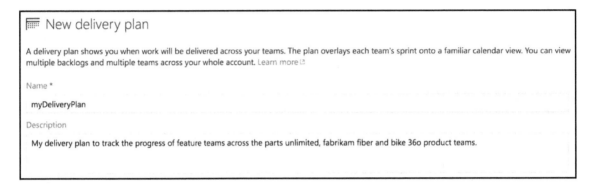

2. Next, select the projects and teams you want to track in the plan, as well as the backlog level. Optionally, specify filter criteria to filter out work items so that they don't show up on the delivery plan. In this case, I've added a filter to ignore bugs. Click **Create** to create the plan:

3. The delivery plan brings the feature backlogs of the selected teams onto the canvas. You'll notice in the following screenshot that the sprint cadence of the PartsUnlimited team is different from the bike 360 and Fabrikam Fiber team, but the delivery plan makes it possible to visualize their feature backlogs on a single canvas:

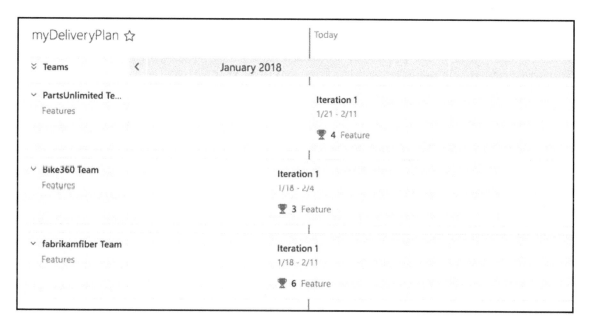

4. Next, click the **Configure plan** settings gear icon on the top right-hand side of the page to personalize the delivery plan. Add **Markers *** for key milestones, such as bug bash, scrum of scrums, team review, and any other key dates:

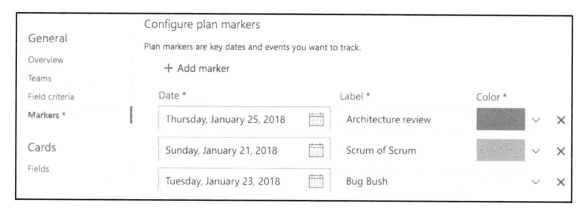

Last but not least, similar to other boards, the plans also support customizing cards. This allows you to surface more information by including more fields in work item cards.

How it works...

With the configuration for the plan complete, the final result is a delivery board that rolls up the work items from multiple teams and projects into a single view along with markers. The board supports all drag and drop operations and makes it really easy to use this view to take actions during planning and tracking sessions. As teams continue to become more distributed and the size/scope of work continues to grow, delivery plans make it easy to visualize your portfolio of teams and projects from across the organization:

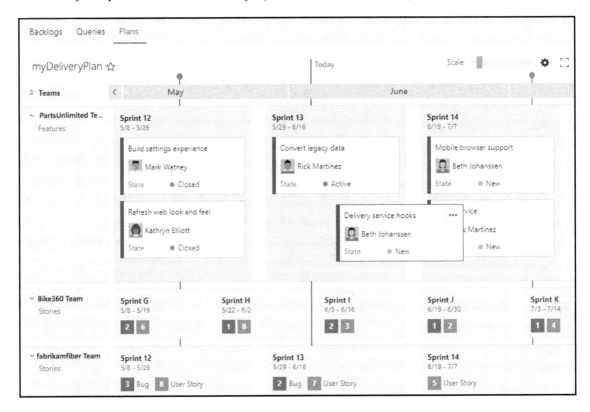

There's more...

The plans view allows you to create as many plans as you want, while the search functionality makes it really easy to search for your plan. The **Mark as favorite feature** allows you to get to your favorite plans quickly.

Dashboards for planning and tracking work

Dashboards in TFS provide a customizable canvas that allows your team to visualize and monitor progress. Dashboards replace the previous **Team Overview** page, providing easy-to-read, real-time information. At a glance, you can make informed decisions without having to drill down into other parts of your team project. Visibility of work is a core concept of Agile software development, and dashboards make it really easy to create an information radiator for your team and stakeholders.

Getting ready

Every team project is created with a default dashboard. You can access the PartsUnlimited dashboard by navigating to the dashboard hub. Anyone with access to the team project, including stakeholders, can view dashboards. Dashboards use widgets to surface information. There is no limit on how many dashboards you can create. Let's start off by creating a new dashboard for sprint 1. At this point, don't add any widgets to the dashboard. Click the **Settings** icon in the top right-hand corner of the page and select the option to auto-refresh the sprint 1 dashboard. Auto-refresh keeps the dashboard up-to-date; it's fantastic if you intend to project the dashboard view on a television screen.

The TFS marketplace features the *Product Vision* widget (`https://marketplace.visualstudio.com/items?itemName=agile-extensions.product-vision`), a free extension that was developed by Agile extensions and allow you to make product vision visible to the whole team by surfacing it to a dashboard via a widget. The sprint countdown widget (`https://marketplace.visualstudio.com/items?itemName=ms-devlabs.CountdownWidget`) is also a free extension and was developed by the Microsoft DevLabs team, and allows you to count down to a configurable moment in time, or down to the end of the current sprint.

How to do it...

Let's perform the following steps:

1. Open the **Sprint 1** dashboard and click the + icon from the lower right-hand side of the page. This launches the **Add widget** pane.

2. Search and add the sprint countdown, product vision, markdown widget, sprint capacity, charts widget, query results widget, sprint burn down, and the sprint overview widget, as shown in the following screenshot:

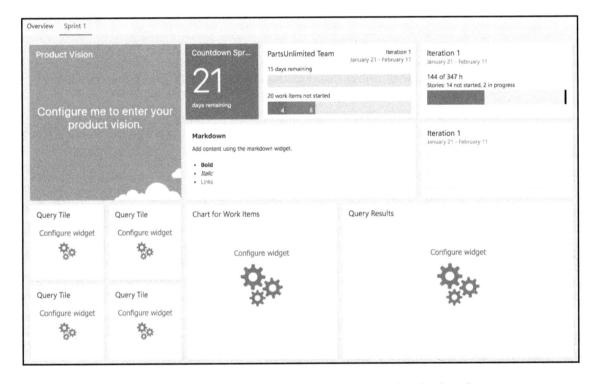

3. With the relevant widgets on the board, click on individual widgets to start configuring them. The **Configure workflow on all the tasks** option is very intuitive, for example, the query tile allows you to configure a work item query to it and specify a styling rule to change the color of the widget based on the number of work items returned by the query. The chart for the work items query allows you to render the results of the work item query as a chart of your choice, with further customization options for colors. The query result returns the work item list for the work item query that was configured by you, giving you the option of which columns to return.

How it works...

Widgets use the TFS REST API to retrieve information. The dashboard canvas allows you to move widgets around and scale them to different sizes. Widgets support interactivity; for example, clicking on the **Query Tile** would take you straight into the **Work Item Query** window. Once the widgets on the dashboard have been configured, you'll see output similar to the following:

There's more...

The TFS marketplace (https://marketplace.visualstudio.com/search?term=widget target=VSTScategory=All%20categorieshosting=onpremisessortBy=Relevance) features a lot of useful widgets, with an evergrowing collection of widgets – some of which will be of interest to you.

Source Control Management 2

Code repositories allow developers to write code confidently. More developers are using source control than ever before. The most obvious benefits of the code repository can be seen when multiple developers are collaborating on code. Many hands in the pot means there's a greater need to manage and understand revisions. Code doesn't exist unless it's committed into source control. Source control is the fundamental enabler of Continuous Delivery. If you ever have to make an argument to support source control, ask the following *have you ever* questions.

- Made changes to the code, realized the mistake, and wanted to revert back?
- Lost some code or had a backup that was too outdated?
- Had to maintain version histories of a product?
- Wanted to see the difference between two (or more) versions of your code?
- Wanted to prove that a particular change broke or fixed a piece of code?
- Wanted to review the version history of some code?
- Wanted to deploy changes to someone else's code?
- Wanted to share your code, or let other people access your code?
- Wanted to see the progress on work being done, and where, when and by whom?
- Wanted to experiment with new features without tampering with working code?

Managing code is an essential part of managing the application life cycle, which spans indiscriminately across programming languages and frameworks. Source-control systems can broadly be distinguished as centralized or distributed. We'll cover the differences between the two, but before that, take a look at this trend chart for SVN versus Git, which was created using Google search data. SVN is a centralized version control system. You'll notice that SVN as a search keyword was very popular during the time of waterfall-based project deliveries. It started losing its popularity to Git (a distributed version control system) during early 2010 when Agile became mainstream. The popularity of Git grew exponentially with the adoption of **Open Source Software** (**OSS**):

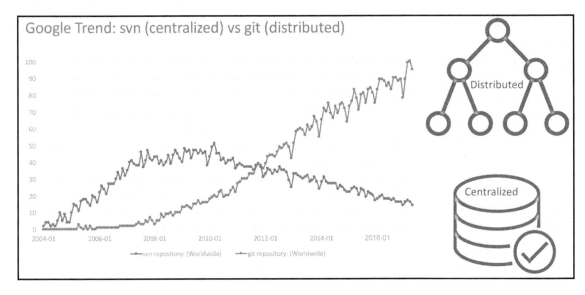

Let's look at both of the version-control systems to understand how they work.

A **Centralized Version-Control System** (**CVCS**) maintains a single **central** copy of your source code on a server repository. When working with a CVCS, the developer downloads the code from the server to a local workspace. Once changes to the code have been made locally, they are pushed to the centralized copy. Since each of the files in the local workspace is connected to the server, the server is aware that they are being modified, which can be useful if you intend to block someone else from making the changes while you are editing the files. Any functions against the repository (such as branching, merging, and shelving) also take place on the server, and require a connection to the server.

Foundation Version Control (**TFVC**) is a centralized version-control system. When working with TFVC using Visual Studio or Eclipse, the IDE is in frequent communication with the server. Basic operations, such as getting the latest code or seeing the full list of history changes, cannot be done without an active connection to the server.

A **Distributed Version Control System** (**DVCS**) does not necessarily rely on a central server to store all the versions of a project's files. Instead, every developer **clones** a copy of a repository and has the full history of the project on their own hard drive. This copy (clone) contains all of the data in the repository – all of the branches and all of the commit history. Git is a distributed version control system. Most operations (except pushing and pulling) can be performed without an active connection to the server.

Both centralized and distributed version control systems have their pros and cons. Consider the strengths of the source control system to determine the viability of using it in your project. CVCS is best suited for very large codebases, where you need granular access control, and especially if you need to audit usage. Consider using CVCS on codebases that are hard to merge:

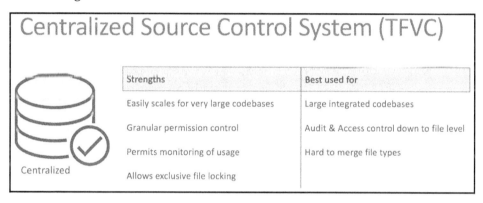

DVCS, on the other hand, is suited for highly distributed teams working across platforms. It provides portable history, and works best with greenfield codebases where the codebase is structured in small modules:

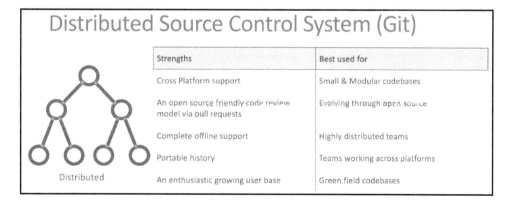

Every business is a technology business, and software is seen as the propeller for innovation. Being able to innovate quickly and cheaply, testing ideas and products with the consumers, refining them, and releasing them on a regular basis has become a competitive advantage. Your speed to convert ideas into working products can sometimes be the difference between success and failure in this very competitive marketplace. Development teams are constantly under pressure to deliver better-quality software faster. The speed is usually a byproduct of a good quality codebase, backed by unit tests. A good source control system can significantly contribute to the quality of the software, but it requires much more than just a good source-control system to drive quality. No code standards, a lack of unit tests, too many tactical implementations, and not addressing underlying architecture issues are major contributors to Technical Debt. Technical debt doesn't hit you overnight—it's a slow and gradual process. Unlike financial debt, technical debt is very hard to recognize. Technical debt slows your ability to deliver value.

In this chapter, we will cover the following recipes:

- Migrating from TFVC to Git keeping with code history
- Accessing Azure DevOps Server Git repositories using SSH
- Importing a Git repository from GitHub into Azure DevOps Server
- Basic Git operations using Visual Studio Code
- Setting up Git branches for continuous delivery
- Pull request for code review using branch policies
- Using Git hooks with Azure DevOps Server
- Managing and storing large files in Git
- Git branching model for Continuous Delivery
- Configuring code search as a search engine
- Using Git forks and sync changes with upstream PR

Migrating from TFVC to Git with code history

To make it easier for you to switch from TFVC to Git, Azure DevOps server now provides an out-of-the-box migration workflow, called **import repository**. The import repository option can be reached from the code hub. This allows you to migrate a TFVC repository into Git with history. However, the tool only allows you to migrate up to 180 days' worth of history from your TFVC repository. Not being able to migrate the entire history from the TFVC repository may be a dealbreaker for some. The following image shows you how to get to the import repository dialogue, the image also shows the migrate history options available to you:

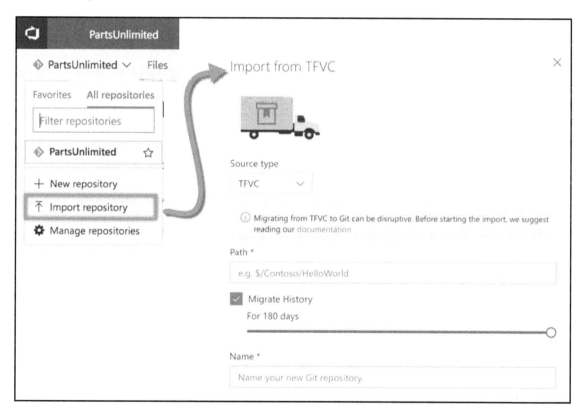

The import repository also allows you to import a Git repository, which is especially useful if you are looking to move your Git repositories from GitHub or any other public or private hosting spaces into Azure DevOps Server.

You may also come across use cases where you need to migrate from the TFVC repository that is hosted in an Azure DevOps server that your new Azure DevOps server doesn't have direct access to through the network. In this recipe, we'll learn how to use the open source command line git-tf to migrate your TFVC projects with complete history into Git, and then publish the local Git repository into a new Git repository in Azure DevOps Server.

Getting ready

In this section, we'll cover how to download and set up git-tf to prepare for the migration:

1. Download the git-tf command-line tools from the Microsoft Download Center (`http://download.microsoft.com/download/A/E/2/AE23B059-5727-445B-91CC-15B7A078A7F4/git-tf-2.0.3.20131219.zip`), and then extract the ZIP file into the `C:\git-tf` folder

2. To access `git-tf` directly from the command line, add the `C:\git-tf` path to your path environment variable

3. Create a folder, `C:\migrated`, to store the migrated repositories

In this example, we'll assume that the host TFVC repository that needs to be migrated is hosted on the `http://myOldAzure DevOps ServerServer/Azure DevOps Server/DefaultCollection` Azure DevOps Server server in the `$/OldTeamProject/App2BeMigrated` folder.

How to do it...

In this section we'll cover the steps for migrating the code from TFVC to git with history:

1. Launch the command line and run the following command; `--deep` is used to extract the entire history from this repository. This operation may take longer to complete, depending on the size and depth of history of the source repository:

```
git-tf clone --deep http://myOldAzure DevOps ServerServer/Azure
DevOps Server/DefaultCollection $/OldTeamProject/App2BeMigrated
C:\migrated\App2BeMigrated
```

2. In the command line, change the directory to `C:\migrated\App2BeMigrated` and run the following command. This will clean the Git metadata from the commit messages:

```
git filter-branch -f --msg-filter "sed 's/^git-Azure DevOps
Server-id:.*;C\([0-9]*\)$/Changeset:\1/g'" -- --all
```

3. Delete the `.git/refs/original` folder in `C:\migrated\App2BeMigrated` to delete the old branches as they are not needed anymore. To publish the local migrated Git repository in Azure DevOps Server, you'll need to create a new Git repository in Azure DevOps Server. To do this, navigate to the PartsUnlimited team project in the team portal and create a new Git code repository, `MyMigratedApp`:

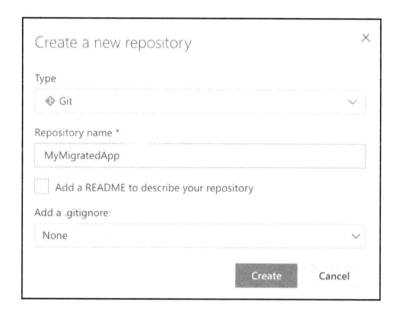

4. Run the following command to add the newly created Git repository as an origin to the migrated Git repository:

```
git remote add origin http://Azure DevOps Server2018/Azure
DevOps
Server/DefaultCollection/PartsUnlimited/_git/MyMigratedApp
```

5. Run the following command to push the new Git repository to the remote origin:

```
git push -u origin -all
```

How it works...

While most of the other commands are pretty self explanatory, the emphasis here is on the --deep switch:

1. By including the --deep switch, the entire history of the TFVC repository is consumed during the migration process. If this keyword is left out, only the most recent changeset will be fetched, which you wouldn't want in the scenario of a full export.

There's more...

Another situation you may keep running into is that the **committer names are different on Azure DevOps Server and Git**. As a rule, Git recognizes committers by their designed email address, while Azure DevOps Server ordinarily utilizes your Windows character. Accordingly, a similar individual may be spoken to by two different **committers** on the Git store. Use the Azure DevOps Server username for the import and the genuine Git client for new submits that are made on the Git storehouse. Utilize the below command to remap the names:

```
git filter-branch -f --commit-filter "
              if [ "$GIT_COMMITTER_NAME" = "<old Azure DevOps Server
user>" ];
              then                    GIT_COMMITTER_NAME="<new name>";
                                      GIT_AUTHOR_NAME="<new name>";
                                      GIT_COMMITTER_EMAIL="<new - email>";
                                      GIT_AUTHOR_EMAIL="<new - email>";
                                      git commit-tree "$@";
              else                    git commit-tree "$@";
              fi" HEAD
```

Accessing Azure DevOps Git repositories using SSH

Azure DevOps Server supports three secure ways to connect to your Git repositories—the first two work over HTTPS and the third option uses SSH:

- Git Credential Manager
- Personal Access Token
- SSH Public Keys

Git credential manager is the preferred option, since it lets you use the same credentials that you use with Azure DevOps Server web portal and also supports multi-factor authentication. In addition to supporting multi-factor authentication with Azure DevOps Server, the credential managers also support two-factor authentication for GitHub repositories. Once authenticated, the credential manager creates and caches a personal access token for future connections to the repo. Git commands that connect to this account won't prompt for user credentials until the token expires or is revoked through Azure DevOps Server. If you are accessing your Azure DevOps Server Git repositories through Team Explorer in Visual Studio, Visual Studio Code, IntelliJ and Android Studio with the Azure DevOps Server Plugin for IntelliJ, and Eclipse (with the Team Explorer Everywhere plugin), you'll be using the Git credentials manager under the hood.

You are probably wondering, "What's the use case for using PAT or SSH keys for authentication?" If you are using an environment that doesn't have an integration plugin available with Azure DevOps Server, configure your IDE to use a Personal Access Token or SSH keys to connect to your repos in Azure DevOps Server. The Git credential manager creates and caches a PAT after initial authentication, which is what it uses for future connections to the repository. The difference here is that if you use PAT for authentication from an environment that doesn't support Git credential manager, then you're responsible for generating and managing the PAT yourself. PATs are a perfect fit when you're trying to authenticate from command-line tools, tasks in build pipelines, or using REST APIs. Personal access tokens are alternate passwords that you create in a secure way using your normal authentication, and they support expiration dates and the scope of access. You can put them into environment variables so that scripts do not hardcode passwords.

If you are coming from a non-Windows ecosystem, you are probably more used to using SSH keys for authentication. SSH keys provide you with secure access to your Git repositories hosted in Azure DevOps Server without having to enter a password. SSH keys work across platforms: you can use one SSH key to connect to multiple systems, such as Azure DevOps Server, Azure DevOps, GitHub, and any other systems that support SSH access. This is especially useful for system administrators who need to access multiple systems and would otherwise find entering passwords tedious. SSH public key authentication works with a pair of generated encryption keys. The public key is shared and used to encrypt messages. The private key is kept safe and secure on your system and is used to read messages encrypted with the public key. As of Visual Studio 2017, Visual Studio provides native support for SSH access to Git repositories.

Now that we are clear on the different types of secure access supported by Azure DevOps Server and when you should use which, let's see how to set up SSH public key access with Azure DevOps Server.

Getting ready

Two important things to do in preparation for setting up SSH:

1. If you are using Windows, install Git for Windows. The Git for windows installation (`http://gitforwindows.org/`) adds a shortcut to Git Bash in the Start menu.
2. When you generate SSH keys they are stored in a default folder in your machine, In this recipe, we'll use Bash to generate the SSH keys. Alternatively, you can use other shell environments to generate SSH keys as well. Be careful if you have any existing SSH keys on your machine, generating SSH keys in the default folder location will overwrite any existing SSH keys in that folder.

How to do it...

In this section we'll go through the commands for generating SSH keys:

1. The following commands will let you create new default SSH keys. Running this command will overwrite any existing default keys. Launch bash and use the `ssh-keygen` command as follows. This produces the two keys that are needed for SSH authentication: your private key (`id_rsa`) and the public key (`id_rsa.pub`):

   ```
   ssh-keygen -C "tarun@contoso.com"

   Generating public/private rsa key pair.
   Enter file in which to save the key (/home/tarun/.ssh/id_rsa):
   /home/tarun/.ssh/id_rsa
   Enter passphrase (empty for no passphrase):
   Enter same passphrase again:
   Your identification has been saved in /home/tarun/.ssh/id_rsa.
   Your public key has been saved in /home/tarun/.ssh/id_rsa.pub.
   ```

    It is important to never share the contents of your private key. If the private key is compromised, attackers can use it to trick servers into thinking the connection is coming from you.

2. Add the public SSH key to the user ID in Azure DevOps Server. To do this, navigate to **Security** first:

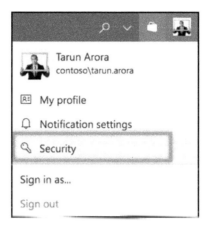

3. Select **SSH public keys**, click **Add**, copy the content of `id_rsa.pub` from the `.ssh` folder, and save your changes:

4. You are now ready to clone the Git repository using your all-new SSH keys. Navigate to the code hub in the parts unlimited team project. You'll notice that the clone dialogue has a clone URL for **HTTP** and **SSH**. Select **SSH** and copy the URL:

5. Run `git clone` from the command line to clone the Git repository using SSH:

```
git clone ssh://azdo2019:22/Azure DevOps
Server/DefaultCollection/PartsUnlimited/_git/MyMigratedApp
```

How it works...

Let's go through the steps to understand how this works:

1. The SSH key setup process prompts you to validate the fingerprint on the SSH public key the first time you use it, this is for your own protection to avoid any malicious use. When you run `git clone` to clone using the SSH URL of the Git repository, you will be prompted to verify that the SSH fingerprint for the server you are connecting to. This is done to protect you from the man-in-the-middle attacks, you can learn more about this at this link at `https://technet.microsoft.com/en-us/library/cc959354.aspx`. Once you accept the host's fingerprint, SSH will not prompt you again unless the fingerprint changes.

2. The `ssh-keygen` command creates a 2,048-bit RSA key for use with SSH. The command gives you an option to add a passphrase for your private key—this provides another layer of security for your private key. If you specify a passphrase, be sure to configure the SSH agent to cache your passphrase so that you don't have to enter it every time you connect.

3. The `ssh-keygen` command in the preceding example has been run with the -c switch. This allows you to add a comment field in the key file – for convenience to the user to help identify the key. The comment can tell what the key is for, or whatever is useful. The comment is initialized to `user@host` when the key is created, but can be changed using the `-c` option.

There's more...

Putty is a very popular telnet client for windows, if instead of using `ssh-keygen` on bash, you plan on using **putty** as your SSH client. You'll need to convert your keys into OpenSSH format, this can be done using PuTTYgen. Simply load the private key into PuTTYgen, go to the **Conversions** menu, and select **Export OpenSSH key**. Then, save the private key file and perform the following steps to set up non-default keys with Azure DevOps server Git repositories. These steps should also be followed if you generate ssh keys using `ssh-keygen`, but don't save them to the default `.ssh` folder in your profile.

The most important step, which is what gets overlooked the most, is that the keys must be in a folder that only you can read or edit. If the folder has wider permissions, SSH will not use the keys. Since these keys have not been generated using the standard process or saved in the default location, you'll need to make SSH aware of these keys. This can be done by running the following command which is used to start the ssh agent.

Windows users need to run the `start-ssh-agent.cmd` command before running the following command:
`ssh-add /home/tarun/myBespokeFolder/.ssh/id_tarun.rsa`

Now, your custom keys are ready to be used for connectivity with Git repositories in Azure DevOps Server.

Importing a Git repository from GitHub into Azure DevOps Server

If you already have a Git repository on GitHub that you want to port to Azure DevOps Server, you'll be delighted to know that Azure DevOps Server natively supports importing a Git repository with history from any Git-hosting platform, including GitHub. In this recipe, you'll learn how to import the parts unlimited GitHub repository with its complete history, including branches and tags, into Azure DevOps Server.

Getting ready

The **PartsUnlimited** GitHub repository (`https://github.com/Microsoft/PartsUnlimited`) that we'll be porting across needs to be accessible from the environment you are accessing in the Azure DevOps Server web portal. In the image below you can see the PartsUnlimited GitHub repository hosted under the Microsoft organization.

The clone URL for this repository can be retrieved by clicking on the green **Clone or download** button in GitHub.

How to do it...

1. Open the Azure DevOps Server parts unlimited team project in the web portal and navigate to the code hub. From the parts unlimited Git repository list, choose to import a repository. In the import window, enter the clone URL of the PartsUnlimited GitHub project and specify a unique name for the target repository to be created, MyPartsUnlimited. Click **Import** to start the import workflow:

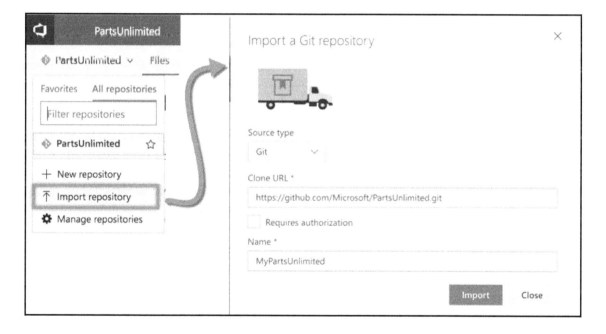

The import process works asynchronously and sends you an email notification once the import has successfully completed. The import process is usually quick, but can take longer, depending on the size and depth of the repository you are importing.

How it works...

Let's see how it works:

1. The Azure DevOps Server **Activity log** and **Job monitoring** page isn't featured in the menu, so not many people are aware of it. Navigate to the Azure DevOps Server activity and job monitor page by browsing to `http://<YourAzure DevOps ServerServer>/Azure DevOps Server/_oi/`. The Azure DevOps **Activity log** lists all recorded activities. The **Job monitoring** page shows the execution processing and history of all jobs that have been submitted to Azure DevOps Server:

2. From the **Job History** view, you'll see that the import Git repository is processed as a job. Subsequent to that, other jobs are executed to send email notifications on completion of the import process and the execution of code sense catchup jobs:

3. The Git repository, with all its history branches and tags, is migrated across from GitHub into a new Git repository in Azure DevOps Server:

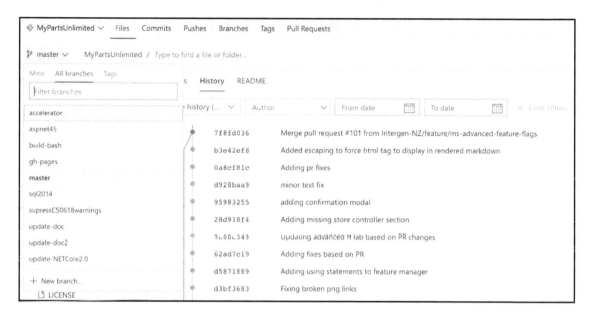

There's more...

The Azure DevOps Server marketplace features the **Commit Network** extension (`https://marketplace.visualstudio.com/items?itemName=swapme3.commitnetwork`). This free extension, created by Swapnil Athawale, brings in visualization capabilities to the branch commits and the flow of code. Visualizations include the following:

- Pie chart of code commits by members
- Flow network of commits
- Graphical representations of work by each member

Basic Git operations using Visual Studio Code

Git and Continuous Delivery is one of those delicious **chocolate & peanut butter** combinations we occasionally find in the software world: two great tastes that taste great together! Continuous Delivery of software demands a significant level of automation. It's hard to deliver continuously if you don't have a quality codebase. Git provides you with the building blocks to really take charge of quality in your codebase; it gives you the ability to automate most of the checks in your codebase even before committing the code into your repository. To fully appreciate the effectiveness of Git, you must first understand how to carry out basic operations on Git, such as clone, commit, push, and pull.

The natural question is, *how do we get started with Git?* One option is to go native with the command line or look for a code editor that supports Git natively. Visual Studio Code is a cross-platform open source code editor that provides a powerful developer tooling for hundreds of languages. To work in the open source, you need to embrace open source tools. In this recipe, we'll start off by setting up the development environment with Visual Studio Code, create a new Git repository, commit code changes locally, and then push changes to a remote repository on Azure DevOps Server.

Getting ready

In this recipe, we'll see how we can initialize a Git repository locally, and then we'll use the ASP.NET Core MVC project template to create a new project and version it in the local Git repository. We'll then use Visual Studio Code to interact with the Git repository to perform basic operations of commit, pull, and push. You'll need to set up your working environment with the following:

- .NET Core 2.0 SDK or later: `https://www.microsoft.com/net/download/macos`
- Visual Studio Code: `https://code.visualstudio.com/download`
- C# Visual Studio Code extension: `https://marketplace.visualstudio.com/items?itemName=ms-vscode.csharp`
- Git: `https://git-scm.com/downloads`
- Git for Windows (if you are using Windows): `https://gitforwindows.org/`

The Visual Studio Marketplace features several extensions for Visual Studio Code that you can install to enhance your experience of using Git:

- **Git Lens** (`https://marketplace.visualstudio.com/items?itemName=eamodio.gitlens`): This extension brings visualization for code history by leveraging Git blame annotations and code lens. The extension enables you to seamlessly navigate and explore the history of a file or branch. In addition to that the extension allows you to gain valuable insights via powerful comparison commands, and so much more.
- **Git History** (`https://marketplace.visualstudio.com/items?itemName=donjayamanne.githistory`): Brings visualization and interaction capabilities to view the Git log, file history, and compare branches or commits.

How to do it...

1. Open the Command Prompt and create a new working folder:

```
mkdir myWebApp
cd myWebApp
```

2. In **myWebApp**, initialize a new Git repository:

```
init git
```

3. Configure global settings for the name and email address to be used when committing in this Git repository:

```
git config --global user.name "Tarun Arora"
git config --global user.email "tarun.arora@contoso.com"
```

 If you are working behind an enterprise proxy, you can make your Git repository proxy-aware by adding the proxy details in the Git global configuration file. There are different variations of this command that will allow you to set up an HTTP/HTTPS proxy (with username/password) and optionally bypass SSL verification. Run the below command to configure a proxy in your global `git config`.

```
git config --global http.proxy
http://proxyUsername:proxyPassword@proxy.server.com:port
```

4. Create a new ASP.NET core application. The new command offers a collection of switches that can be used for language, authentication, and framework selection (more details can be found on Microsoft docs: `https://docs.microsoft.com/en-us/dotnet/core/tools/dotnet-new?tabs=netcore2x`):

`dotnet new mvc`

Launch Visual Studio Code in the context of the current working folder:

`code .`

5. When the project opens up in Visual Studio Code, select **Yes** for the **Required assets to build and debug are missing from 'MvcMovie'. Add them?** warning message. Select **Restore** for the **There are unresolved dependencies** info message. Hit *F5* to debug the application. Then, myWebApp will load in the browser, as shown in the following screenshot:

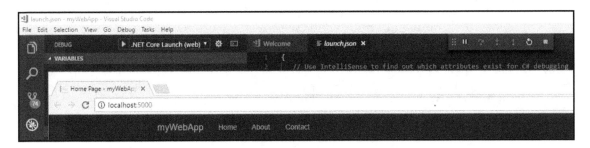

You'll notice that the .vscode folder has been added to your working folder. To avoid committing this folder into your Git repository, you can include this in the .gitignore file. With the .vscode folder selected, hit *F1* to launch the command window in Visual Studio Code, type gitIgnore, and accept the option to include the selected folder in the .gitIgnore file:

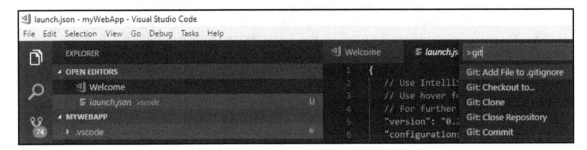

6. To stage and commit the newly created myWebApp project to your Git repository from Visual Studio Code, navigate to the Git icon from the left panel. Add a commit comment and commit the changes by clicking the checkmark icon. This will stage and commit the changes in one operation:

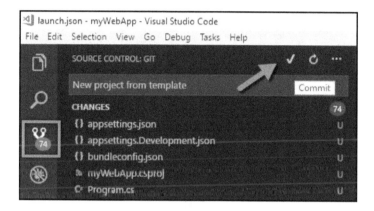

7. Open Program.cs; you'll notice that Git lens decorates the classes and functions with the commit history and also brings this information inline to every line of code:

8. To share your Git repository with others, it needs to be published to a remote repository. Create a new Git repository in the Azure DevOps Server's partsunlimited team project and call it myWebApp. Don't initialize the Git repository by adding a readme.md file.

If you have a reinitialized repository on the server that you want to associate with an unrelated local Git repository, you'll need to merge unrelated histories – refer to the *There's more* section to learn how to do this.

9. Add the newly created Git repository in the Azure DevOps Server as the remote for the local Git repository:

```
git remote add origin http://Azure DevOps Server2018/Azure
DevOps Server/DefaultCollection/PartsUnlimited/_git/MyWebApp
```

10. In order to validate the URL of the remote git branch run the following command:

```
git origin -v
```

Visual Studio Code detects that the local Git repository is associated with a remote Git repository in Azure DevOps Server. It gives you the option to push the local changes to the origin right from within the Visual Studio Code status bar:

How it works...

The easiest way to understand how the steps work is to check the history of the operation. Let's have a look at how to do this...

Navigate to the `myWebApp` Git repository in Azure DevOps Server's `partsunlimited` web portal, and then click on **History** to see the history of changes that have been pushed from the local to the server:

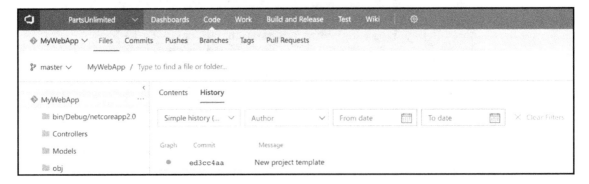

There's more...

If the Git repository was initialized at the time of creation by having a new README.md file added to it, then the Git repository on the server and the local will have a history that is unrelated:

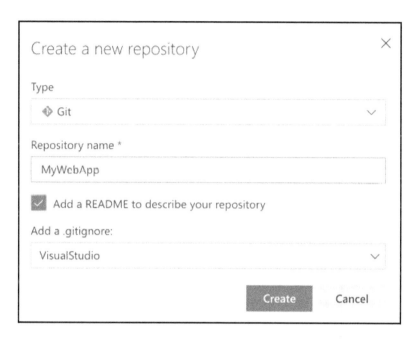

In this situation, you'll have to explicitly link the local branch with the branch on the remote. Associate the local branch with an upstream branch:

```
git branch --set-upstream-to=origin/master
```

Visual Studio Code detects that a remote has been added for this local Git repository and that the local branch and the upstream branch are not in sync. Since the history in the remote repository and the history in the local repository aren't related yet, use the --allow-unrelated-histories switch to pull the changes from the remote repository into the local repository:

```
git pull origin master --allow-unrelated-histories
```

Push the changes from your local repository into the remote by clicking on the push icon in the Visual Studio Code status bar:

Navigate to the `myWebApp` Git repository in Azure DevOps Server's `partsunlimited` web portal, then click on `History` to see the history of changes. The graph of history reflects that the code histories of the local repository and the remote were not related before being pushed into the remote repository:

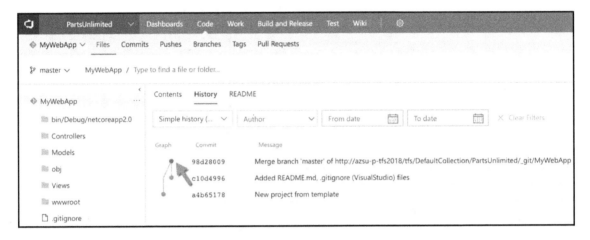

Pull request for code review using branch policies

Code issues that are found sooner are both easier and cheaper to fix. Therefore, development teams strive to push code quality checks as far left into the development process as possible. As the name suggests, branch policies give you a set of out-of-the-box policies that can be applied to the branches on the server. Any changes being pushed to the server branches need to comply with these policies before the changes can be accepted. Policies are a great way to enforce your team's code quality and change-management standards. In this recipe, you'll learn how to configure branch policies on your master branch.

Getting ready

The out-of-the-box branch policies include several policies, such as build validation and enforcing a merge strategy. In this recipe, we'll only focus on the branch policies that are needed to set up a code-review workflow.

How to do it...

1. Open the branches view for the `myWebApp` Git repository in the parts unlimited team portal. Select the **master** branch, and from the pull-down context menu, choose **Branch policies**:

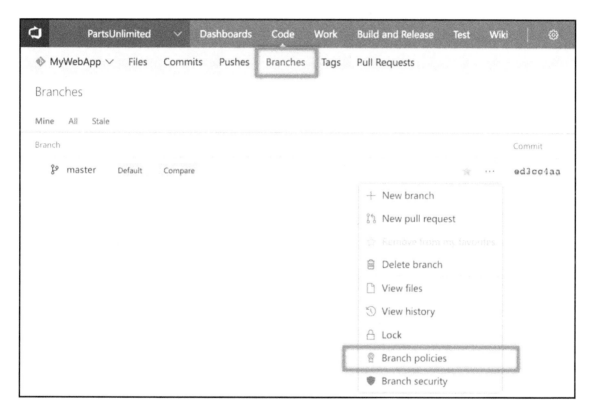

2. In the policies view, check the option to protect this branch:

3. This presents the out-of-the-box policies. Check this option to select a minimum number of reviewers. Set the **minimum number of reviewers** to 1 and check the option to reset the code reviewer's votes when there are new changes:

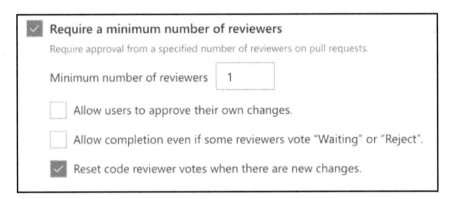

The **Allow users to approve their own changes** option allows the submitter to self-approve their changes. This is OK for mature teams, where branch policies are used as a reminder for the checks that need to be performed by the individual.

4. Use the review policy in conjunction with the comment resolution policy. This allows you to enforce that the code review comments are resolved before the changes are accepted. The requester can take the feedback from the comment and create a new work item and resolve the changes. This at least guarantees that code review comments aren't just lost with the acceptance of the code into the master branch:

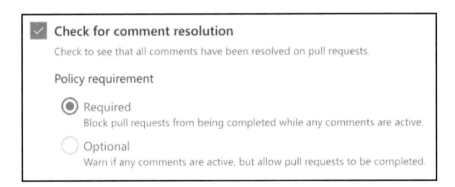

5. A code change in the team project is instigated by a requirement. If the work item that triggered the work isn't linked to the change, it becomes hard to understand why the changes were made over time. This is especially useful when reviewing the history of changes. Configure the **Check for linked work items** policy to block changes that don't have a work item linked to them:

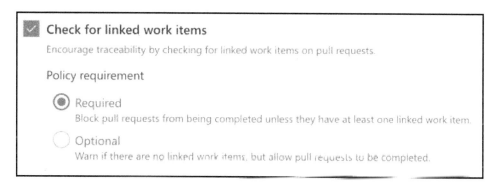

6. Select the option to automatically add code reviewers when a pull request is raised. You can map which reviewers are added based on the area of the code being changed:

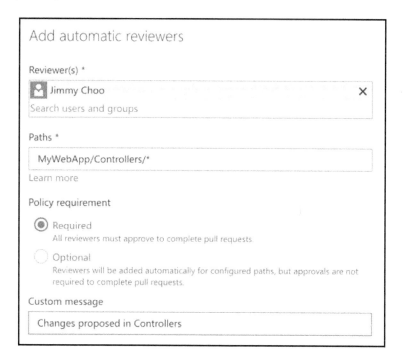

How it works...

With the branch policies in place, the master branch is now fully protected. The only way to push changes to the master branch is by first making the changes in another branch and then raising a pull request to trigger the change-acceptance workflow. From one of the existing user stories in the work item hub, choose to create a new branch. By creating a new branch from a work item, that work item automatically gets linked to the branch. You can also include more than one work item with a branch as part of the create workflow:

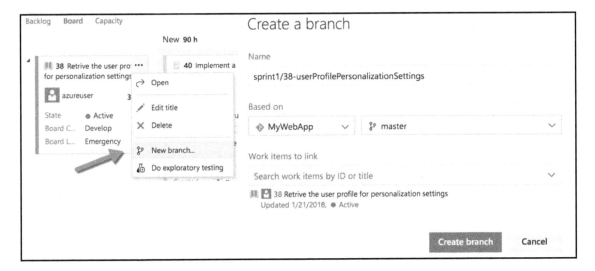

> Prefix / in the name when creating the branch to make a folder for the branch to go in. In the preceding example, the branch will go in the `sprint1` folder. This is a great way to organize branches in busy environments.

With the newly created branch selected in the web portal, edit the `HomeController.cs` file to include the following code snippet and commit the changes to the branch. In the image below you'll see that after editing the file, you can directly commit the changes by clicking the commit button.

The file path control in team portal supports search. Start typing `Home` in the file path to see all the files in your Git repository under that directory starting with these letters. They will show up in the file path search results dropdown.

```
Contents    Highlight changes                                          🖫 Commit...

 1  using System;
 2  using System.Collections.Generic;
 3  using System.Diagnostics;
 4  using System.Linq;
 5  using System.Threading.Tasks;
 6  using Microsoft.AspNetCore.Mvc;
 7  using mywebapp.Models;
 8
 9  namespace mywebapp.Controllers
10  {
11      public class HomeController : Controller
12      {
13          public IActionResult Index()
14          {
15              return View();
16          }
17
18          private string JoinTwoStrings(string one, string two)
19          {
20              var NewString = string.Concat(one, two);
21              return NewString;
22          }
```

The code editor in web portal has several new features in Azure DevOps Server 2018, such as support for bracket matching and toggle white space, and so on. You can load the command palette by pressing *F1*. Among many other new options, you can now toggle the file using a file mini-map, collapse and expand, as well as other standard operations.

To push these changes from the new branch into the master branch, create a pull request from the pull request view. Select the new branch as the source and the master as the target branch. The new pull request form supports markdown, so you can add the description using the markdown syntax. The description window also supports @ mentions and # to link work items:

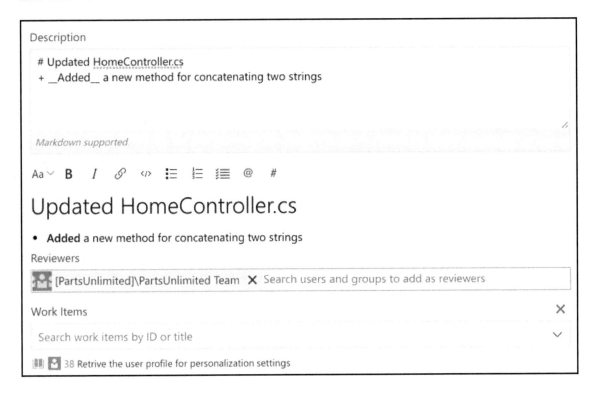

The pull request will be created; the overview page summarizes the changes and the status of the policies. The **Files** tab shows you a list of changes, along with the difference between the previous and the current versions. Any updates that are pushed to the code files will show up in the updates tab, and a list of all the commits is shown under the **Commits** tab:

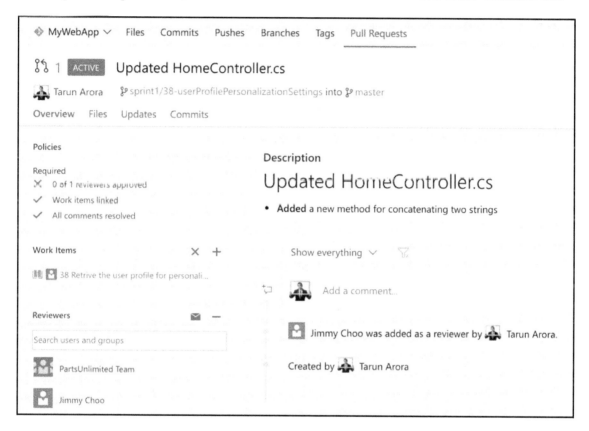

Open the **Files** tab: this view supports code comments at the line level, file level, and overall. The comments support both @ for mentions and # to link work items, and the text supports markdown syntax:

The code comments are persisted in the pull request workflow; the code comments support multiple iterations of reviews and work well with nested responses. The reviewer policy allows for a code review workflow as part of the change acceptance. This is a great way for the team to collaborate on any code changes being pushed into the master branch. When the required number of reviewers approve the pull request, it can be completed. You can also mark the pull request to auto-complete after your review. This auto-completes the pull requests once all the policies have been successfully compiled to.

There's more...

Have you ever been in a state where a branch has been accidentally deleted? It can be difficult to figure out what happened. Azure DevOps Server now supports searching for deleted branches. This helps you understand who deleted it and when, the interface also allows you to recreate the branch it if you wish.

To cut out the noise from the search results, deleted branches are only shown if you search for them by their exact name. To search for a deleted branch, enter the full branch name into the branch search box. It will return any existing branches that match that text. You will also see an option to search for an exact match in the list of deleted branches. If a match is found, you will see who deleted it and when. You can also restore the branch. Restoring the branch will recreate it at the commit to which is last pointed. However, it will not restore policies and permissions.

Using Git hooks with Azure DevOps Server

Ryan Hellyer accidentally leaked his Amazon AWS access keys to GitHub and woke up to a $6,000 bill the next morning. Wouldn't you just expect a source control as clever as Git to stop you from making such a blunder? Well, in case you didn't know, you can put Git Hooks to work to address not just this but many similar scenarios. In the spirit of pushing quality left into the development process, you want to enable developers to identify and catch code quality issues when they are developing the code locally in their repository, even before raising the pull request to trigger the branch policies. Git hooks allow you to run custom scripts whenever certain important events occur in the Git life cycle, such as committing, merging, and pushing. Git ships with a number of sample hook scripts in the `repo\.git\hooks` directory.

Since Git snares simply execute the contents on the particular occasion type they are approached, you can do practically anything with Git snares. Here are a few instances of where you can utilize snares to uphold arrangements, guarantee consistency, and control your environment:

- Enforcing preconditions for merging
- Verifying work Item ID association in your commit message
- Preventing you and your team from committing faulty code
- Sending notifications to your team's chatroom (Teams, Slack, HipChat)

In this recipe, we'll look at using the pre-commit Git hook to scan the commit for keywords from a predefined list to block the commit if it contains any of these keywords.

Getting ready

Let's start by exploring client-side Git hooks. Navigate to
the `repo\.git\hooks` directory – you'll find that there a bunch of samples, but they are
disabled by default. For instance, if you open that folder, you'll find a file called `pre-commit.sample`. To enable it, just rename it to pre-commit by removing
the `.sample` extension and make the script executable. When you attempt to commit
using `git commit`, the script is found and executed. If your pre-commit script exits with a
`0` (zero), you commit successfully; otherwise, the commit fails:

If you are using Windows, simply renaming the file won't work. Git will fail to find the
shell in the designated path as specified in the script. The problem is lurking in the first line
of the script, that is, in the **shebang** declaration:

```
#!/bin/sh
```

On Unix-like OSes, the #! tells the program loader that this is a script to be interpreted,
and `/bin/sh` is the path to the interpreter you want to use, which is `sh` in this case.
Windows is definitely not a Unix-like OS. Git for Windows supports Bash commands and
shell scripts via Cygwin. By default, what does it find when it looks
for `sh.exe` at `/bin/sh`? Yup, nothing-nothing at all. Fix it by providing the path to
the sh executable on your system. I'm using the 64-bit version of Git for Windows, so my
shebang line looks like this:

```
#!C:/Program\ Files/Git/usr/bin/sh.exe
```

How to do it...

Let's go back to the example we started with—how could have Git hooks stopped Ryan Hellyer from accidentally leaking his Amazon AWS access keys to GitHub? You can invoke a script at pre-commit using Git hooks to scan the increment of code being committed into your local repository for specific keywords:

1. Replace the code in this pre-commit shell file with the following code:

```
#!C:/Program\ Files/Git/usr/bin/sh.exe
matches=$(git diff-index --patch HEAD | grep '^+' | grep -Pi
'password|keyword2|keyword3')
if [ ! -z "$matches" ]
then
    cat <<\EOT
Error: Words from the blacklist were present in the diff:
EOT
  echo $matches
  exit 1
fi
```

You don't have to build the full keyword scan list in this script. Instead, you can branch off to a different file by referring it here that you could simply encrypt or scramble if you wanted to.

How it works...

In the script, Git diff-index is used to identify the code increment being committed. This increment is then compared against the list of specified keywords. If any matches are found, an error is raised to block the commit; the script returns an error message with the list of matches. In this case, the pre-commit script doesn't return 0 (zero), which means the commit fails.

There's more...

The `repo\.git\hooks` folder is not committed into source control, so you may wonder how you share the goodness of the automated scripts you create with the team. The good news is that, from Git version 2.9, you now have the ability to map Git hooks to a folder that can be committed into source control. You could do that by simply updating the global settings configuration for your Git repository:

```
git config --global core.hooksPath '~/.githooks'
```

If you ever need to overwrite the Git hooks you have set up on the client side, you can do so by using the no-verify switch:

```
git commit --no-verify
```

You can also use PowerShell scripts in your Git hooks – refer to the walkthrough on how to implement it here: `https://www.visualstudiogeeks.com/DevOps/UsingPowerShellForGitHooksWithVstsGitOnWindows`.

See also

So far, we have looked at the client-side Git hooks on Windows, Azure DevOps Server also exposes server-side hooks. Azure DevOps Server uses the same mechanism to create pull requests. You can read more about the git.push server-side event here: `https://docs.microsoft.com/en-us/vsts/service-hooks/events#git.push`.

Managing and storing large files in git

It is not uncommon for projects to have include high quality images and videos that are large in size. If you have large files in your repository, such as images and videos, Git will keep a full copy of the file in the repo every time you commit a change to the file. Git is ultimately versioning the file, if many versions of these files exist in your repo, they will dramatically increase the time to check out, branch, fetch, and clone the code.

Luckily git has solved this problem using Git **Large File System** (**LFS**). LFS is an extension to Git; it replaces large files, such as audio samples, videos, datasets, and graphics, with text pointers inside Git, while storing the file's contents on a remote server which commits data that describes the large files in a commit to your repo, and stores the binary file contents into separate remote storage.

When you clone and switch branches in your repo, Git LFS automatically downloads the correct version from that remote storage. Your local development tools will transparently work with the files as if they were committed directly to your repo.

Git LFS provides your teams with a seamless experience, as they can use the familiar end-to-end Git workflow no matter whether they work on small or large files. LFS files can be as big as you need them to be. As of version 2.0, Git LFS now also supports file-locking (`https://github.com/git-lfs/git-lfs/wiki/File-Locking`) to help your team work on large, undefiable assets, such as videos, sounds, and game maps.

You should be aware of a few things before using Git LFS:

- Every Git client used by your team must install the Git LFS client and understand its tracking configuration (`https://github.com/github/git-lfs/tree/master/docs`).
- If the Git LFS client is not installed and configured correctly, you will not see the binary files committed through Git LFS when you clone your repo. Git will download the data that describes the large file (which is what Git LFS commits to the repo) and not the actual binary file. Committing large binaries without the Git LFS client installed will push the binary to your repo.
- Git cannot merge the changes from two different versions of a binary file even if both versions have a common parent. If two people are working on the same file at the same time, they must work together to reconcile their changes to avoid overwriting the other's work. Git LFS provides file-locking to help. Users must still take care to always pull the latest copy of a binary asset before beginning work.
- Azure DevOps server currently does not support using SSH in repos with Git LFS tracked files.

Getting ready

In order to use Git LFS (`https://git-lfs.github.com/`), you need to download and install it once:

```
git lfs install
```

How to do it...

For Git LFS to work, it needs to know what file types you want to be tracked using Git LFS. Git LFS stores this setting in the .gitattributes file. This file is committed to the repository; this way everyone on your team that uses Git will be using the same LFS configuration. Let's get started:

1. Configure Git LFS to track all MP4 files:

   ```
   git lfs track "*.mp4"
   ```

2. Track the changes in your .gitattribute file:

   ```
   git add .gitattributes
   ```

3. Commit and push the changes in your .gitattribute file to the remote repository:

   ```
   git commit -m "Track all mp4 files in git LFS"
   git push origin master
   ```

How it works...

Validate the version of Git LFS in your environment:

```
> git lfs version
git-lfs/2.3.4 (GitHub; windows amd64; go 1.8.3; git d2f6752f)
```

Verify the changes in the .gitattribute file:

```
\MyWebApp> type .gitattributes
*.mp4 filter=lfs diff=lfs merge=lfs -text
```

Create a folder to store videos and store an MP4 video in this folder:

```
\MyWebApp> mkdir videos
\MyWebApp> cd videos
\MyWebApp> copy c:\tmp\HandsOnDemo-vLog.mp4 .\videos
```

Check the size of the video file (the video size is over 640 MB):

```
MyWebApp\videos> dir HandsOnDemo-vLog.mp4

02/07/2018 11:53 AM 6,472,920 HandsOnDemo-vLog.mp4
                 1 File(s) 6,472,920 bytes
```

Stage the changes and check the status:

```
MyWebApp> git add .

MyWebApp>git status
On branch master
Your branch is up-to-date with 'origin/master'.

Changes to be committed:
  (use "git reset HEAD <file>..." to unstage)

        new file: videos/HandsOnDemo-vLog.mp4
```

When committing changes, Git LFS may give you an error message. Your username must be of the form DOMAIN\user. It is currently tarun.arora@contoso.com. This happens because Git is using Kerberos to authenticate and LFS does not support Kerberos, so you will get errors that say **Your user name must be of the form DOMAIN\user** To get out of this state, you will need to remove the Kerberos credential and let Git pick up a new NTLM credential instead. To do this, simply remove your Git credentials from the Windows Credential Manager.

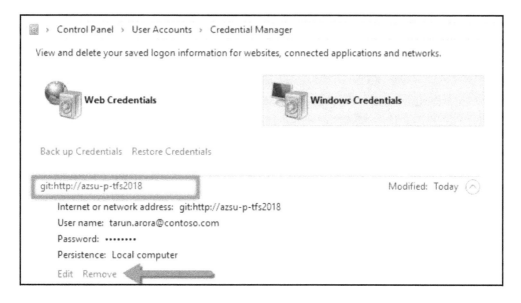

Commit the video to your local repository:

```
MyWebApp> git commit -m "Vlab for hands on demo"
[master 47b4370] Vlab for hands on demo
 1 file changed, 3 insertions(+)
 create mode 100644 videos/HandsOnDemo-vLog.mp4
```

Push the changes to the remote repository. Git LFS will kick in as it detects configuration settings for .mp4 type files:

```
MyWebApp> git push remote origin

Locking support detected on remote "origin". Consider enabling it with:
  $ git config lfs.http://Azure DevOps Server2018/Azure DevOps
Server/DefaultCollection/PartsUnlimited/_git/MyWebApp.git/info/lfs.locksver
ify true
Git LFS: (1 of 1 files) 6.17 MB / 6.17 MB
Counting objects: 4, done.
Delta compression using up to 8 threads.
Compressing objects: 100% (3/3), done.
Writing objects: 100% (4/4), 444 bytes | 444.00 KiB/s, done.
Total 4 (delta 1), reused 0 (delta 0)
remote: Analyzing objects... (4/4) (11 ms)
remote: Storing packfile... done (42 ms)
remote: Storing index... done (68 ms)
To http://azsu-p-Azure DevOps Server2018/Azure DevOps
Server/DefaultCollection/PartsUnlimited/_git/MyWebApp
    9304fa1..47b4370 master -> master
```

To investigate the contents of the commit history, use the -p switch with the Git log command:

```
MyWebApp> git log -p

commit 47b4370d539f85eeb765b45a51021dbd51c33634 (HEAD -> master,
origin/master, origin/HEAD)
Author: tarun arora <tarun.arora@outlook.com>
Date: Wed Feb 7 12:12:50 2018 +0000

    Vlab for hands on demo

diff --git a/videos/HandsOnDemo-vLog.mp4 b/videos/HandsOnDemo-vLog.mp4
new file mode 100644
index 0000000..d67c622
--- /dev/null
+++ b/videos/HandsOnDemo-vLog.mp4
@@ -0,0 +1,3 @@
+version https://git-lfs.github.com/spec/v1
```

```
+oid
sha256:62388612f4e5f2abe80d50fa24a4160dd0de3dc20dee75762a7135549c164a6c
+size 6472920
```

The important part of the commit log details is the Git LFS URL for the `HandsOnDemo-vLog.mp4` file. The GitHub URL included for the version value only defines the LFS pointer file type, and is not a link to your binary file. The URL tracks the version of Git LFS you're using, followed by a unique identifier for the file (OID). It also stores the size of the final file.

See also

We've been talking about storing large files in a Git repository. if you have a Git repository that is too big due to the architecture of the product you will find that normal Git operations, such as clone and commit, take too long. Microsoft has innovated the virtualization of Git repositories to address an internal problem found in adopting Git for the Windows product development team that has Git repositories which are over hundreds of GB in size. Microsoft has contributed this innovation to the open source under the GVFS project. **Git Virtual File System** (**GVFS**) is the open source system that enables Git to operate at enterprise-scale. It makes using and managing massive Git repositories possible. GVFS virtualizes the filesystem beneath your Git repository so that Git tools see what appears to be a normal repository when, in fact, the files are not actually present on disk. GVFS only downloads files as they are needed. GVFS also manages Git's internal state so that it only considers the files you have accessed, instead of having to examine every file in the repository. This ensures that operations, such as status and checkout, are as fast as possible. Learn more about GVFS here: `https://gvfs.io/`.

Git branching model for continuous delivery

The purpose of writing code is to ship enhancements to your software. A branching model that introduces too much process overhead does not help in increasing the speed with which you can get changes out to customers. It is therefore important to come up with a branching model that gives you enough padding to not ship poor-quality changes but at the same time not introduce too many processes to slow you down. The internet is full of branching strategies for Git; while there is no right or wrong, a perfect branching strategy is one that works for your team! In this recipe, we'll learn how to use a combination of feature branches and pull requests to always have a ready-to-ship master branch and how to sync bug fixes fixed in fix of fail branches back into master to avoid regression.

Getting ready

Let's cover the principles of what is being proposed:

- The master branch:
    - The master branch is the only way to release anything to production.
    - The master branch should always be in a ready-to-release state.
    - Protect the master branch with branch policies.
    - Any changes to the master branch flow through pull requests only.
    - Tag all releases in the master branch with Git tags.
- The feature branch:
    - Use feature branches for all new features and bug fixes.
    - Use feature flags to manage long-running feature branches.
    - Changes from feature branches to the master only flow through pull requests.
    - Name your feature to reflect their purpose, like so:

    List of branches:

    ```
    features/feature-area/feature-name
    users/username/description
    users/username/workitem
    bugfix/description
    features/feature-name
    features/feature-area/feature-name
    hotfix/description
    ```

- Pull requests:
    - Review and merge code with pull requests.
    - Automate what you inspect and validate as part of pull requests.
    - Track pull request completion duration and set goals to reduce the time it takes.

In this recipe, we'll be using the `myWebApp` we created in the *Pull Request for code review using branch policies* recipe. If you haven't already, follow that recipe to lock down the master branch using branch policies. In this recipe, we'll also be using two very popular extensions from the marketplace:

- **The VSTS CLI** (`https://marketplace.visualstudio.com/items?itemName=ms-vsts.cli`): This is a new command-line experience for Azure DevOps (AzDo) and **Azure DevOps Server** (**AzDos**), and was designed to seamlessly integrate with Git, CI pipelines, and Agile tools. With the VSTS CLI, you can contribute to your projects without ever leaving the command line. VSTS CLI runs on Windows, Linux, and Mac.

- **Git Pull Request Merge Conflict** (`https://marketplace.visualstudio.com/items?itemName=ms-devlabs.conflicts-tab`): This open source extension that was created by Microsoft DevLabs allows you to review and resolve pull request merge conflicts on the web. Before a Git pull request can complete, any conflicts with the target branch must be resolved. With this extension, you can resolve these conflicts on the web, as part of the pull request merge, instead of performing the merge and resolving conflicts in a local clone.

In order to use the VSTS-CLI, you'll need to log in with your PAT token. To make full use of the VSTS CLI, you should check the **All scopes** option when generating the PAT. Since the URL of the Azure DevOps Server instance needs to be used in most commands, it's best to store it as a variable and reference it when required. You can get a list of all the Git repositories in the parts unlimited team project:

```
$Azure DevOps Server =  "https://Azure DevOps
Server2018.westeurope.cloudapp.azure.com/Azure DevOps Server"
vsts login --token xxxxxxx --instance $Azure DevOps Server
$prj = "PartsUnlimited"
vsts code repo list --instance $i --project $prj --output table
```

```
vsts code repo list --instance $i --project $prj --output table
ID                                       Name            Default Branch    Project
----------------------------------       ------------    --------------    --------------
9b08d519-37a6-4aed-84e6-3a2712f742a9     MyWebApp        master            PartsUnlimited
b2c65132-d148-49e0-81aa-ce106fbf3747     PartsUnlimited                    PartsUnlimited
```

The VSTS CLI supports returning the results of the query in JSON, JSONC, table, and TSV format. You can configure your preference by using the VSTS configure command.

How to do it...

1. After you've cloned the master branch into a local repository, create a new feature branch, `myFeature-1`:

```
myWebApp> git checkout -b feature/myFeature-1
Switched to a new branch 'feature/myFeature-1'
```

2. Run the Git branch command to see all the branches. The branch showing up with an asterisk is the currently-checked-out branch:

```
myWebApp> git branch
* feature/myFeature-1
  master
```

3. Make a change to the `Program.cs` file in the `feature/myFeature-1` branch:

```
myWebApp> notepad Program.cs
```

4. Stage your changes and commit locally, then publish your branch to the remote server:

```
myWebApp> git status

On branch feature/myFeature-1
Changes not staged for commit:
  (use "git add <file>..." to update what will be committed)
  (use "git checkout -- <file>..." to discard changes in working
directory)
 modified: Program.cs

myWebApp> git add .

myWebApp> git commit -m "Feature 1 added to Program.cs"

[feature/myFeature-1 70f67b2] feature 1 added to program.cs
 1 file changed, 1 insertion(+)

myWebApp> git push -u origin feature/myFeature-1

Delta compression using up to 8 threads.
Compressing objects: 100% (3/3), done.
Writing objects: 100% (3/3), 348 bytes | 348.00 KiB/s, done.
Total 3 (delta 2), reused 0 (delta 0)
remote: Analyzing objects... (3/3) (10 ms)
remote: Storing packfile... done (44 ms)
remote: Storing index... done (62 ms)
```

```
To http://Azure DevOps Server2018/Azure DevOps
Server/DefaultCollection/PartsUnlimited/_git/MyWebApp
 * [new branch] feature/myFeature-1 -> feature/myFeature-1
Branch feature/myFeature-1 set up to track remote branch
feature/myFeature-1 from origin.
```

The remote shows the history of the changes:

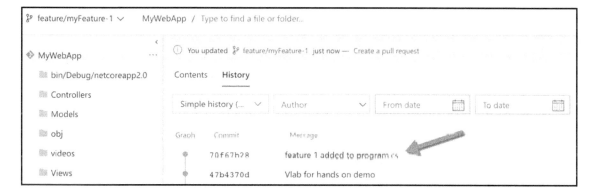

5. Create a new pull request (using the VSTS CLI) to review the changes in the `feature-1` branch:

```
> vsts code pr create --title "Review Feature-1 before merging
to master" --work-items 38 39 `
                 -d "#Merge feature-1 to master" `
                 -s feature/myFeature-1 -t master -r myWebApp -p
$prj -i $i
```

Use the `--open` switch when raising the pull request to open the pull request in a web browser after it has been created. The `--delete-source-branch` switch can be used to delete the branch after the pull request is complete. Also, consider using `--auto-complete` to complete automatically when all policies have passed and the source branch can be merged into the target branch.

The team jointly reviews the code changes and approves the pull request:

The master is ready to release, team tags master branch with the release number:

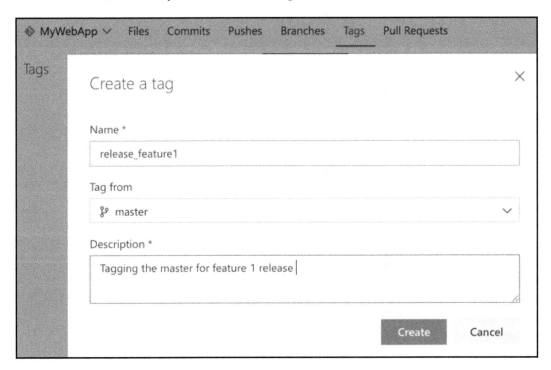

6. Start work on Feature 2. Create a branch on remote from the master branch and do the checkout locally:

```
myWebApp> git push origin origin:refs/heads/feature/myFeature-2

Total 0 (delta 0), reused 0 (delta 0)
To http://azsu-p-Azure DevOps Server2018/Azure DevOps
Server/DefaultCollection/PartsUnlimited/_git/MyWebApp
 * [new branch] origin/HEAD -> refs/heads/feature/myFeature-2

myWebApp> git checkout feature/myFeature-2

Switched to a new branch 'feature/myFeature-2'
Branch feature/myFeature-2 set up to track remote branch
feature/myFeature-2 from origin.
```

7. Modify Program.cs by changing the same line of code that was changed in feature-1:

```
public class Program
{
    // Editing the same line (file from feature-2 branch)
    public static void Main(string[] args)
    {
        BuildWebHost(args).Run();
    }

    public static IWebHost BuildWebHost(string[] args) =>
        WebHost.CreateDefaultBuilder(args)
            .UseStartup<Startup>()
            .Build();
```

8. Commit the changes locally, push them to the remote repository, and then raise a pull request to merge the changes from feature/myFeature-2 to the master branch:

```
> vsts code pr create --title "Review Feature-2 before merging
to master" --work-items 40 42 `
            d "#Merge feature-2 to master" `
            -s feature/myFeature-2 -t master -r myWebApp -p
$prj -i $i
```

With the pull request in flight, a critical bug is reported in production against the `feature-1` release. In order to investigate the issue, you need to debug against the version of code that's currently being deployed in production. To investigate this issue, create a new `fof` branch using the `release_feature1` tag:

```
myWebApp> git checkout -b fof/bug-1 release_feature1

Switched to a new branch 'fof/bug-1'
```

9. Modify `Program.cs` by changing the same line of code that was changed in the `feature-1` release:

```
// Editing this file from [feature-fof branch]
public static void Main(string[] args)
{
    BuildWebHost(args).Run();
}

public static IWebHost BuildWebHost(string[] args) =>
    WebHost.CreateDefaultBuilder(args)
        .UseStartup<Startup>()
        .Build();
```

10. Stage and commit the changes locally, then push changes to the remote repository:

```
myWebApp> git add .
myWebApp> git commit -m "Adding FOF changes"
myWebApp> git push -u origin fof/bug-1

To http://azsu-p-Azure DevOps Server2018/Azure DevOps
Server/DefaultCollection/PartsUnlimited/_git/MyWebApp
 * [new branch] fof/bug-1 -> fof/bug-1
Branch fof/bug-1 set up to track remote branch fof/bug-1 from
origin.
```

11. Immediately after the changes have been rolled out to production, tag the `fof\bug-1` branch with the `release_bug-1` tag, then raise a pull request to merge the changes from `fof/bug-1` back into the master:

```
> vsts code pr create --title "Review Bug-1 before merging to
master" --work-items 100 `
        -d "#Merge Bug-1 to master" `
        -s fof/Bug-1 -t master -r myWebApp -p $prj -i $i
```

As part of the pull request, the branch is deleted; however, you can still reference the full history to that point using the tag:

With the critical bug fix out of the way, let's go back to the review of the `feature-2` pull request. The **Branches** page makes it clear that the `feature/myFeature-2` branch is one change ahead of the master and two changes behind the master:

If you tried to approve the pull request, you'll see an error message informing you of a merge conflict:

12. The Git Pull Request Merge Conflict resolution extension makes it possible to resolve merge conflicts right in the browser. Navigate to the **Conflicts** tab and click on `Program.cs` to resolve the merge conflicts:

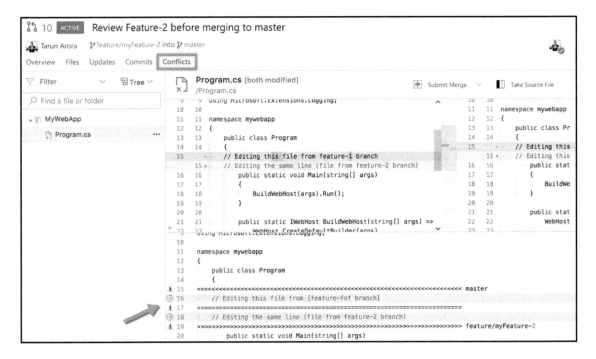

The user interface gives you the option to take the source version, target version, or add custom changes and review and submit the merge. With the changes merged, the pull request is completed.

How it works...

In this recipe, we learned how the Git branching model gives you the flexibility to work on features in parallel by creating a branch for each feature. The pull request workflow allows you to review code changes using the branch policies. Git tags are a great way to record milestones, such as the version of code that was released; tags give you a way to create branches from tags. We were able to create a branch from a previous release tag to fix a critical bug in production. The branches view in the web portal makes it easy to identify branches that are ahead of the master, and forces a merge conflict if any ongoing pull requests try to merge to the master without first resolving the merge conflicts. A lean branching model such as this allows you to create short-lived branches and push quality changes to production faster.

Configuring code search as a search engine

Search engines have become such an integral part of our life that we just expect to be able to search for everything. Noticing this, Microsoft has delivered an intelligent, integrated search experience that allows for semantic search across all your code repositories and projects in the team project collection. Code search is pre-installed as an extension in the Azure DevOps Server web portal. The search functionality is very intuitive; you can learn more about the advanced search capabilities on Microsoft docs: `https://docs.microsoft.com/en-us/vsts/search/code/advanced-search`. In this recipe, we'll learn how to configure code search as a search engine in Google Chrome.

Getting ready

While code search works natively in the web portal on all browsers, across devices and platforms, configuring code search as a search engine is only supported in Google Chrome. This recipe requires that you have Google Chrome installed on the machine where you intend to set up code search as the default search engine in the browser.

How to do it...

1. Open Google Chrome, navigate to **Settings**, and then click on **Manage search engines**:

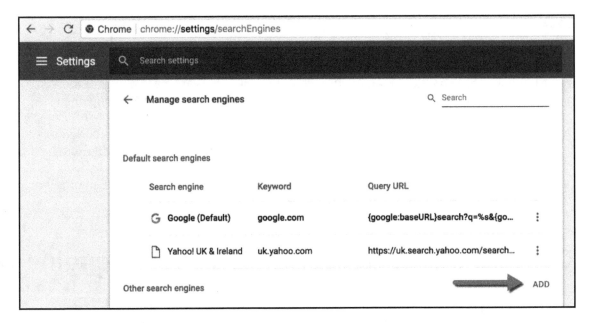

2. Click on **ADD** to add a new search engine and set the name as `Azure DevOps Server Code Search`, which is a keyword that will invoke the search engine and the code-search URL. The `%s` in the URL is replaced with the search keyword. The `Azure DevOps Serverc` keyword triggers this specific search engine:

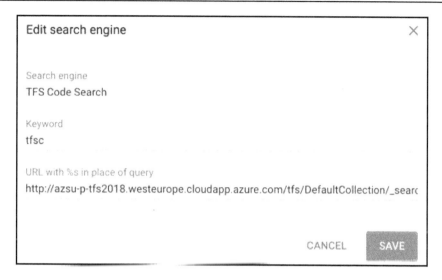

```
http://<Azure DevOps Server>/Azure DevOps
Server/<collection>/_search?type=Code&lp=apps-account&text=%s&_a=contents
```

How it works...

Open Google Chrome and type `Azure DevOps Server` (follow this with a space) in the search box to trigger the Azure DevOps Server Code Search engine. Follow this with the keyword you intend to search across the code base and hit *Enter*:

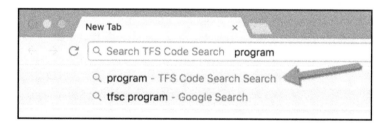

You'll see that the search keyword is replaced with the `%s` in the search engine URL we configured earlier in this recipe:

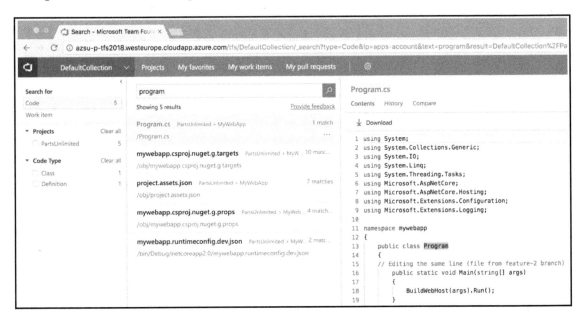

There's more...

Search in Azure DevOps Server allows you to search code semantically; for example, you can filter the search results to functions, classes, callers, and more. In addition, you can right-click on the search result to find the references and caller, see the file history, and compare it with previous versions:

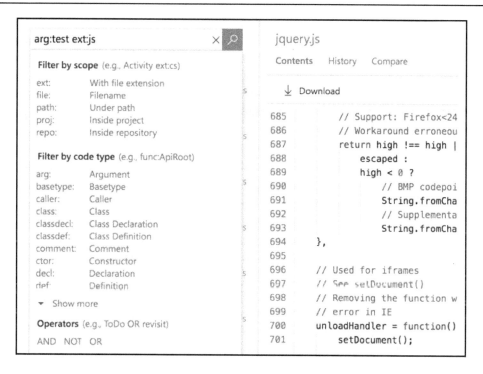

Using Git forks and sync changes with upstream PR

People fork repositories when they want to change the code in a repository they don't have write access to. Clearly, if you don't have write access, you really aren't part of the team contributing to that repository, so why would you want to modify the code repository? In our line of work, we tend to look for technical reasons to improve something.

You may find a better way of implementing the solution or may simply want to enhance the functionality by contributing to or improving an existing feature. Personally, I fork repositories in the following situations:

- I want to make a change.
- I think the project is interesting and may want to use it in the future.
- I want to use some or all of the code in that repository as a starting point for my own project.

Software teams are encouraged to contribute to all projects internally, not just their own software projects. Forks are a great way to foster a culture of inner open source. Forks are a recent addition to the Azure DevOps Server-hosted Git repositories. In this recipe, we'll learn how to fork an existing repository and contribute changes back upstream via a pull request.

Getting ready

A fork starts with all the contents of its upstream (original) repository. When you create a fork in the Azure DevOps Server, you can choose whether to include all branches or limit them to only the default branch. A fork doesn't copy the permissions, policies, or build definitions of the repository being forked. After a fork has been created, the newly created files, folders, and branches are not shared between the repositories unless you start a pull request. Pull requests are supported in either direction: from fork to upstream, or upstream to fork. The most common direction for a pull request will be from fork to upstream.

How to do it...

1. Choose the **Fork** button (1), then choose the project where you want the fork to be created (2). Give your fork a name and choose the **Fork** button (3):

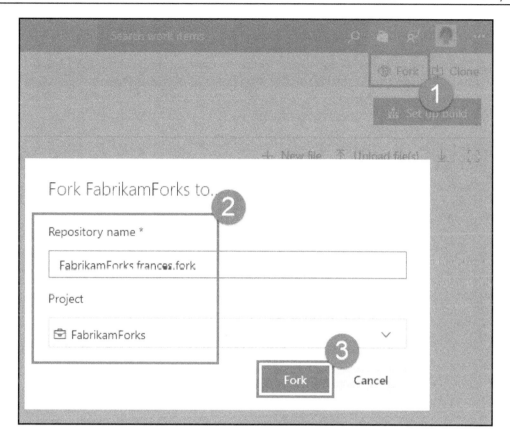

2. Once your fork is ready, clone it using the **command line** (https://docs.
   microsoft.com/en-us/vsts/git/tutorial/clone?tabs=command-line) or an
   IDE, such as **Visual Studio** (https://docs.microsoft.com/en-us/vsts/git/
   tutorial/clone). The fork will be your origin remote. For convenience, you'll
   want to add the upstream repository (where you forked from) as a remote
   named upstream. On the command line, type the following:

   ```
   git remote add upstream {upstream_url}
   ```

   It's possible to work directly in the master – after all, this fork is your personal
   copy of the repo. We recommend, you still work in a topic branch, though. This
   allows you to maintain multiple independent workstreams simultaneously. Also,
   it reduces confusion later when you want to sync changes into your fork.

3. Make and commit your changes as you normally would. When you're done with the changes, push them to origin (your fork).

4. Open a pull request from your fork to the upstream repository. All the policies, required reviewers, and builds will be applied in the upstream repo. Once all the policies are satisfied, the PR can be completed and the changes become a permanent part of the upstream repo:

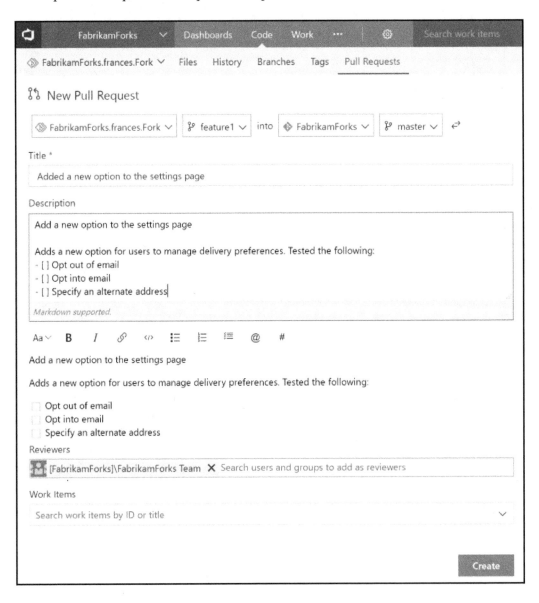

5. When your PR is accepted into upstream, you'll want to make sure your fork reflects the latest state of the repo. We recommend rebasing on the upstream's master branch (assuming that the master is the main development branch). On the command line, run the following:

```
git fetch upstream master
git rebase upstream/master
git push origin
```

How it works...

The forking workflow lets you isolate changes from the main repository until you're ready to integrate them. When you're ready, integrating code is as easy as completing a pull request.

3
Build and Release Agents

The build system in Azure DevOps Server known as Azure Pipelines is an open source, cross-platform, extensible, task-based execution system with a rich web interface that allows us to author, queue, and monitor builds. The new JSON-based build system was first introduced in TFS 2015, and it has since been rewritten for the .NET Core CLR as one code base in C#. The modern platform continues to evolve through the open source ecosystem, with new features and enhancements rolling out every other week. The build system is set to evolve further with the new multi-phase builds and a build-definition-as-code functionality that was introduced through YAML-based builds in Azure DevOps. These features have been recently introduced into Azure DevOps Server with the update 1 of Azure DevOps server 2019. In the following screenshot you can see the evolution of the build system over the last 10 years:

Generation	Name	Configuration	Introduced in
Generation 1	MS Build	XML	TFS 2005
Generation 2	XAML Build	WWF	TFS 2010
Generation 3	TFBuild	JSON	TFS 2015

The build system allows you to install multiple agents on a host. An agent can be registered to an agent pool. An **agent pool** can be mapped out to a queue which can be scoped to a project. The following diagram illustrates the architecture of the new build system:

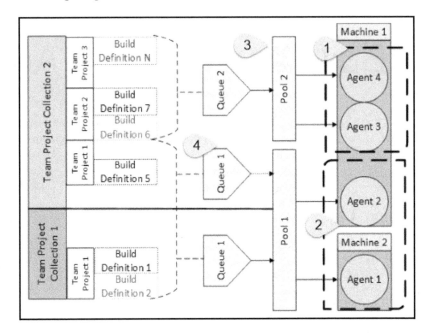

Let's review the diagram:

- Multiple agents can be configured on one machine
- Agents from across different machines or multiple agents on the same machine can be grouped into a pool. This allows you to host more than 1 instance of the agent on a host, helping you maximize the utilization of a server.
- Each pool can have only one queue, which is mapped to a project.

We'll cover some great features for configuring and automating the build system setup that will help you scale your build system efficiently.

In this chapter, we will cover the following recipes:

- Unattended configuration of build agents using PowerShell
- Downloading agents using the GitHub release API
- Configuring deployment groups
- Configuring the agent to use a proxy
- Analyzing build usage data
- Automating agent pool maintenance
- Configuring build and release retention policies
- Agent capabilities and build demands for special builds
- Managing agent permissions using role-based access

Unattended configuration of build agents using PowerShell

Azure DevOps Server Build and Release agents are the engines of your build system; the size of the infrastructure translates to the speed at which you can run and scale the build process. As you ramp up the use of the build system to automate Continuous Integration pipelines, you are going to need more agents. An automated process to add and remove build agents allows you to scale up and scale down the agents on demand. The build system has native support for unattended installation. In this recipe, we'll learn how to configure a build agent programmatically in an unattended mode using PowerShell.

Getting ready

To configure a build agent, you should be a member of the build administrators group and an administrator on the target machine. If the target machine is Windows 10 or beyond (x64), all the prerequisites will already be in place. If the target machine is Windows 7 to Windows 8.1, or Windows Server 2008 R2 SP1 to Windows Server 2012 R2 (64-bit), you will need to ensure that PowerShell version 3 or newer is available on the target system. Even though not technically required by the agent, many build scenarios require that Visual Studio be installed to get all the tools. It is recommended that you use Visual Studio 2015 or later.

Microsoft has open sourced its build system on GitHub under the `Microsoft/azure-pipelines-agent` project name. You can download the latest version of the agent directly from the GitHub repository (`https://github.com/Microsoft/azure-pipelines-agent`) or from the **Agent Pools** page under the collection administration page in the team portal:

How to do it...

1. Launch PowerShell in elevated mode and execute the following command:

```
> mkdir tfs_a1 && cd tfs_a1

tfs_a1> Add-Type -AssemblyName System.IO.Compression.FileSystem
;
[System.IO.Compression.ZipFile]::ExtractToDirectory("$HOME\Down
loads\vsts-agent-win-x64-2.129.0.zip", "$PWD")
```

 In the preceding command, replace the version of the agent (`vsts-agent-win-x64-2.129.0.zip`) with the version you intend to configure.

2. Configure the agent to run as a Windows service:

```
tfs_a1> .\config.cmd --unattended `
>> --url http://tfs2018.westeurope.cloudapp.azure.com/tfs `
>> --auth pat --token xxxxxxxx `
>> --pool default --agent tfs_a1 `
>> --runAsService --windowsLogonAccount contoso\zz_tfs-build --
windowsLogonPassword xxxxx

>> Connect:
```

```
Connecting to server ...

>> Register Agent:

Scanning for tool capabilities.
Connecting to the server.
Successfully added the agent
Testing agent connection.
2018-02-15 11:05:52Z: Settings Saved.
```

How it works...

In the preceding command, we are simply creating a new directory and then instructing the ZIP file to be extracted in this new directory:

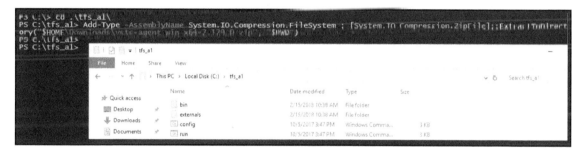

To configure the agent in unattended mode, all the configuration for the installation needs to be specified through the command-line switches. In the `--unattended` command, we are simply passing the details of the Azure DevOps server's URL, the type of authentication to use, and the pool the agent needs to be configured into. When selecting the authentication type as PAT, you'll need to pass the PAT account that will be used by the agent to authenticate with TFS. In addition, you have the option of running the agent as a Windows service under a Windows domain account, which is what we are passing through in the `--runAsService`, `--windowsLogonAccount`, and `--windowsLogonPassword` switches.

 In order to use basic authentication while configuring the agent, you need to have a secure connection (SSL) with the TFS server. If you don't have a secure connection, the preceding command will fail with an error message: **Basic authentication requires a secure connection to the server.**

If you do not have SSL configured for your TFS server, you can configure the agent using integrated authentication. Once the command has been successfully executed, you'll see the agent show up in the Agent Pools page, as shown in the following screenshot:

```
tfs_a1> .\config.cmd --unattended `
>> --url http://tfs2018.westeurope.cloudapp.azure.com/tfs `
>> --auth integrated `
>> --pool default `
>> --agent tfs_a1
```

Downloading agents using the GitHub release API

In a big move to embrace open source, Microsoft transitioned a lot of its key projects to GitHub. By developing products in an open source and contributing back to the open source communities, Microsoft is starting to change its negative public perception. This has resulted in some very surprising partnerships and an overall growth story for Microsoft, which is reflected in its stock price going up significantly over the last couple of years.

The `azure-pipelines-agent` and `azure-pipelines-tasks` projects are also hosted on GitHub. *How does this benefit you?* You can see all of the product's code, see the quality and architecture of the patterns used, have visibility of the product roadmap, contribute to the product's development, and engage with the product team by raising feedback and issues through GitHub. Both experimental and long-term supported versions of the agents are released on GitHub. Based on the pace at which the product is evolving, it is likely that the agent version you are running today will be superseded by a newer version tomorrow with more desirable features. Luckily, the GitHub release API supports programmatic invocation, so you never have to manually check for updates.

In this recipe, we'll learn how to use PowerShell to query the GitHub release API for the latest version of the agent. Upon finding a long-term supported version of the agent, how to download the agent in a designated folder path. You can optionally extend this solution to include the PowerShell script from the previous recipe to create an end-to-end automated process for downloading, unpacking, and installing agents programmatically using PowerShell scripting.

Getting ready

The release API for GitHub is well-documented at `https://developer.github.com/v3/repos/releases/`. The API supports various functions, including the ability to get all releases for a repository, get a specific release, get a release by tag name, and most importantly, to get the latest release. In this recipe, we'll be using the get latest release functionality:

```
https://api.github.com/repos/Microsoft/azure-pipelines-agent/releases/latest
```

If you invoke this URL in a browser, you'll get a JSON response that includes most of the properties we'll be leveraging in our PowerShell script. The body of the response also includes the `https://vstsagentpackage.azureedge.net/agent` URL. A download URL can be dynamically generated for the platform of your choice using the version of the release derived using `tag_name`:

How to do it...

1. Launch PowerShell, and then use the `Invoke-RestMethod` cmdlet to call the GitHub release API to get the latest release of the agent:

```
# Get the latest release of the agent from the GitHub API
$latestRelease = Invoke-RestMethod
                 -Uri
"https://api.github.com/repos/Microsoft/azure-pipelines-agent/r
eleases/latest"
Value of "tag_name" : "v2.129.0"
```

2. The `tag_name` property shows the name of the tag. By simply removing the first character, you'll get the version number of the agent:

```
$v = $latestRelease.name.Substring(1,
$latestRelease.tag_name.Length-1)
Value of $v : "2.129.0"
```

3. Dynamically construct the URL needed to download the agent. As you can see in the command below the string is being concatenated to create the download URL of the agent for the Windows platform:

```
$latestReleaseDownloadUrl =
"https://vstsagentpackage.azureedge.net/agent/" `
+ $v + "/vsts-agent-win-x64-" + $v + ".zip"

Value of $latestReleaseDownloadUrl =
https://vstsagentpackage.azureedge.net/agent/2.129.0/vsts-agent
-win-x64-2.129.0.zip
```

4. Create a new temporary folder; if it doesn't exist, force the creation of the temporary directory:

```
$agentTempFolderName = Join-Path
$env:temp([System.IO.Path]::GetRandomFileName())

If(!(test-path $agentTempFolderName))
{
    New-Item -ItemType Directory -Force -Path
$agentTempFolderName
}
```

5. Call the `Invoke-WebRequest` cmdlet with the agent-download URL to download the agent into the newly created temporary directory:

```
# Download the agent to the temp directory
Invoke-WebRequest -Uri $latestReleaseDownloadUrl -Method Get `
-OutFile "$agentTempFolderName\agent.zip"
```

6. The `agent` will be downloaded into the newly created temporary folder:

How it works...

Bringing it all together, in this section we'll look at the complete script and how it works. The script is wrapped up in a try catch block for error handling, and a retry procedure has been added for resilience. In the following script, the `Invoke-RestMethod` cmdlet is used to get the latest version of the agent from GitHub. The result is then consumed to generate a download installer for the Windows-based agent. The agent is downloaded to a temporary folder and the script checks whether the temporary folder is already in place; if not, it creates the temporary folder before using the `Invoke-WebRequest` cmdlet to download the agent to the temporary folder:

```
$retryCount = 3
$retries = 1
$agentTempFolderName = Join-Path
$env:temp([System.IO.Path]::GetRandomFileName())
Write-Verbose "Downloading Agent install files" -verbose
do
{
    try
    {
        Write-Verbose "Trying to get download URL for latest agent
release..."
        # Get the latest release of the agent from the GitHub API
        $latestRelease = Invoke-RestMethod -Uri `
"https://api.github.com/repos/Microsoft/vsts-agent/releases/latest"
        # Format the name to create a download URL for windows
        $v = $latestRelease.name.Substring(1, $latestRelease.name.Length-1)
        $latestReleaseDownloadUrl =
```

```
"https://vstsagentpackage.azureedge.net/agent/" `
                                   + $v + "/vsts-agent-win-x64-" + $v
+ ".zip"

        # Validate that the temp directory exists or create it
         If(!(test-path $agentTempFolderName)){
             New-Item -ItemType Directory -Force -Path
$agentTempFolderName
        }
        # Download the agent to the temp directory
        Invoke-WebRequest -Uri $latestReleaseDownloadUrl `
                               -Method Get -OutFile
"$agentTempFolderName\agent.zip"
        Write-Verbose "Download agent successfully on attempt $retries" -
Verbose
        break
    }
    catch
    {
        $exceptionText = ($_ | Out-String).Trim()
        Write-Verbose "Exception occurred downloading agent: `
                            $exceptionText in try number $retried" -
Verbose
        $retries++
        Start-Sleep -Seconds 30
    }
}
while ($retries -le $retryCount)
```

In case there is an exception, the exception is caught and there is logic to retry the download. A total of 3 retries are attempted at an interval of 30 seconds before exiting the script.

Configuring deployment groups

An application environment is composed of multiple servers in different roles, such as web, application, and database. Scaled out versions of these environments could have multiple servers front-ended by load balancers and availability groups. While agents in agent pools give you a way to deploy your application, you are responsible for bringing together the agents in the agent pool to deploy to your environment.

In this model, you are responsible for managing the complexity of how the deployment impacts the environment, such as orchestrating the rotation of the web servers as they are being upgraded. In this model, it's hard to answer simple questions such as the version of the release deployed on a machine. Microsoft has significantly enhanced the machine groups feature that it first introduced in TFS 2015 and rebranded as deployment groups.

Simply put, deployment groups are a collection of agents collectively representing an application environment, such as Dev, UAT, Pre-Prod, or Production. Each machine in the deployment group has an agent; metadata can be associated with the agent by adding tags. The deployment group can then be queried for this tag to return a list of agents that match the tags. This makes deploying to a multi-server web tier very easy. As the framework is aware of all the agents with the `WebServer` tag, you can specify a deployment rule to roll out the deployment on a small subset of web servers and stop in case of any failures. All the native agent capabilities are still available to you – for example, you can view live logs for each server as a deployment takes place, and download logs for all servers to track your deployments to individual machines. The deployment group records the version of the release that was deployed in an environment and on the individual servers in the deployment group as well. Deployment groups also provide a security context, so you can add users and give them appropriate permissions to administer, manage, view, and use the group.

 The host machine can have one or more agents deployed on it, and each agent can be associated with a different deployment group. This gives you the ability to use shared environments exclusively through their own deployment groups.

Deployment groups are not visible to build pipelines; they are only meant to be used in release pipelines. While we'll be covering how to use deployment groups in `Chapter 7`, *Azure Artifacts and Dependency Management,* we'll learn how to configure the Azure DevOps agent into a deployment group.

Getting ready

To create a deployment group, you need to be a member of the build administrator and release administrator group; membership to the project-collection administrator group also gives you permission to perform this action across multiple team projects in a collection.

How to do it...

In this section we'll cover the steps to setup an agent into a deployment group:

1. Navigate to the build and release hub in the PartsUnlimited team project portal. Click on **Deployment Groups** and add a new deployment group, `ps-test-01`:

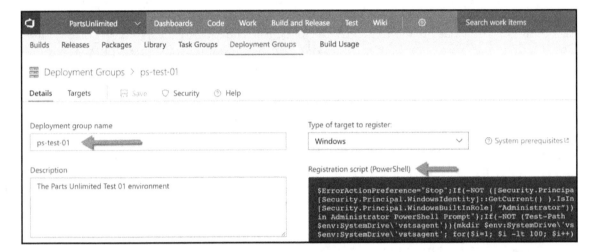

2. Copy the PowerShell script, then navigate to the target machine you intend to add to this deployment group. Run PowerShell in elevated mode and execute the script. The script downloads the agent and configures the agent as a deployment group. Run this script on other machines you intend to join this deployment group:

3. Flip over to the **Targets** tab for the `ps-test-01` deployment group in the PartsUnlimited team portal. This will show you the list of all the target machines joined into this deployment group:

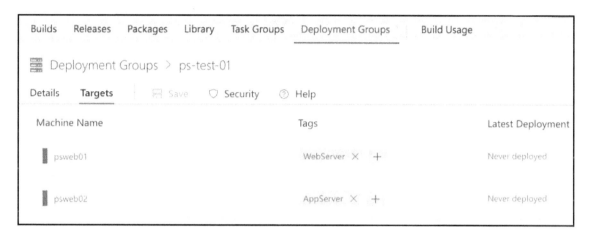

How it works...

Let's look at the deployment-group-registration script in more detail. The error preference for this script is set to stop, implying the script will stop execution on the first failure:

```
$ErrorActionPreference="Stop";
```

Validate that the user executing the script is part of the administrator role on the host machine:

```
If(-NOT
([Security.Principal.WindowsPrincipal][Security.Principal.WindowsIdentity]:
:GetCurrent() ).IsInRole( [Security.Principal.WindowsBuiltInRole]
"Administrator"))
{ throw "Run command in Administrator PowerShell Prompt"};
```

Validate that the `vstsagent` folder exists in the `System` directory on the host machine. If not, create a new directory for `vstsagent` and navigate to that directory. If an agent already exists in the directory, create a new `agent` folder with a different name:

```
If(-NOT (Test-Path $env:SystemDrive\'vstsagent'))
{mkdir $env:SystemDrive\'vstsagent'};
cd $env:SystemDrive\'vstsagent';
```

```
for($i=1; $i -lt 100; $i++){$destFolder="A"+$i.ToString();
if(-NOT (Test-Path ($destFolder))){mkdir $destFolder;cd
$destFolder;break;}};
```

Download `agent.zip` and unzip it into the newly created `agent` folder:

```
$agentZip="$PWD\agent.zip";
(New-Object Net.WebClient).DownloadFile(
'https://go.microsoft.com/fwlink/?linkid=858950', $agentZip);
Add-Type -AssemblyName
System.IO.Compression.FileSystem;[System.IO.Compression.ZipFile]::ExtractTo
Directory( $agentZip, "$PWD");
```

Configure the agent as a deployment group, use the host machine name to name the agent, and configure the agent to run as a Windows service. Join the agent in the `ps-test-01` deployment group in the `PartsUnlimited` team project:

```
.\config.cmd --deploymentgroup --agent $env:COMPUTERNAME --runasservice --
work '_work' --url 'http://tfs2018.westeurope.cloudapp.azure.com/tfs/' --
collectionname 'DefaultCollection' --projectname 'PartsUnlimited' --
deploymentgroupname "ps-test-01" --auth Integrated;
Remove-Item $agentZip;
```

Remove the agent installer file from the `agent` directory:

```
Remove-Item $agentZip;
```

You can use the `--unattended` switch we saw in the *Unattended configuration of build agents using PowerShell* recipe to configure the deployment group in unattended mode. This is useful if you want to push the configuration of deployment groups remotely on target machines.

Configuring the agent to use a proxy

Enterprises that host their infrastructure on-premise or in a hybrid cloud setup tend to use a multi-level security approach. This usually involves one or more firewalls that protect the infrastructure from external traffic, and a web proxy to control the intranet and internet traffic. In such a scaled setup, traffic generated from the agent may be blocked from connecting to the Azure DevOps server if it is not routed through the proxy. Luckily, the Azure DevOps agent infrastructure supports proxy configuration natively. In this recipe, we'll learn how to configure a web proxy during agent configuration.

Getting ready

Ensure you've downloaded the latest version of the agent locally on the target machine where you intend to install and configure the agent. You'll need to be part of the build administrators group in Azure DevOps Server to be able to connect the agent as well as an administrator on the target machine to be able to install the agent. The TFS agent is programmed to pick up the proxy settings configured in the `.proxy` file in the `agent` folder. Therefore, for the agent to pick up the proxy settings, you will need to create a `.proxy` file in the agent install folder ahead of configuring the agent.

How to do it...

1. Navigate to the location where the agent has been downloaded and unzipped:

   ```
   > cd c:\tfs_a1
   tfs_a1>
   ```

2. Create a `.proxy` file with the proxy URL:

   ```
   echo http://theProxyServer:443 > .proxy
   ```

 The preceding configuration is sufficient if the proxy doesn't require authentication. This is usually the case if you are using a Windows domain account to run the agent. However, if you are running the agent under the default network credential or the user running the agent is required to authenticate with a proxy, you'll need to perform the following additional steps.

3. Provide the proxy credentials to TFS using environment variables. TFS treats these credentials as secrets and then masks the values before passing them into the job output:

   ```
   set VSTS_HTTP_PROXY_USERNAME=myProxyUser
   set VSTS_HTTP_PROXY_PASSWORD=myProxyPassword
   ```

How it works...

With the proxy configured in the `root` folder of the build agent, you can use `config.cmd`, as demonstrated in the recipe Unattended configuration of build agents using PowerShell, to configure the agent. The agent automatically picks up the proxy configuration; if the proxy configuration requires authentication, the agent uses the `VSTS_HTTP_PROXY_USERNAME` and `VSTS_HTTP_PROXY_PASSWORD` environment variables to authenticate with the proxy. Any build jobs that you run thereafter will print the proxy URL being used by the agent in the build output.

Analyzing build usage data

Wouldn't it be great if you could get insights into how the build system is being used? For example, which projects are using builds more than others, which definitions are consuming most build time, and top build users. After all, data is the new currency, and you should feel empowered to make empirical data-driven decisions. This is especially useful if you plan to evolve the build pools and queues with empirical usage data trends. In this recipe, we'll learn how to get insights into the usage of the build system using an open source extension available in the marketplace.

Getting ready

The marketplace features the **Build Usage** extension (`https://marketplace.visualstudio.com/items?itemName=ms-devlabs.BuildandTestUsage`). This open source extension, released by the Microsoft DevLabs team, provides insights into the build infrastructure usage at different granularities. Install this extension in the project collection you plan to analyze the data for.

How to do it...

1. Navigate to the collection administration page and open the **Build Usage** page. **All Team Projects** gives you a headline of the total build usage across the collection. You can drill into the specific team projects to see the build usage by users, definitions, and agent pools. The data can be filtered to this month, last month, the last six months, or a custom period:

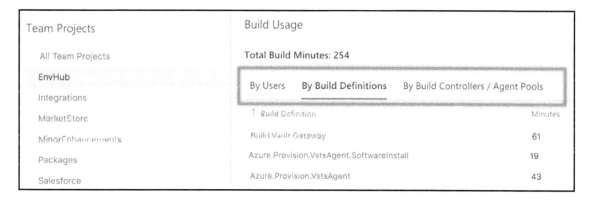

2. Click the **Export** button to export the results into a CSV file, which you can then use for further analysis offline. In addition, the extension also includes a dashboard widget.

How it works...

The extension is open source; you can take a look at the extension's code implementation on GitHub at: `https://github.com/ALM-Rangers/build-usage-widget-extension/blob/master/vsts-buildusage/src/build.ts`. The extension uses the build REST API to get a list of all the build definitions across the collection and then all builds recorded against those definitions. It then processes this data by aggregating the properties to show a view of usage by projects, definition, user, and agent pool:

```
public getBuildExecutions(projectId: string, startDate: Date, finishDate: Date, successCallback, errorCallback): void {
    let builds = this.getBuilds(projectId, startDate, finishDate);

    builds.then(
        (builds) => {
            let totalTime: number = 0;
            let buildDataSource = new Array<BuildDetails>();

            for (let i = 0; i < builds.length; i++) {
                let build: Tfs_Build_Contracts.Build = builds[i];
                let buildDefinition: string = build.definition.name;
                let buildController: string = (build.controller == null ? build.queue.pool.name : build.controller.name);
                let minutes: number = (build.finishTime.valueOf() - build.startTime.valueOf()) / 1000 / 60;
                totalTime += minutes;

                buildDataSource.push(new BuildDetails(build.requestedFor.displayName, minutes, buildDefinition, buildContro
            }
            successCallback({ totalTime: totalTime, buildDataSource: buildDataSource });
        },
        (error) => {
            errorCallback(error);
        }
    );
}
```

See also

The Azure DevOps marketplace also features the *Export as PDF* extension (`https://marketplace.visualstudio.com/items?itemName=onlyutkarsh.ExportAsPDF`). This free extension, created by Utkarsh Shigihalli, allows you to export the build definition steps, triggers, history, and so on in a neat report so that you can print or share it with colleagues. The extension is especially useful if you intend to document the build setup for training or knowledge-transfer purposes:

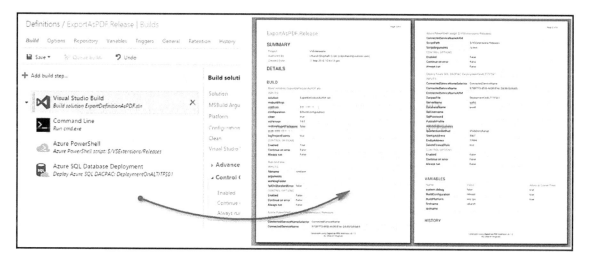

Automating agent pool maintenance

Each build and release pipeline creates a directory under the agent working directory to store the source code, artifacts, and test results. Some builds consume more space than others; as projects evolve, some builds are used more than others. As you may have guessed, this results in agent maintenance activity to clear out the agent work directory. While you wouldn't want to remove everything from the directory, you would certainly be looking to remove some of the less-used build folders. Luckily, the agent comes with out-of-the-box support for pool maintenance. In this recipe, we'll learn how to configure the agent-pool maintenance schedule to automatically free up storage from the agent work directory by removing unused build folders.

Getting ready

To configure the agent pool maintenance, you need to be part of the build collection administrator group or in the administrator role for the specific agent pool.

How to do it...

In this section we'll look at the steps needed to configure the automated maintenance of the agent pool:

1. Navigate to the collection administration page and open the agent pools page.
2. Select the default agent pool or any other agent pool and click settings to configure the maintenance schedule. Set the schedule to run every day and remove all build and release agent directories that haven't been used in the last **5** days:

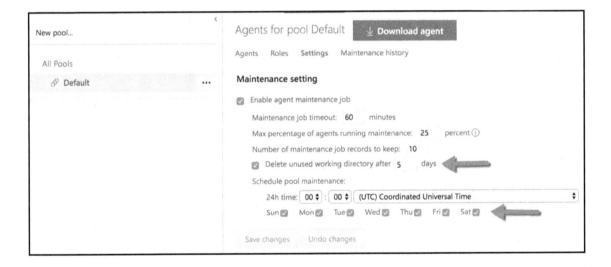

How it works...

To trigger the maintenance schedule in an ad hoc manner, right click the agent pool, from the context menu select queue agent maintenance. When you trigger agent pool maintenance, this queues a new build job, the results of which are published in the build **Maintenance history**. As per the settings configured, the job only takes the specified percentage of agents out for maintenance, so the pool can still be used for builds and releases:

Since `azure-pipeline-agent` is open source on GitHub, you can see the code of the product. The `RunMaintenanceOperation` function in the `BuildDirectoryManager` class (`https://github.com/Microsoft/azure-pipeline-agent/blob/f9e5bb7337fb51ace995cafeeaa8665cad638a84/src/Agent.Worker/Build/BuildDirectoryManager.cs`) goes through each of the build and release directories under the agent work directory to identify when it was last used. If it meets the criteria, it's marked for garbage collection. All folders marked for garbage collection are deleted, and the overall storage space is reported at the end of the job's execution. If you download the agent maintenance logs, you will see this reflected in the maintenance log:

```
##[section]Starting: Maintenance
Current agent version: '2.117.1'
Agent is running behind proxy server: 'http://proxy-azsu.com:8080'
##[section]Starting: Initialize Job
Download all required tasks.
##[section]Finishing: Initialize Job
##[section]Starting: Maintenance
##[section]Start maintenance: Delete unused build directories
Discover stale build directories that haven't been used for more than 5 days.
Directory expiration limit: 5 days.
Current UTC: 2018-02-17T12:14:05.0198621Z
Evaluate BuildDirectory tracking file: C:\AZSU-D-DTL1-007_A1\_work\SourceRootMapping\3c8ed95b-7485-43dd-b028-0d646c24fb87\1\SourceFolder.json
The last time build directory 'C:\AZSU-D-DTL1-007_A1\_work\33' been used is: 08/11/2017 11:51:35 +01:00
Mark tracking file 'C:\AZSU-D-DTL1-007_A1\_work\SourceRootMapping\3c8ed95b-7485-43dd-b028-0d646c24fb87\1\SourceFolder.json' for GC, since it hasn't been used for 5 days.
Evaluate BuildDirectory tracking file: C:\AZSU-D-DTL1-007_A1\_work\SourceRootMapping\3c8ed95b-7485-43dd-b028-0d646c24fb87\102\SourceFolder.json
```

There's more...

To help you keep the agents updated with the latest product version, Azure DevOps Server offers you the ability to upgrade within the **Agent Pools** page directly, without having to go through the process of removing and reconfiguring agents. To do this, you need to be part of the collection build administrator group or in the administrator role for the agent pool you intend to perform this operation on. From the pool context menu, simply select **Update All Agents**. This will temporarily take the agents in the pool out, download the latest version of the agent, and upgrade in-situ:

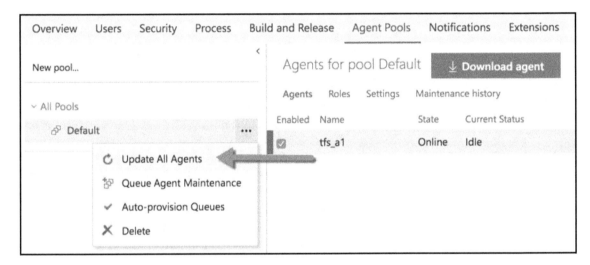

Configuring build and release retention policies

In the *Automating agent pool maintenance* recipe, we learned how to configure maintenance schedules on the agent machines. While that helps free up space on the agent machine, there is maintenance activity required on the Azure DevOps Server to free up space by removing unwanted builds and releases. An average build artifact, test results, and associated metadata is in the range of 50 MB.

If the build is run 20 times a day for 30 days, this will generate about 29 GB worth of assets! While Azure DevOps Server does a great job in compressing and storing this data in blob storage, it is best to offload what you don't need. In this recipe, we'll learn how to configure a retention policy for both builds and releases at the collection level to automatically remove builds and releases that match this criteria. We'll also learn how to overwrite the default retention policy for a specific build or release definition.

Getting ready

To administer build resources for the collection, you need to be a member of the Project Collection Build Administrators group.

How to do it...

1. Navigate to the collection administration page and open the **Build and Release** page
2. Keep the **Minimum Retention Policy** as is, and change the default configuration for the maximum retention to 15 days and the minimum to keep to 5
3. Change the days to keep the build record after deletion to 10

The retention policy applies to all builds in a Team Project Collection. There may, however, be a few builds that you would like to retain longer than the maximum retention enforced by the global policy. This can be achieved by marking a build or release for indefinite retention. Browse to the specific build that you would like to exclude from the retention policy, right-click the build, and set the **retain indefinitely** flag on the build. In the image below you can see the editable settings to configure the retention period.

Overview   Users   Security   Process   **Build and Release**   Agent Pools   Notifications   Extensions

Settings   Resource limits

Maximum Retention Policy

Days to keep:	15
Minimum to keep:	5
Delete build record:	true
Delete source label:	false
Delete file share:	true
Delete symbols:	true
Delete test results:	true
Branch filters:	All

Default Retention Policy

Days to keep:	10
Minimum to keep:	1
Delete build record:	true
Delete source label:	false
Delete file share:	true
Delete symbols:	true
Delete test results:	true
Branch filters:	All

Permanently Destroy Builds

Days to keep build record after deletion:	10

How it works...

TFS has a set of background jobs that are scheduled to run to manage various operations within TFS. You can access the TFS job monitoring page by browsing to `_oi/jobmonitoring page http://<tfsInstance>/tfs/_oi/_jobmonitoring`. The build and retention policy is also orchestrated as a job. Builds and releases that match these criteria, with the exception of those marked for indefinite retention, will be removed.

It is also possible to overwrite the global build and release policy at a build and release level, which can be done from the retention tab in a build or release definition. With the ability to apply branch filters, you can specify different retention schedules for different types of branches. For example, the topic branch builds can be removed more frequently compared to the master branch. You may want to remove the source label for topic branches, but not necessarily for the master branch:

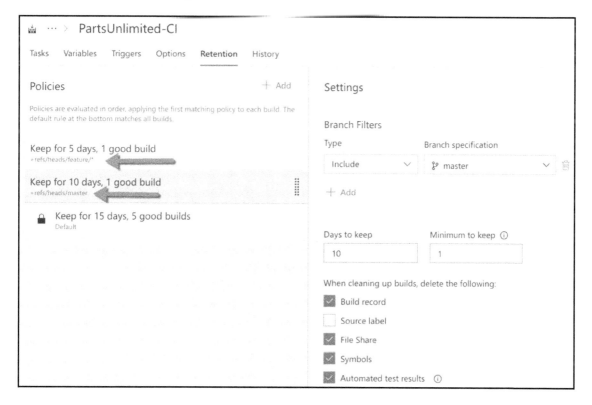

Agent capabilities and build demands for special builds

The build and test execution of an application depends on the specific version of the framework. For example, an application may have a component that depends on DotNetCore 1.0 and another component may depend on DotNetCore 2.0. The build system gives you the ability to define demands in a build definition and specify capabilities in the agent queues. This creates a build that you can route to an agent queue by simply mapping the demand to the capabilities. The framework leverages this capability internally; during the agent setup, the agent collects a list of software and frameworks installed on the host machine. These can be seen in the agent queue or **Agent pools** page under the **Capabilities** tab. In this recipe, we'll learn how to add custom capabilities in the agent queues and demand that in-build definitions target specific agent queues.

Getting ready

To configure the agent capabilities, you need to be part of the build administrator group or in the administrator role for the specific agent queue.

How to do it...

1. Navigate to the admin portal for the PartsUnlimited team project, select the **Agent queues** page, and click on the **Capabilities** tab. The page displays a list of system capabilities, which shows you a list of all the software and frameworks set up on the host machine. In **USER CAPABILITIES**, click to add a custom capability. This gives you a key-pair; specify the `dotnetcore` name in the key and the number 1 in the value, and then save the changes:

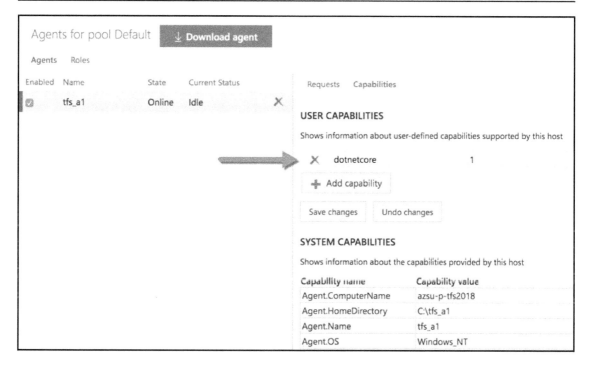

2. Navigate to the build hub in the PartsUnlimited team portal. Add a new build definition and choose an empty build template. In the **Options** tab, under the **Demands** section, add two demands: one that checks for the `dotnetcore` key and another that checks for the version:

How it works...

When you queue a new build, the build pipeline queries the system capabilities of the queue and determines whether there is an available agent in the queue that meets the build demands. If no agent is found, you will be notified via a warning message. If you queue the build regardless, it will fail at the configured timeout interval if no agent is found that meets the demands in the build definition. At build-queue-time, you have an option to add, remove, or overwrite the build demands:

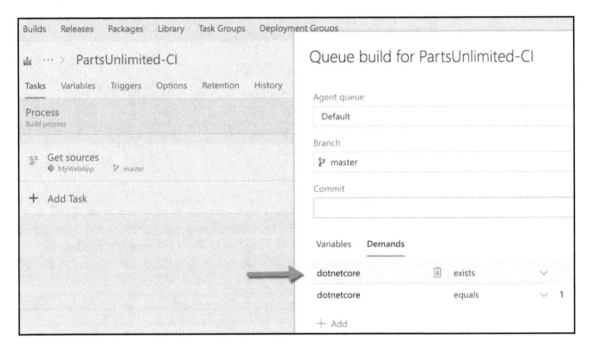

Managing agent permissions using role-based access

The build system provides *role-based access control* instead of exposing the underlying permissions directly. In this recipe, we'll learn how to permission build resources at the pool and the queue level.

Getting ready

To manage the all pools membership, you need to be a member of the Team Foundation Administrators Group. Membership to the Team Project Collection Administrator Group is required to manage the permissions for individual pools. In order to manage the permissions for the queues, you need to be a member of the Project Collection Build Administrators Group. Build Definition Administration requires membership to the Build Administrators Group.

How to do it...

1. Launch the collection administrator page and navigate to the **Agent pools** page. Click on all pools, then add the service account(s) that you intend to use in the agent pool **Service Account** role:

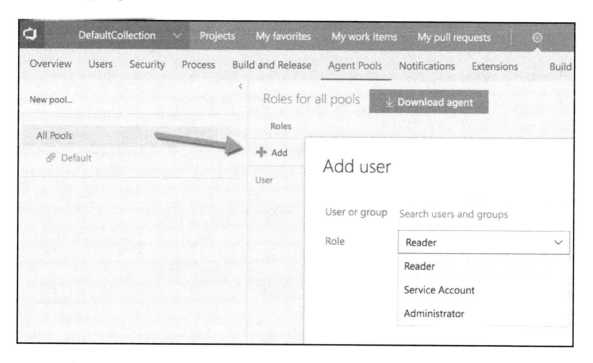

2. To add a user as a reader to a specific pool, click on the specific pool and add the user account or group to that specific pool:

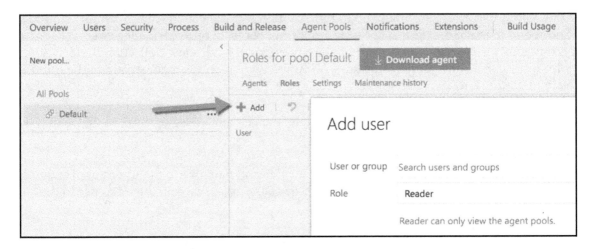

How it works...

As illustrated in the following diagram, the new build system contains a hierarchical role-based access-control model:

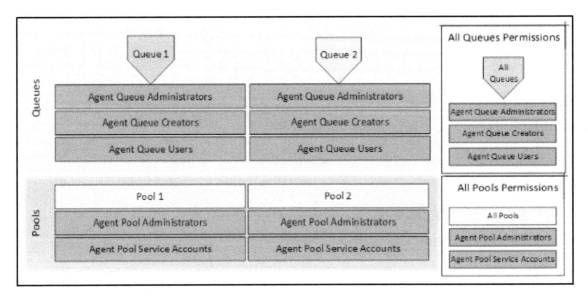

Let's look at each of the roles and the accesses they offer:

- **All queues**:
    - **Agent Queue Administrators**: Users in this role have the ability to manage all queues within the project collection.
    - **Agent Queue Creators**: Users in this role have the ability to create new queues. If there is no pool with the same name as the queue, one will be provisioned at queue-creation-time and the caller will be added as an administrator of both the queue and the corresponding pool. If a pool with the same name already exists, the caller must have the *Manage* permission (must be a pool administrator) on the pool to create a new queue that uses the pool.
    - **Agent Queue Users**: Users in this role have the ability to use all queues for the entire collection. This means that they can assign the queues to be used by definitions in the Build space.

- **Individual queues**:
    - **Agent Queue Administrators**: Same as the preceding role, but the permissions are restricted to the specific queue
    - **Agent Queue Users**: Same as the preceding role, but the permissions are restricted to the specific queue

- **All pools**:
    - **Agent Pool Administrators**: Users in this role have the ability to manage all pools within the entire account
    - **Agent Pool Service Accounts**: Users in this role have the ability to connect to the pool and receive messages regarding Build jobs, including control messages such as *update yourself* and *cancel this job*.

- **Individual pools**:
    - **Agent Pool Administrators**: Same as the preceding role, but the permissions are restricted to the specific pool
    - **Agent Pool Service Accounts**: Same as the preceding role, but the permissions are restricted to the specific pool

4
Continuous Integration and Build Automation

As a developer compiling code and running unit tests gives you assurance that your code changes haven't had an impact on the existing codebase. Integrating your code changes into the source control repository enables other to validate their changes with yours. As a best practice teams integrate into the shared repository several times a day to reduce the risk of introducing breaking changes or worst overwriting each other's.

 Continuous Integration (**CI**) is a development practice that requires developers to integrate code into a shared repository several times a day. Each check-in is verified by an automated build, allowing teams to detect problems early.

The Automated build running as part of the CI process is often referred to as the CI build. While there isn't a clear definition of what the CI build should do, at the very minimum it is expected to compile code and run unit tests. Running the CI build on a non-developer isolated workspace helps identify dependencies that may otherwise go unnoticed late into the release process. We can talk endlessly about the benefits of CI; the key here is that it enables you to have potentially deployable software at all times.

Deployable software is the most tangible asset to customers.

Moving from concept to application, in this chapter we'll learn how to leverage the build tooling in Azure DevOps Server to set up a quality focused Continuous Integration process.

In this chapter, we will cover the following recipes:

- Configuring one build definition for all branches of a Git repository
- Reflecting the branch quality in the build name
- Using web deploy to create a package in an ASP.NET build pipeline
- Organizing build output into separate folders
- Configuring assembly version info in build pipelines
- Setting up a build pipeline for a .NET core application
- Setting up a build pipeline for Node.js application
- Setting up a build pipeline for your database projects
- Integrating SonarQube in build pipelines to manage technical debt

Configuring one build definition for all branches of a Git repository

The Git branching model and pull request workflow makes it so easy to manage the flow of code that you will get accustomed to creating a topic branch for each new item of work. **Continuous Integration** is table stakes for any organization looking to move into a DevOps way of working. Associating a Continuous Integration flow with every new Git topic branch you create can be cumbersome, as you'll need to create a new build definition for each Git branch.

This becomes an operational nightmare if the topic branches are short-lived. In this recipe, we'll learn how to use one build definition to build all your Git branches in a team project.

Getting ready

You need to be a member of the build administrator group in the team project. The build administrator group gives you permissions to administer build resources. Members can manage test environments, create test runs, and manage builds.

Create the following Git branches in your team project:

- **master**: Mainline for production
- **develop**: Integration for all features
- **feature/myFeature-1**: Feature development branch

How to do it...

1. Navigate to the **Builds** and **Releases** hub in the parts unlimited team portal. From the **Builds** page, click **New** to create a new build definition.
2. Select the empty process to start with an empty build definition.
3. Name the build definition `partsunlimited.web`, choose the **Default** agent queue, and save the build definition, as shown in the following screenshot:

In the **Get sources** step, you'll see that the build is configured to use the MyWebApp Git repository and the master branch, which signifies that this build definition is linked to the master branch of the MyWebApp Git repository only. However, it is a little-known secret that this setting can be overridden.

4. Navigate to the **Triggers** tab in the build definition and enable the **Continuous Integration** trigger for this build definition, as shown in the following screenshot:

After enabling the **Continuous Integration** trigger, you can now see you have the option to configure the branches this **Continuous Integration** trigger is configured against.

5. In the branch specification, type * and hit *Enter*. Save the build definition:

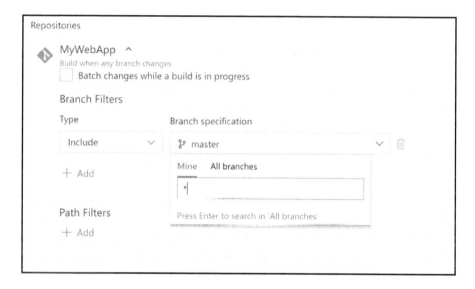

The branch specification drop-down menu does not have an option to select all; you'll need to type * in the branch selector search box and hit the *Enter* key immediately. If this does not work, disable and re-enable the **Continuous Integration** trigger, select the branch selector drop-down, type *, and press *Enter*. This will enforce this build to be configured for a **Continuous Integration** trigger for all Git branches of the Git repository.

While the build definition is defaulted to the master branch in the **Get sources** step, it will get the source from the branch the **Continuous Integration** is triggered from.

6. By changing the **Continuous Integration** filter to *, this build definition is now configured to work with all branches of the Git repository:

You can optionally add multiple branches using the **+ Add** link if you only intend to configure a build definition for multiple Git branches and not all of them.

How it works...

To better understand how this works, in this section we'll test the configuration and go through its implementation. Let's start by testing that the build definition is correctly configured to work against all branches in the MyWebApp Git repository. Navigate to the code hub, open the MyWebApp Git repository, and select the feature/myFeature-1 branch. Edit the Program.cs file by adding a comment. Commit the changes to trigger the CI build for this branch:

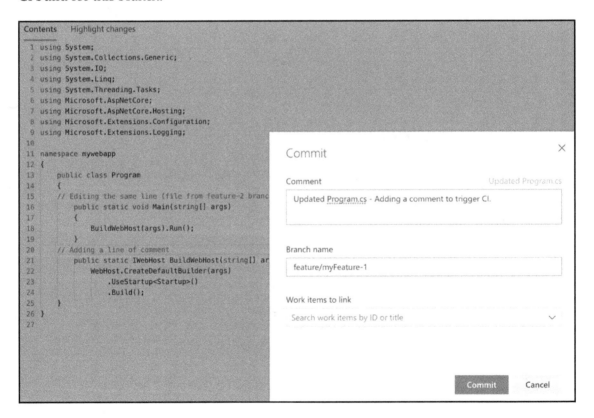

Navigate to the build hub and open the `partsunlimited.web` build definition. You'll notice that the CI build execution was triggered from the last commit for the `feature/myFeature-1` branch:

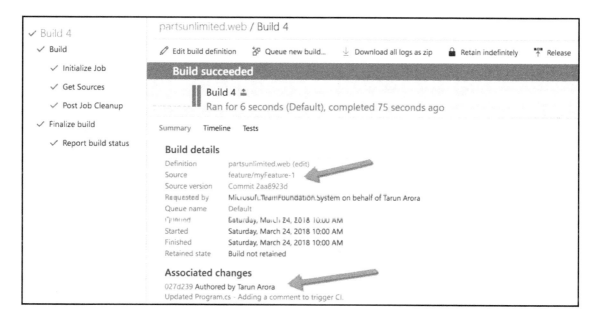

Repeat these steps for the develop and master branch now. You'll notice that the same build definition gets triggered and gets the sources from the correct branch by simply using the **Continuous Integration** trigger:

See also

This approach can be extended to link one build definition to a release definition to release multiple branches into an environment. By using release artifact filters, you can lock down the topic branches to dev test environments only.

Reflecting the branch quality in the build name

Most software changes evolve from an alpha release quality to a beta release quality before they are ready to be shipped. This is often reflected in how the code moves between Git branches. Builds coming out of a topic branch where the change is still being matured are mostly alpha quality, while a first cut of the develop branch (as the changes are being integrated) where you are still soliciting feedback may be classed as beta quality before it's moved up to master, from where you tend to do production quality releases. In this recipe, we'll learn how to use the name of the branch to flag the quality of the build by appending it to the build name.

Getting ready

This is an extension to the *Configuring one build definition for all branches of a git repository* recipe. If you haven't already, configure a build definition to trigger all branches for the `MyWebApp` Git repository.

How to do it...

1. Navigate to the build view in the parts unlimited team portal and edit the `partsunlimited.web` build definition.In the **Options** tab, change the **Build number format** to `0.1.$(DayOfYear)$(Rev:.r)`, as shown in the following screenshot:

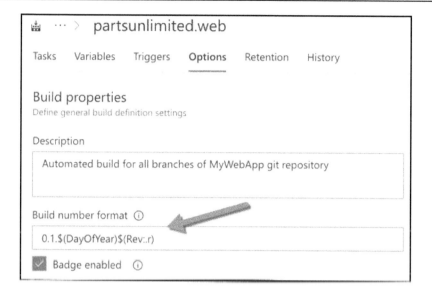

The build number provides various macros out of the box. More details on the predefined variables that can be used to construct the build number can be found here: `https://docs.microsoft.com/en-us/vsts/build-release/concepts/definitions/build/options?view=vsts#build-number-format`.

2. Click **+ Add Task** to add a new task to the build task list. Search for the **PowerShell** task and add it to the build pipeline, as shown in the following screenshot:

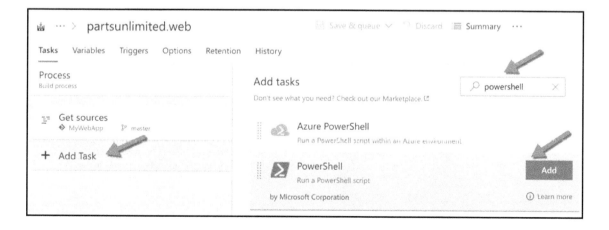

3. Click on the **PowerShell** task to configure it. Change the display name to `Add branch quality to build name`. Change the type of script to inline script and add the following code snippet into the task as inline script. Click **Save** to save the updates to the build definition:

```
write-host $env:BUILD_SOURCEBRANCHNAME
if ($env:BUILD_SOURCEBRANCHNAME -eq "Develop"){
    Write-Output ("##vso[build.updatebuildnumber]" +
$env:BUILD_BUILDNUMBER+"-beta")
    Write-host "setting version as -beta"
}
else{
    if($env:BUILD_SOURCEBRANCHNAME -ne "master"){
        Write-Output ("##vso[build.updatebuildnumber]" +
$env:BUILD_BUILDNUMBER+"-alpha")
        Write-Output "setting version as -alpha"
    }
}
```

4. To test the script, make changes to the `feature/myFeature-1`, `develop`, and `master` branches. This will trigger the build definition as it's associated with the CI build for all of these branches. In the following screenshot, you can see that the branch quality flag has been appended to the build number:

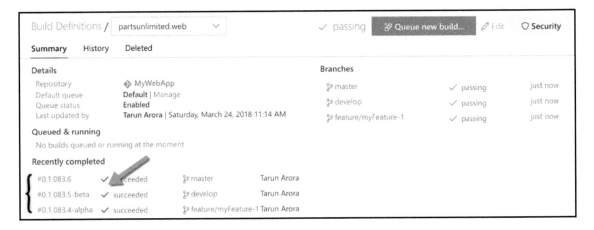

How it works...

Let's look at what the script is doing. The build exposes a number of predefined variables. This includes a combination of system variables used internally by the build system itself and helper variables that can be used to manage the build workflow. A list of all the predefined variables can be found here: `https://docs.microsoft.com/en-us/vsts/build-release/concepts/definitions/build/variables?view=vststabs=batch`.

The value of the `BUILD_SOURCEBRANCHNAME` build variable is read to identify if the source branch that triggered the build definition is `develop`. If so, the `BUILD_BUILDNUMBER` build variable is postfixed with `-beta`. For all other source branches (except master), the build number is updated as `-alpha`. However, in order to update the build variable, the build system uses the following format:

```
Write-Output "##vso[task.setvariable
variable=build.variablename;issecret=bool]new value"
```

The statement is a simplified implementation of this format to update the build variable that's used for the build number:

```
Write-Output ("##vso[build.updatebuildnumber]" + $env:BUILD_BUILDNUMBER+"-
alpha")
```

Using web deploy to create a package in an ASP.NET build pipeline

The build system in Azure DevOps Server ships a set of pre-canned build templates with all the necessary build tasks and configuration to help you get off the ground without having to learn how the build system works. If you are creating an application that uses the web project type in Visual Studio, then you'll be delighted to know that there is a build template you can apply to set up a build pipeline for your web application. In this recipe, we'll use the ASP.NET build template to create a build pipeline. In addition to building and testing the web app, this pipeline also creates a web deploy package that can be used to deploy to any web server, including Azure hosted app services.

Getting ready

Create a new Git repository—MyModernWebApp—in the parts unlimited team project. Create a new ASP.NET MVC project using Visual Studio and commit the changes to the master branch in the newly created Git repository.

How to do it...

1. Navigate to the build view in the **PartsUnlimited** team portal. Create a new build definition by clicking the **+ New** button. This will show you a list of all the pre-canned build templates.
2. From the featured section, apply the ASP.NET build template, as shown in the following screenshot:

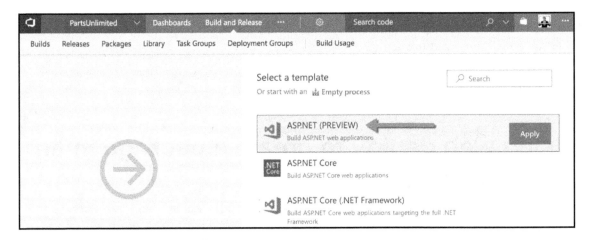

3. Name the build modern.webapp, select the default agent queue, and save the build definition. As you look around in the build definition, you'll see that the pre-canned pipeline has all the necessary tasks to restore the NuGet packages, as well as build, test, and publish a build artifact. The NuGet restore build task is configured to execute all .sln files from the source. The test step, on the other hand, is configured to operate on all DLL files that can be found in the bin folder using the *test*.dll convention and the publish artifact step publishes the bin folder of all projects associated to the solution. The build solution step also has a set of MSBuild arguments. It is these MSBuild arguments that trigger the generation of the Web Deploy package.

4. Queue a new build for this build definition without making any changes to the pre-canned build template:

```
/p:DeployOnBuild=true /p:WebPublishMethod=Package
/p:PackageAsSingleFile=true /p:SkipInvalidConfigurations=true
/p:PackageLocation="$(build.artifactstagingdirectory)\\"
```

You'll be able to see live updates of the build execution from the build console. The logs are still available after the build execution and are especially useful when troubleshooting build failures. Once the build execution completes, you'll see the following view:

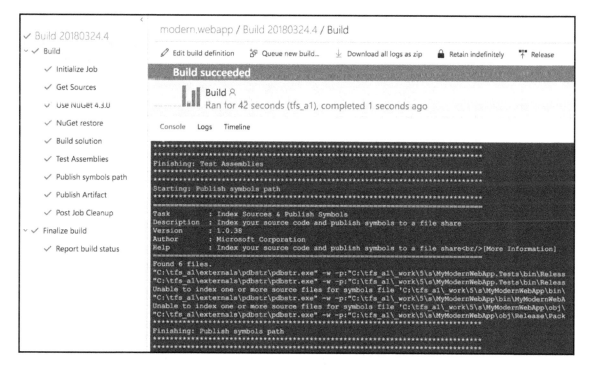

5. Navigate into the build summary view by clicking the build number in the build crumb. This view gives you the gist of the associated changes, test results, timeline of build execution (details of time spent on each step), and the artifacts section.

6. Click on the **Artifacts** section to see the web deploy package generated by this build execution:

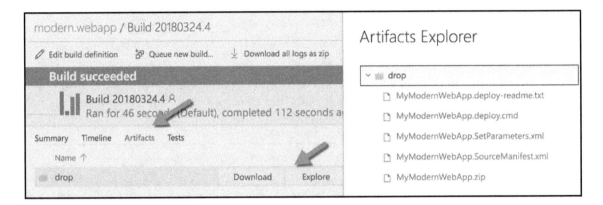

How it works...

MSBuild ships with a set of command-line switches: /p: simply means property of MSBuild. The following MSBuild properties are used in the build step of the pipeline to create the web deploy package, these are explained in the section below:

```
/p:DeployOnBuild=true /p:WebPublishMethod=Package
/p:PackageAsSingleFile=true /p:SkipInvalidConfigurations=true
/p:PackageLocation="$(build.artifactstagingdirectory)\\"
```

- DeployOnBuild: This property is used to signal that the web project needs to be packaged in this build.
- WebPublishMethod: This property ensures that the output of the publish method is a package. This property supports other publish methods such as publishing to the filesystem or elsewhere using MSDeploy.
- PackageAsSingleFile: This property is used to signal that the package be zipped up into a single output file.
- SkipInvalidConfigurations: This tells the build engine to generate one or more warning if the build encounters an invalid configuration.
- PackageLocation: This takes the path where the package needs to be generated. We're using the default build variable to signal that the package should be copied into the build artifact staging directory, so that the next step in the build pipeline can pick the package from this location and publish the build artifact and attach it to the build.

There's more...

The Azure DevOps Server marketplace features the Build Traffic Lights extension: `https:/ /marketplace.visualstudio.com/items?itemName=4tecture.BuildTrafficLights`. This free extension, developed by **4tecture**, allows you to add build traffic lights to your dashboard to visualize the state of a specific build definition and its builds. Continuous Integration is the foundation to Continuous Delivery, and showing the visibility of the CI pipeline on the team dashboard is a good way to encourage people to maintain a healthy CI pipeline:

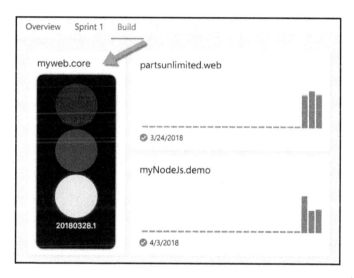

Organizing build output into separate folders

In the DevOps way of working, teams are encouraged to adopt the right tools and practices earlier in the development lifecycle to minimize waste later. While the pre-canned build templates make it really easy to get started with build pipelines, the generic configuration bloats the build artifact and adds folders that you don't necessarily care about. The ones that you do care about are folded into multiple hierarchies. While it isn't necessarily a problem immediately, when you start to consume the build output in release pipelines, much of the release pipeline effort is spent in organizing the build output correctly. In the spirit of pushing more software development activities left into the lifecycle and minimizing waste, let's see how easy it is to organize the build output into relevant folders from the outset.

Getting ready

In this section we'll go through the pre-requisites for this recipe:

1. Extend the `MyModernWebApp` solution by adding two new projects of type (.NET Standard) console application and calling the first one `ExecutionEngine.Service` and the other one `MessagingEngine.Service`.

2. Commit the changes and sync them up to the origin/master in the `MyModernWebApp` Git repository:

3. In the build view, click the **+ New** button to create a new build pipeline using the .NET Desktop pre-canned template.

4. Choose the default agent queue, name the build definition `modern.app.framework`, and queue a new build using this definition.

When the build completes, look at the build artifact: you'll see that the build output has uploaded the test project as an artifact. The build output of `ExecutionEngine.Service` and `MessagingEngine.Service` is tucked into `bin/release` folders.

This only gets messier as you associate more projects to the solution:

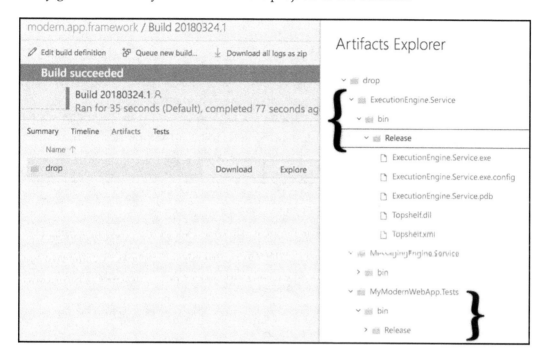

Review the `modern.app.framework` build definition. You'll notice that the build pipeline only has one copy step and one publish step. As you can see, it is configured to copy everything from the source folder that matches the express `**\bin\$(BuildConfiguration)\**` in the artifact staging directory:

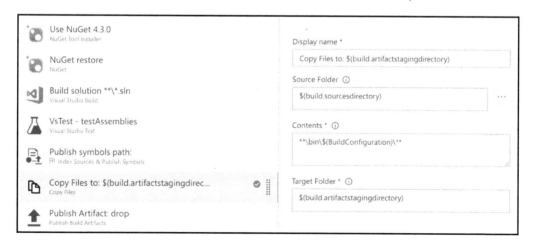

Now that you have a sense of the problem, let's see how easy it is to take back control of the build output.

How to do it...

1. Navigate to and edit the `modern.app.framework` build definition.
2. Instead of overloading just one copy step to copy everything, we'll use multiple copy steps. The source folder location needs to be fully qualified to the exact location path from where the binaries need to be copied:

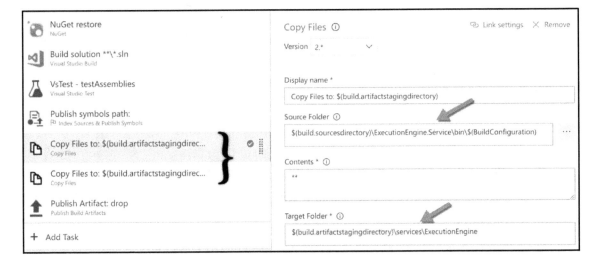

How it works...

Queue a build for the `modern.app.framework` definition; you'll now notice that the build output is a lot more organized. This has been done by removing the generic copy step and replacing it with two purposeful copy steps that fully qualify the source folder location and the target folder location. As a result, the test project DLL files haven't been uploaded as a build artifact.

The two service projects are nicely organized under the services project without being cryptically folded under the `bin/release` configuration:

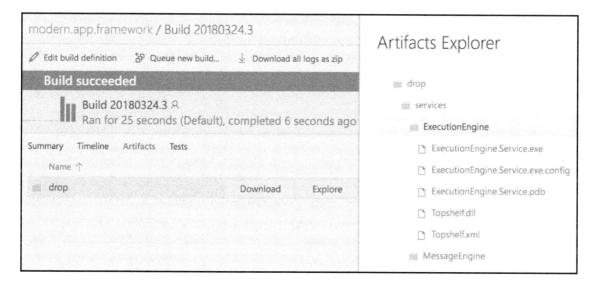

Configuring assembly version info in build pipelines

Azure DevOps Server provides a high level of traceability that makes it really easy to track builds generated from a build definition through to pull request, to code changes, and finally, back to work items. This traceability is, however, lost at the point when the binaries are generated through the build. Wouldn't it be great if you could look at the binaries deployed in an environment and identify the build they originated from? This could prove to be really useful when testing for regression issues. You can also take it a step further and display the binary version in the application, so when users log issues against your application they can also report the version of the application they are seeing the issues in. In this recipe, we'll learn how to configure the build number in the assemblies generated through a build pipeline.

Getting ready

The marketplace features the **Assembly Info** extension. This open source task, created by Bleddyn Richards, allows you to set assembly information such as version, copyright, trademark, and so on, right from within the build pipeline. Install the assembly info extension in your team project collection: `https://marketplace.visualstudio.com/items?itemName=bleddynrichards.Assembly-Info-Task`.

How to do it...

1. Navigate to the build view in the parts unlimited team portal and edit the previously created `modern.webapp` build definition.
2. Click **+ Add** to add the newly installed Assembly Info task into the `modern.webapp` build pipeline:

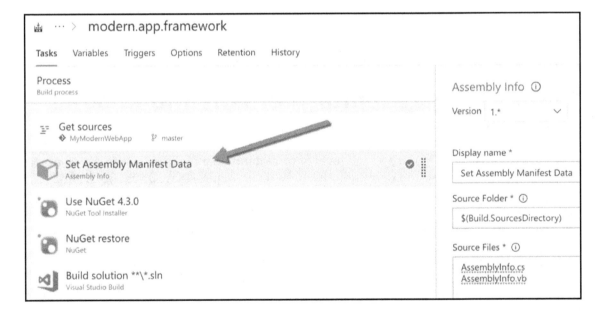

3. In the **Options** tab, it is recommended that you configure the build number to a `digit.digit.digit.digit` assembly number format. However, if you have a different naming convention for the build number, then you can still version the binaries by using a semantic assembly version that you can control directly in the build pipeline:

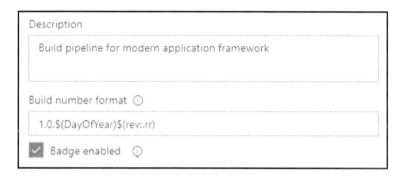

Leave the default configuration for the source files to `AssembyInfo.cs` and `AssembyInfo.vb`.

4. Update the **Manifest Attributes** and the **Informational Attributes** in the task to what you want to reflect in the generated assemblies:

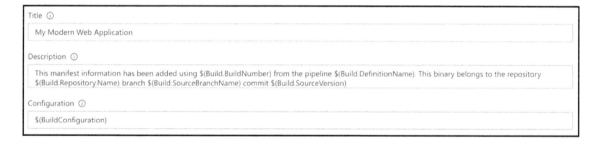

Also, update the information attribute section of the **Assembly Info** task:

And, finally, update the **Identity Attributes**:

You can use the pre-defined build variables to add more contextual information in the Assembly Info injected in the assemblies generated through the build pipeline. Information on the pre-defined build variables can be found in the Microsoft docs at `https://docs.microsoft.com/en-us/vsts/build-release/concepts/definitions/build/variables?view=vststabs=batch.`

How it works...

1. Trigger a new build and wait for it to complete execution.

2. Download the build artifact and see the assembly property. This should correctly reflect the configuration specified by you in the Assembly Info task:

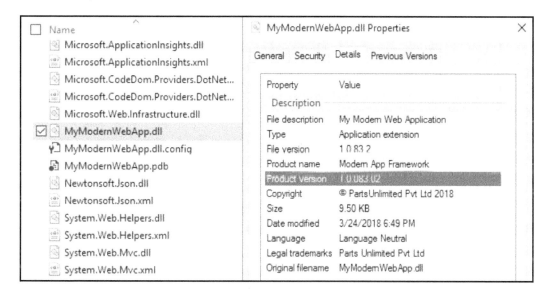

3. The Assembly Info task exposes the following fields via the build task. The following table shows you how these map back to the attributes in the `AssemblyInfo` file:

Field	Attribute	Function
Title	AssemblyTitle	Provides a friendly name for the assembly
Product	AssemblyProduct	Provides the product information for the assembly
Description	AssemblyDescription	Provides a short description that summarizes the nature and purpose of the assembly
Company	AssemblyCompany	Provides the company name for the assembly
Copyright	AssemblyCopyright	Provides the assembly or product copyright information
Trademark	AssemblyTrademark	Provides the assembly or product trademark information
Culture	AssemblyCulture	Provides information on what culture the assembly supports

Field	Attribute	Function
Configuration	AssemblyConfiguration	Provides the build configuration for the assembly, such as debug or release
Version number	AssemblyVersion	Provides an assembly version for the application
File version number	AssemblyFileVersion	Provides a file version for the application
Informational version	AssemblyInformationalVersion	Provides a text version for the application

Setting up a build pipeline for a .NET core application

Microsoft introduced .Net Core back in 2016. It has evolved from a framework in preview to a framework that is running business-critical workloads in production. .Net core is an open source, cross-platform, high-performing framework for modern, cloud-based, internet-connected applications. While one had to handcraft build tasks for .Net core applications in its early days, the tooling has now caught up with the pace of change in .Net core. Azure DevOps Server fully supports .Net core and allows you to go from zero to DevOps in a few clicks. In this recipe, we'll learn how to set up a build pipeline for a .NET Core application that can build, unit test, and package the output as an artifact.

Getting ready

In this recipe, we'll be using a simple .Net core application that comprises a few unit tests. To get started, simply import the .Net core sample GitHub repository `https://github.com/MicrosoftDocs/pipelines-dotnet-core` into the parts unlimited team project.

How to do it...

1. Navigate to the build view in the parts unlimited team project. Click **+ New** to create a new build definition and apply the **ASP.NET Core** template:

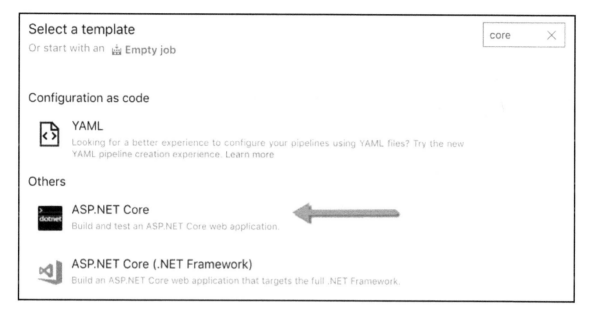

2. Configure the agent queue to use the default queue and the **Get sources** step to the code repository you've imported the .Net core sample repository into.

3. Name the definition `myweb.core` and save the build definition. The template is pre-canned with all the relevant configuration to build and unit test a .Net core application. Queue a new build to see the build definition in action:

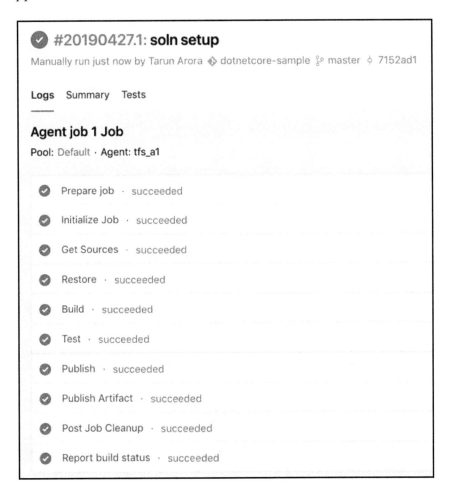

How it works...

Let's double-click the build process to understand the inner workings of the pipeline better. Start with the restore step. This simply restores all the package dependencies specified in the `csproj` file:

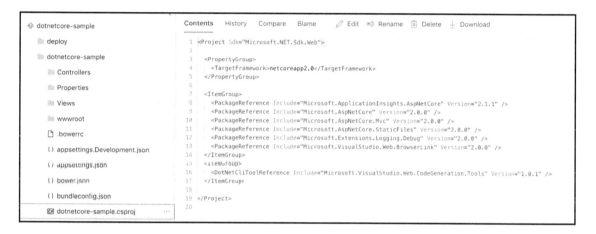

You can also restore package references from NuGet. Use an accompanying `NuGet.config` file in your repository to manage the references to internal or public NuGet feed. More information on how to set this up can be found on Microsoft docs: `https://docs.microsoft.com/en-us/dotnet/core/tools/dotnet-restore?tabs=netcore2x`. Version 2 of the VSTS .Net core restore task supports specifying the NuGet feed configuration in the task directly.

The build and test task simply uses the .Net core build engine to build all `csproj` files in the repository. The test task uses a wildcard search to look for all `csproj` files that include the name `*test*`. The build and test task allows you to specify additional arguments, for example, the configuration to build in. The publish task finally creates a package that you can optionally ZIP and include the project name in:

Working through the earlier steps, you'll notice that the .Net core tooling is wrapped up into one single VSTS build task that allows you to simply select the command you intend to perform. The task supports the following commands:

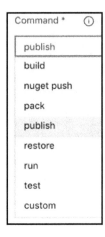

There's more...

The Azure DevOps Server marketplace features the **Diagnostics Tasks**, which can be found here: `https://marketplace.visualstudio.com/items?itemName=andremarques023.DiagnosticTasks`. This free extension, developed by André Marques de Araújo, provides you with a set of useful tasks for both build and release pipelines. The log variables task is extremely useful, especially when you are working through debugging build issues. Team build brings a number of predefined variables that can be used in build (and release) definitions and scripts. Variables are generated by the agent in the scope of a particular job (prior to it starting) or generated on the server side and sent to the agent as part of the job. This task logs these variables to the console:

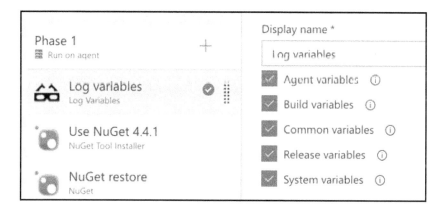

Setting up build pipeline for a Node.js application

Node.js is a cross-platform, open source platform built on Chrome's JavaScript runtime for fast and scalable server-side and networking applications. It is very popular for both frontend as well as server-side programming. In this recipe, you'll learn how to set up a CI pipeline for a Node.js application using gulp.

Getting ready

The focus of the recipe is to help you understand the construction of a CI pipeline for a Node.js application. To abstract the complexity of the node application out of the recipe, we'll be using a demo code repository from GitHub. To get started, simply import the following code base from `https://github.com/nilaydshah/MochaTypescriptTest-101/` into your team foundation server. You can also create a new Node.js code repository in Visual Studio code using the instructions in this blog post: `https://blogs.msdn.microsoft.com/nilayshah/2018/01/07/unit-testing-node-application-with-typescript-in-vs-code-%E2%80%8A-%E2%80%8A-using-mocha-chai-mochawesome-gulp-travis/`:

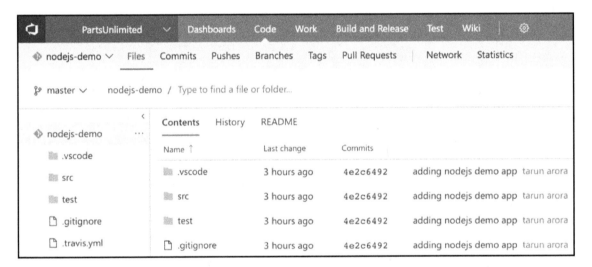

How to do it...

1. Navigate to the build view in the parts unlimited team project. Click **+ New** to create a new build definition and apply the **Node.js With gulp** template:

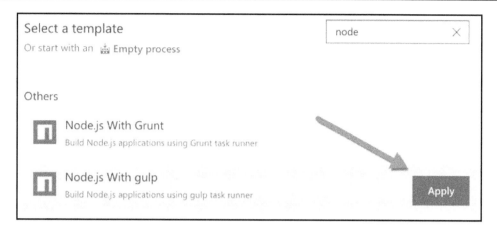

2. Configure the agent queue to use the default queue and change the default archive type to ZIP. This pre-canned template includes a task to run `gulpfile` in the repository.

3. Name the definition `myNodeJs.demo` and save the build definition. The configuration in place is sufficient to build and package a Node.js application and queue a new build to see the build definition in action:

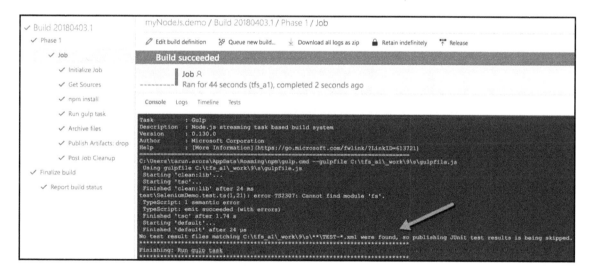

4. While the build is successful, the pipeline isn't executing the test in the repository. To configure the test execution, update `package.json`, append the below code snippet.

   Include the `mocha-junit-reporter` dependency in `package.json`:

   ```
   "mocha-junit-reporter": "^1.17.0"
   ```

   Add a `test` script block to execute mocha tests with `mocha-junit-reporter`:

   ```
   "scripts": {
       "test": "mocha lib/test/**/*.js --reporter mocha-junit-
   reporter --reporter-options    mochaFile=./TestResults/TEST-
   RESULT.xml"
       }
   ```

5. Edit the `myNodeJs.demo` pipeline and add a NPM task after the gulp task, configure it to run the `custom` task type, and set the **Command and arguments** to `test`.

6. Uncheck test execution in the run gulp task, as the newly added NPM custom task will be doing this for us:

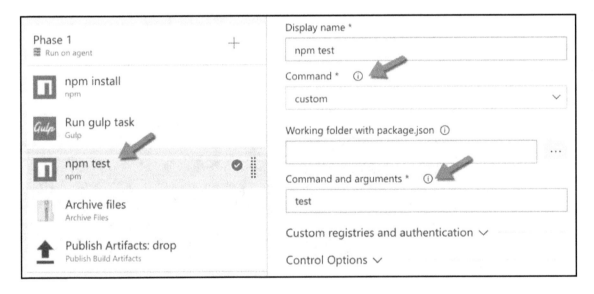

7. To publish the test results into the build output, add the `publish test results` task after the NPM test task.

8. Configure the test results filename to `**\TEST-RESULT.xml`:

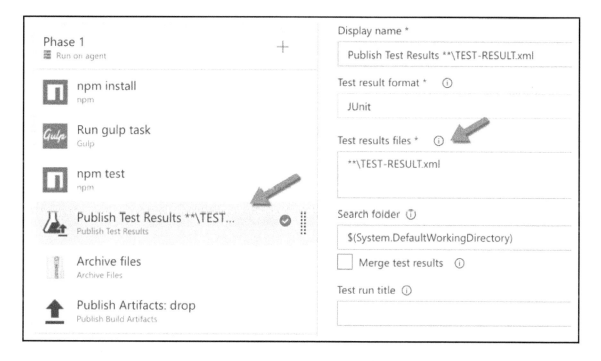

9. Queue a new build to see your Node.js continuous integration pipeline in action. The pipeline will build, run tests, publish test results, and package the output into a ZIP file that will be attached as an artifact with the build:

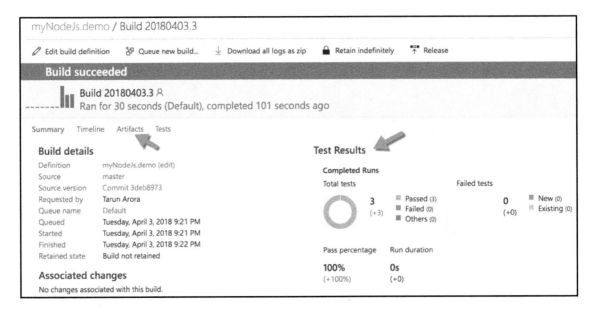

How it works...

The `package.json` file is the glue in the Node.js build pipeline. Let's double-click in the build pipeline to understand how this is working under the hood. The first task in the `npm install` pipeline reads `package.json` to identify the application dependencies and restores the packages into the build environment. In the package management chapter, we'll also learn how to plug in a private NPM feed to the build pipeline to restore the package dependencies:

The run gulp task executes the `gulpfile.js` file. Gulp is a JavaScript task runner that lets you automate tasks such as bundling and minifying libraries and stylesheets. In this case, gulp creates a TypeScript project using the configuration settings in `tsconfig.json`. Most of this is the standard configuration that you can use across multiple node projects:

```
master ∨      nodejs-demo / gulpfile.js

Contents   History   Compare   Blame

1  "use strict";
2  var gulp = require('gulp');
3  var ts = require('gulp-typescript');
4  var del = require('del');
5  var tsProject = ts.createProject("tsconfig.json");
6
7  // task to clean all files in lib (which is out folder for containing all javascripts)
8  gulp.task("clean:lib", function() {
9      return del(['lib/**/*']);
10 });
11
12 // task to build(transpile) all typescripts into javascripts in lib folder
13 gulp.task("tsc", function () {
14     return tsProject.src()
15         .pipe(tsProject())
16         .js.pipe(gulp.dest("lib"));
17 });
18
19 // adding default tasks as clean and build
20 gulp.task('default', ['clean:lib','tsc'], function () {
21 });
```

Sidebar:
- nodejs-demo
  - .vscode
  - src
  - test
  - .gitignore
  - .travis.yml
  - chromedriver
  - chromedriver.exe
  - JS gulpfile.js
  - LICENSE
  - {} package-vsts.json
  - {} package.json
  - M↓ README.md
  - {} tsconfig.json

The `package.json` file also includes the custom script to test the application. This calls the mocha test framework and specifies the test output format as `TEST-RESULT.xml`. The output file generated here is compatible with the open test result syntax supported by the build system:

```
"scripts": {
  "test": "mocha lib/test/**/*.js --reporter mocha-junit-reporter --reporter-options mochaFile=./TestResults/TEST-RESULT.xml"
},
```

This allows the build systems to consume the `TEST-RESULT.xml` file through the publish test result task and process it to render the test results visually as part of the build output. Finally, the archive task takes the output processed through the gulp task executor and packages it up into a ZIP file, which is then published as an artifact into the build.

There's more...

You can optionally use the **Node Tool Installer** task to configure the version of Node used by your build pipeline. This task allows you to specify the configuration of the node version to be used in the build pipeline; it accepts the less than, equal to, and greater than expressions. The task finds or downloads and caches the specified version of Node.js and adds it to the path on the build agent host machine:

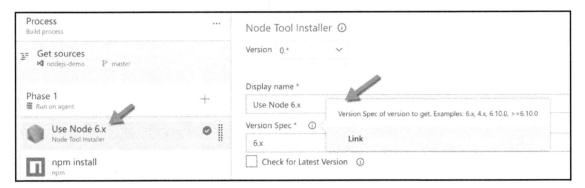

Setting up a build pipeline for your database projects

A continuous integration pipeline ensures code and related resources are integrated regularly and tested by an automated build system. CI is becoming a standard in modern software development. While teams are quick to set up a CI pipeline for their application, the database usually gets sidelined in this equation. The benefits of CI can be applied to brownfield as well as greenfield databases. In this recipe, we'll learn how to set up a pipeline for a database project that generates a `dacpac` file as a build artifact.

 A DAC is a self-contained unit of SQL Server database deployment that enables data-tier developers and database administrators to package SQL Server objects into a portable artifact called a DAC package, also known as a **DACPAC**.

Getting ready

The focus of the recipe is to help you understand the construction of a pipeline for a database project. If you don't have a database project for your database already, you can generate a database project from an existing database using the steps listed here: `https://msdn.microsoft.com/en-us/library/hh864423(v=vs.103).aspx`. In this recipe, we'll be using a simple demo database project from GitHub: `https://github.com/Microsoft/sql-server-samples.git`. To get started, simply import the GitHub repository into the parts unlimited team project:

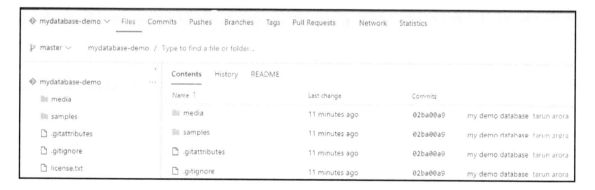

We'll be using the `wwi-ssdt` solution, which already includes the `WideWorldImporters.sqlproj` database project sample:

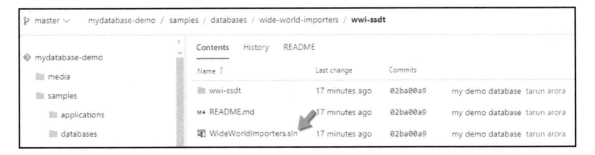

How to do it...

1. Navigate to the build view in the parts unlimited team project. Click **+ New** to create a new build definition and apply the .NET Desktop build template:

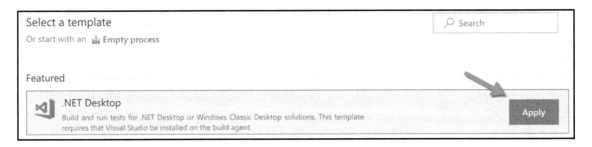

2. Configure the agent queue to use the default queue and, in the process, update the path of the solution file to `samples/databases/wide-world-importers/wwi-dw-ssdt/WideWorldImportersDW.sln`.

3. Name the definition `myDb.demo` and save the build definition:

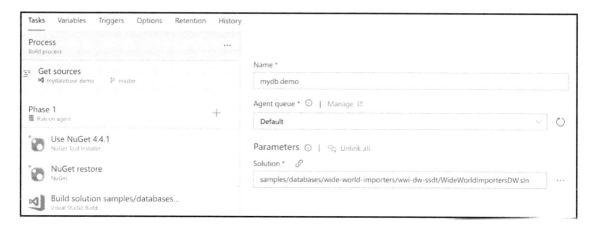

The configuration in place is sufficient to build and package an SQL database project; queue a new build to see the build definition in action. The build successfully generates a `dacpac` file and attaches it as an artifact:

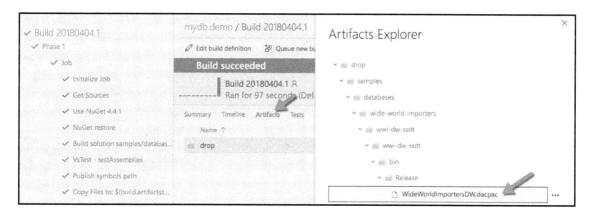

How it works...

Open the `samples/databases/wide-world-importers/wwi-dw-ssdt/WideWorldImportersDW.sln` solution in visual studio, right-click on the `WideWorldImporters.dbproj` file, and view properties. In the **Build** tab you'll see that the project is configured to generate an output (`dacpac`) in the `bin\Release` or `bin\Debug` folder:

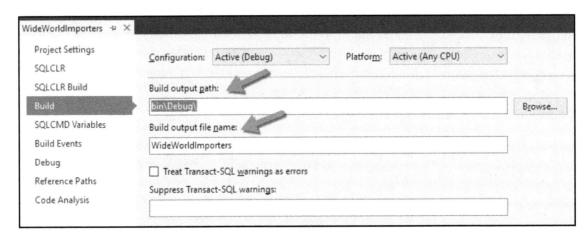

The build pipeline uses the same setting to generate the `dacpac` file. Download the `dacpac` file generated in the build artifact and rename its extension from `.dacpac` to `.zip`. You'll notice that it simply contains the database model wrapped up into an XML file and the post-deployment scripts in a `postdeployment.sql` file:

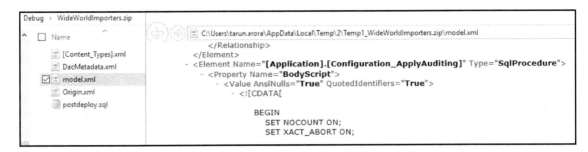

The `dacpac` file can be used at deploy time to compare the database against the current state of the schema to generate the incremental delta script for deployment. Refer to *Deploying the database to Azure SQL using the release pipeline* recipe in `Chapter 6`, *Continuous Deployments*, to learn how to deploy dacpac to a sql azure database using Azure Pipelines.

Integrating SonarQube in build pipelines to manage technical debt

Technical debt can be classified as the measure between the codebase's current state and an optimal state. Technical debt saps productivity by making code hard to understand, easy to break, and difficult to validate, in turn creating unplanned work, ultimately blocking progress. Technical debt is inevitable! It starts small and grows over time through rushed changes, lack of context, and lack of discipline. Organizations often find that more than 50% of their capacity is sapped by technical debt. The hardest part of fixing technical debt is knowing where to start. SonarQube is an open source platform that is the de facto solution for understanding and managing technical debt. In this recipe, we'll learn how to leverage SonarQube in a build pipeline to identify technical debt.

Getting ready

SonarQube is an open platform to manage code quality. As such, it covers the seven axes of code quality as illustrated in the following diagram. Originally famous in the Java community, SonarQube now supports over 20 programming languages. The joint investments made by Microsoft and SonarSource make SonarQube easier to integrate with TFBuild and better at analyzing .NET-based applications. You can read more about the capabilities offered by SonarQube here: `http://www.sonarqube.org/resources/`

In this recipe, we'll be analyzing the technical debt in one of the .Net core sample repositories in the `partsunlimited` team project. If you don't already have an instance of SonarQube, then set one up by following the instructions here: `https://github.com/SonarSource/sonar-.net-documentation/blob/master/doc/installation-and-configuration.md`.

To get started with SonarQube, you'll also need to install the SonarQube build tasks to your Azure DevOps Server Team Project collection from the marketplace: `https://marketplace.visualstudio.com/items?itemName=SonarSource.sonarqube`:

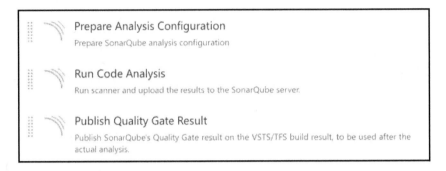

How to do it...

1. Navigate to the build view in the parts unlimited team project.
2. Choose to edit the `modern.webapp` build definition, click **+**, and add the following tasks: **Prepare analysis on SonarQube** and **Run Code Analysis**.
3. Click on the **Prepare analysis on SonarQube** task and click **+ New** to configure the SonarQube service endpoint to be used:

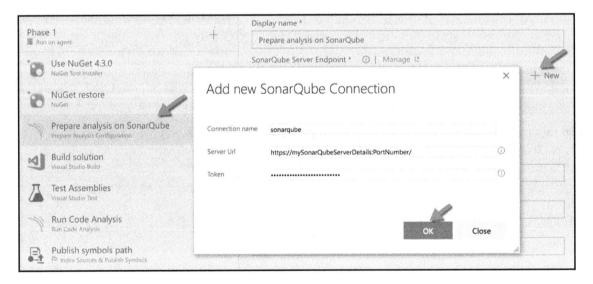

The **Run Code Analysis** task needs to be placed after the build solution and test assemblies task for it to include the build and test binaries (test results and code coverage) in the analysis.

4. The prepare analysis task further needs three configurations, namely the project key, project name, and project version. Fill these out as highlighted in the following screenshot:

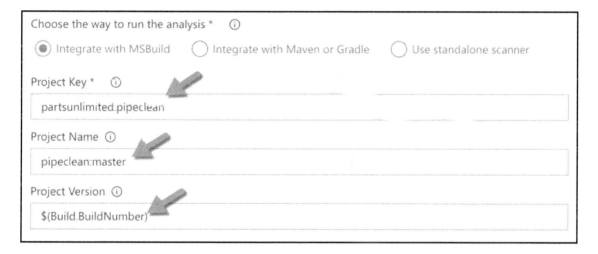

The project version is configured to use the pre-configured $(Build.BuildNumber) variable, which will give you traceability between the builds in the team foundation server and the analysis reports in SonarQube.

5. Queue a new build and wait for the build execution to complete:

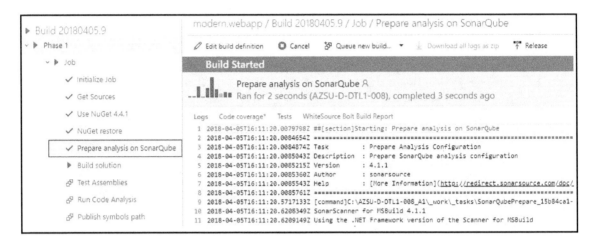

The build has successfully run, completed the SonarQube analysis, and pushed the results into your SonarQube instance.

How it works...

The build tasks provided by SonarQube provide the underlying plumbing to leverage the correct analyzers, generate the analysis report, and publish it to the SonarQube instance specified in the build pipeline. The service endpoint created for SonarQube keeps track of all the requests that make use of this service endpoint:

Result	Type	Definition	Name	Time started	Time finished ↓
⚠ Succeeded with issues	Build	modern.webapp	20180405.6	4/5/2018 2:13 PM	4/5/2018 2:14 PM
✕ Failed	Build	modern.webapp	20180405.5	4/5/2018 1:59 PM	4/5/2018 2:00 PM
✕ Failed	Build	modern.webapp	20180405.4	4/5/2018 12:54 PM	4/5/2018 12:57 PM

To lock down access to service endpoints, you can add users in user and administrator roles. Only members of the service endpoint have permissions to consume the service endpoint.

As the analysis is complete, navigate to SonarQube; you'll see a new project has been created using the details from the prepare analysis task:

The analysis includes the version number, which maps back to the build number the analysis was kicked off from:

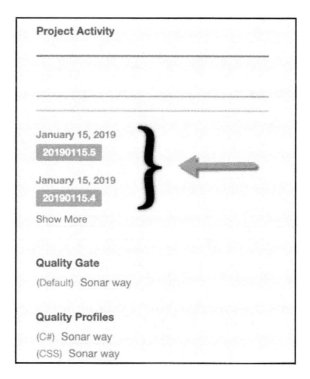

The analysis shows that there are three major issues; click on the issues to see more details about them. This view gives you the option to slice and dice the issues by various categories. It's possible to click on the issue and see the offending line of code with details of how this can be fixed:

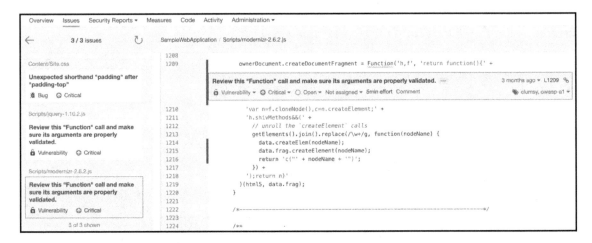

The measures in SonarQube give you the ability to get a better all-around view of the quality of your application. For example, in the duplication measure it is demonstrated that the application is plagued by 17% of code that can be refactored to more shared functions, as in its current state it's simply duplicated:

There's more...

You can optionally edit the pipeline to include the **Publish Quality Gate Results** task in the pipeline. This task publishes a summary of the SonarQube code analysis results into the build summary view.

5
Continuous Testing

Software teams are constantly under pressure to deliver more, faster. End users expect software to simply work. Low-quality software just isn't acceptable. But you may ask what the right level of quality is. Quality is a very subjective term; it is, therefore, important for teams to agree on a definition of quality for their software. Teams that are unable to define quality usually end up testing for coverage.

Microsoft has made some bold bets with Azure DevOps Server 2019. Rather than continue to invest in features that have a very high cost of ownership and low usability footprint, Microsoft has instead decided to deprecate those features and instead focus the energy elsewhere. Let's see what's changing:

- **Microsoft Test Manager (MTM)**: The toolkit in Azure DevOps Server provides tooling for both manual and automated testing. A key part of that tooling used to be MTM. MTM was first introduced with TFS 2010. It enabled testers to plan, track, and run manual tests, exploratory tests, and automated tests. While MTM fully integrated with TFS, it did not offer integration with other testing platforms, nor did it offer APIs for extensibility. Microsoft's ambition over the last few years has been to support every developer, every app, and every platform; that isn't possible with tooling that can't be run on non-Windows platforms. As a result, over the years, test tooling has gradually moved out of MTM onto the web, which is now called Test Hub. As it stands, Test Hub is a fully-featured test management solution spanning all stages of the testing life cycle. It works on all platforms (such as Linux, macOS, and Windows) and all browsers (such as Edge, Chrome, and Firefox). You can easily get started using manual testing features right from your Kanban board and use it for more advanced manual testing capabilities.

The following screenshot shows a feature-level comparison between web-based test features and the client-based MTM. With feature parity between Test Hub and MTM, no new versions of MTM will be released. Microsoft Test Manager 2017 (which shipped with Microsoft Visual Studio 2017) is the last version and will be supported up to January 1, 2020:

Test planning capability	Web-based test features	Client-based Microsoft Test Manager
Create test plan	☑	☑
Create/Manage suites	☑	☑
Add/remove tests from test suite	☑	☑
Assign individual testers to test plan/test suite	☑	☑
Create/edit/assign configurations	☑	☑
Clone test plan/test suite*	☑	☑
Add tests from other test suites*	☑	☑
Order manual tests within suites (RBS, QBS, Static)	☑	☒
Export test plans and test suites	☑	☒
View test case references across test suites	☑	☒
Assign multiple testers to test plans and test suites for user acceptance testing	☑	☒

- **Load testing**: Load testing helps you ensure that your apps can scale and do not go down when peak traffic hits. Although Microsoft has been shipping load-testing tools and their cloud-based load-testing service for many years, the adoption has not been growing. Some of the factors contributing to this are as follows: load testing is typically initiated for seasonal events; load testing is more meaningful for products operating at scale; and application complexity can sometimes make it difficult to adopt an off-the-shelf service without a high level of customization. With a high level of investment required to maintain the load testing functionality and a very low adoption rate, Microsoft has announced the deprecation of load testing in its product. Visual Studio 2019 will be the last version of Visual Studio with web performance and load test features, and the corresponding Azure DevOps cloud-based load testing service will shut down on March 31, 2020. You can read more about the announcement and the specifics of the deprecation timeline here: `https://devblogs.microsoft.com/devops/cloud-based-load-testing-service-eol/`.

- **Coded UI testing**: Automated tests that drive your application through its UI are known as **Coded UI Tests** (**CUITs**) in Visual Studio. These tests include functional testing of the UI controls. They let you verify that the whole application, including its user interface, is functioning correctly. Coded UI Tests are particularly useful where there is validation or other logic in the user interface, for example, in a web page. They are also frequently used to automate an existing manual test. In addition to supporting record and playback for web applications, Coded UI only supported Windows-based desktop applications. Coded UI tests worked particularly well for greenfield applications with native controls. The success rate on automation dropped with third-party controls and legacy implementations. With a greater push for cross-platform support, Microsoft has acknowledged that open source frameworks such as Selenium and Appium are the better answer here. Microsoft has therefore announced that Coded UI tooling for automated UI-driven functional testing is being deprecated. Visual Studio 2019 is the last version where the Coded UI Test will be available. Microsoft recommends using Selenium (`https://docs.seleniumhq.org/`) for testing web apps and Appium with WinAppDriver (`https://github.com/Microsoft/WinAppDriver`) for testing desktop and UWP apps.

With the deprecation of MTM, load testing, and Coded UI Testing, you are probably thinking: where is Microsoft investing in testing? I'll answer that question, but let's first look at this interesting shift. To speed up the software delivery loop, software testing needs to be incorporated into the continuous integration pipeline. In order to do this, software testing needs to shift left in the development processes. Test-driven development enables developers to write code that's maintainable, flexible, and easily extensible. Code backed by unit tests helps identify change impact and empowers developers to make changes confidently. In addition to this, functional testing needs to be automated. This enables software testers to focus on high-value exploratory testing rather than just coverage of the test matrix. The DevOps movement at large supports bringing testing into the continuous integration pipeline. As a result, the next wave of investment is going into improving the testing story within pipelines, specifically around unit testing: more support for testing frameworks and enriching the analytics from test execution.

Through the recipes in this chapter, we'll learn how to leverage pipelines to execute tests and perform distributed test execution.

In this chapter, we will cover the following recipes:

- Running NUnit tests using Azure Pipelines
- Using feature flags to test in production
- Distributing multi-configuration tests against agents
- Configuring parallel execution of tests using Azure Pipelines
- Running SpecFlow tests using Azure Pipelines
- Analyzing test execution results from Runs view
- Exporting test artifacts and test results from Test Hub
- Charting testing status on dashboards in the team portal

Running NUnit tests using Azure Pipelines

NUnit is one of the many open source testing frameworks popular with cross-platform developers. In this recipe, we'll learn how easy it is to create a pipeline for NUnit-based tests and publish the test execution results in Azure DevOps Server.

Getting ready

In this section, we'll use the .NET CLI to create a new solution and a new class library project, and install the NUnit test template.

These are the prerequisites:

- .NET Core 2.1 SDK or later versions
- A text editor or code editor of your choice

Follow these steps:

1. Launch Command Prompt and create a new folder called `ContinuousTesting`:

   ```
   mkdir ContinuousTesting
   cd ContinuousTesting
   ```

2. Create a new solution:

   ```
   dotnet new sln -n prime
   ```

3. Create a new `PrimeService` directory:

   ```
   mkdir PrimeService
   ```

4. Set `PrimeService` as the current directory and create a new project:

   ```
   dotnet new classlib
   ```

5. Rename `Class1.cs` to `PrimeService.cs`. Start by copying this failing implementation of the `PrimeService` class:

   ```
   using System;
   namespace Prime.Services
   {
   public class PrimeService
   {
   public bool IsPrime(int candidate)
   {
   throw new NotImplementedException("Please create a test
   first");
   }
   }
   }
   ```

6. Change the directory back to the `ContinuousTesting` directory. Run the following command to add a reference of the class library project to the solution:

   ```
   dotnet sln add PrimeService/PrimeService.csproj
   ```

7. Before you can use NUnit from the `dotnet` CLI, you'll need to install NUnit. This can easily be done by running the following command:

```
dotnet new -i NUnit.DotNetNew.Template
```

8. Next, create a directory for `Test` under the `ContinuousTesting` directory, and call it `PrimeService.Tests`:

```
mkdir PrimeService.Tests
```

9. Create a new `nunit` test project and add a reference for this test project into solution. The test project will also need a reference to the class library:

```
dotnet new nunit
dotnet sln add ./PrimeService.Tests/PrimeService.Tests.csproj
dotnet add reference ../PrimeService/PrimeService.csproj
```

Let's follow the **Test-Driven Development (TDD)** approach. Start off by writing one failing test and then make it pass by writing the implementation for it. In the `PrimeService.Tests` directory, rename the `UnitTest1.cs` file to `PrimeService_IsPrimeShould.cs` and replace its entire contents with the following code:

```
using NUnit.Framework;
using Prime.Services;
namespace Prime.UnitTests.Services
{
 [TestFixture]
 public class PrimeService_IsPrimeShould
 {
 private readonly PrimeService _primeService;
public PrimeService_IsPrimeShould()
 {
 _primeService = new PrimeService();
 }
[Test]
 public void ReturnFalseGivenValueOf1()
 {
 var result = _primeService.IsPrime(1);
Assert.IsFalse(result, "1 should not be prime");
 }
 }
}
```

The [TestFixture] attribute denotes a class that contains unit tests. The [Test] attribute indicates that a method is a test method. Save this file. From the command line, execute dotnet test; this builds the tests and the class library and then executes the tests. The NUnit test runner contains the program entry point to run your tests. dotnet test starts the test runner using the unit test project you've created.

Your test fails. You haven't created the implementation yet. Make this test pass by writing the simplest code in the PrimeService class that works:

```
public bool IsPrime(int candidate)
{
 if (candidate == 1)
 {
 return false;
 }
 throw new NotImplementedException("Please create a test first");
}
```

In the ContinuousTesting directory, run dotnet test again. The dotnet test command runs a build for the PrimeService project and then for the PrimeService.Tests project. After building both projects, it runs this single test. It passes.

Now that we have a working .Net core service and NUnit-based unit test, commit the code into a Git repository (be sure to use a gitignore file to avoid staging files you don't need). Create a remote continuoustesting.demo repository in the **Parts Unlimited** team project. Push the code into the master branch on the remote.

How to do it...

1. Navigate to the **Build** view in the Parts Unlimited team project.
2. Click **+New** to create a new pipeline and apply the dotnetcore template. Name the pipeline nunit.demo.

3. Select the repository as `continuoustesting.repo` and the branch as master:

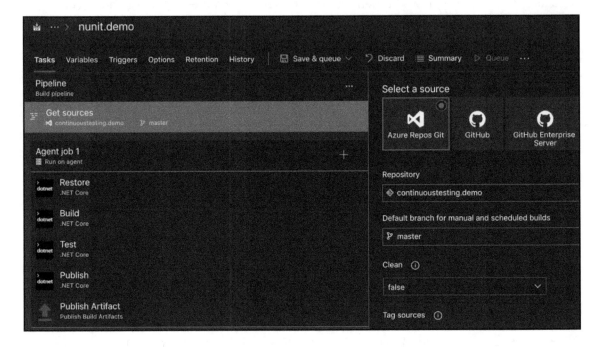

4. Click on the **Test** step in the pipeline and ensure that the **Path to project(s)** field uses the wildcard `**/*[Tt]ests/*.csproj` search value and the **Publish test results and code coverage** option is checked:

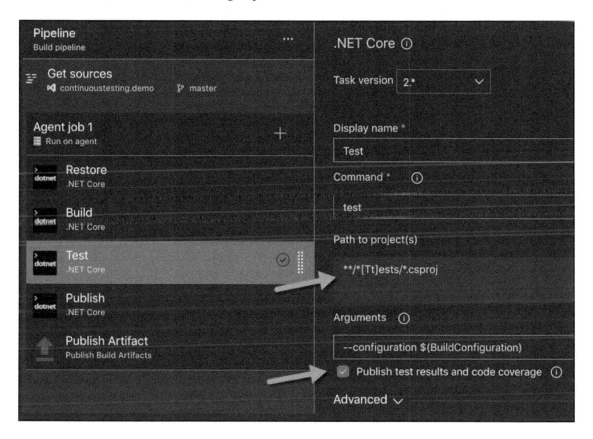

5. Click on the **Publish** task and uncheck **Publish Web Projects**, as the sample solution is a class library and not a web project:

6. Save and queue the build to run and wait for the pipeline to complete execution:

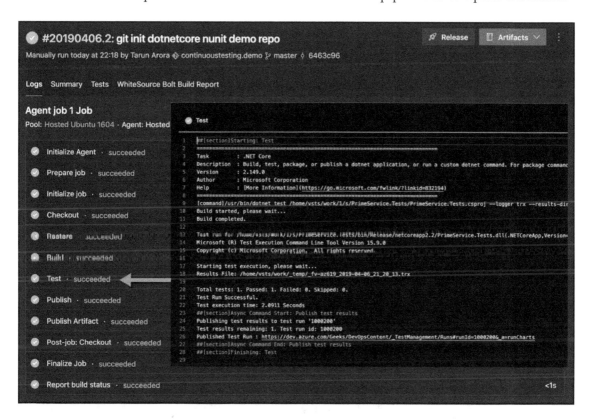

7. Click on the **Tests** tab to see the test execution results:

How it works...

This was simple! You didn't have to add any reference to the NUnit test runner in the pipeline or worry about parsing the NUnit test results back into a format that is understood by the pipeline. The Azure DevOps service does a lot of work behind the scenes to make it seamless. To understand how it works, let's start by zooming into the **Restore** step in the pipeline. The pipeline reads the `csproj` reference to the NUnit test adapter:

```xml
<Project Sdk="Microsoft.NET.Sdk">

  <PropertyGroup>
    <TargetFramework>netcoreapp2.2</TargetFramework>

    <IsPackable>false</IsPackable>
  </PropertyGroup>

  <ItemGroup>
    <PackageReference Include="nunit" Version="3.11.0" />
    <PackageReference Include="NUnit3TestAdapter" Version="3.12.0" />
    <PackageReference Include="Microsoft.NET.Test.Sdk" Version="15.9.0" />
  </ItemGroup>

  <ItemGroup>
    <ProjectReference Include="..\PrimeService\PrimeService.csproj" />
  </ItemGroup>

</Project>
```

As a result, the test runner is downloaded:

```
Restore  924    Writing lock file to disk. Path: /home/vsts/work/1/s/PrimeService/obj/project.assets.json
         925    Writing cache file to disk. Path: /home/vsts/work/1/s/PrimeService/obj/PrimeService.csproj.nuget.cache
Build    926    Restore completed in 742.43 ms for /home/vsts/work/1/s/PrimeService/PrimeService.csproj.
         927    GET https://api.nuget.org/v3-flatcontainer/microsoft.net.test.sdk/index.json
         928    GET https://api.nuget.org/v3-flatcontainer/nunit/index.json
Test     929    GET https://api.nuget.org/v3-flatcontainer/nunit3testadapter/index.json
         930    OK https://api.nuget.org/v3-flatcontainer/nunit/index.json 18ms
Publi    931    OK https://api.nuget.org/v3-flatcontainer/microsoft.net.test.sdk/index.json 43ms
         932    GET https://api.nuget.org/v3-flatcontainer/nunit/3.11.0/nunit.3.11.0.nupkg
Publi    933    GET https://api.nuget.org/v3-flatcontainer/microsoft.net.test.sdk/15.9.0/microsoft.net.test.sdk.15.9.0.nupkg
```

Then it is installed through the **Restore** step in the pipeline:

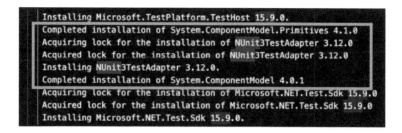

Next, let's look at how the test results from the test execution were parsed into the test run results:

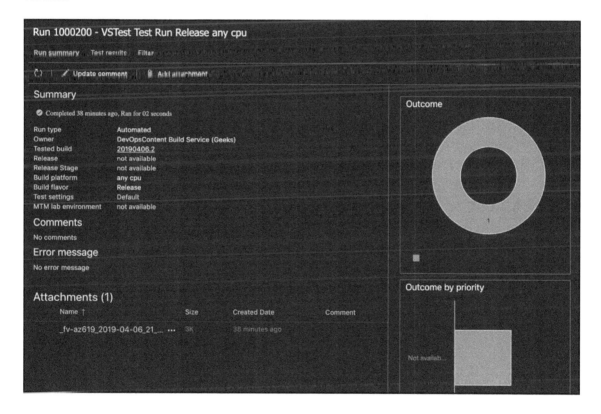

Azure Pipelines are highly extensible and provide a wide range of extensibility points. The test task out-of-the-box supports the following test result formats: CTest, JUnit, NUnit 2, NUnit 3, Visual Studio Test (TRX), and xUnit 2. The test task is executed through the pipeline supports parsing the test results from any test execution framework as long as the test framework can publish the test results in any of these supported formats. All the advanced concepts of searching test results using wildcard search as well as merging test results are handled by the pipeline itself.

Using feature flags to test in production

We are in an era of continuous delivery, where we are expected to quickly deliver software that is stable and performant. We see development teams embracing a suite of continuous integration/delivery tools to automate their testing and QA, all while deploying at an accelerated cadence. No matter how hard we try to mitigate the risk of software delivery, almost all end-user software releases are strictly coupled with some form of code deployment. This means that companies must rely on testing and QA to identify all issues before a release hits production. There are two key challenges when testing features in test environments:

- Testing in test environments can be challenging if your test scenarios depend on production-quality data. It can take a lot of effort to create this kind of data in test environments and it's likely you'll still miss out on key test scenarios, since in some cases the effort involved in creating this data outweighs the benefits.
- The other most common scenario is doing user testing, inspecting, and adapting the functionality of your product based on usage data. End users may be invested in the success of your product, but it can get increasingly difficult to get constant feedback on every functionality in a test environment.

Once a release is in production, it is basically out in the wild. Without proper controls, rolling back to previous versions becomes a code deployment exercise, requiring engineering expertise and increasing the potential for downtime. One way to mitigate risk in feature releases is to introduce feature flags (feature toggles) into the continuous delivery process. These flags allow features (or any code segment) to be turned on or off for particular users. Feature flags are a powerful technique, allowing teams to modify system behavior without changing code. Innovation is the key to success, and success depends on hypothesis testing through experimentation. By adopting a culture of continuous experimentation, features can be tested by creating an instrumented minimal viable product rapidly and released to a subset of customers in production for testing; this enables the team to make fact-based decisions and quickly evolve toward an optimal solution.

In this recipe, we'll learn how to get into a true continuous testing culture by leveraging feature flags.

Getting ready

1. Create a new web application using the ASP.NET Web Application template in Visual Studio, name it MyWebApp, and save it in a new folder called featuretoggle.demo:

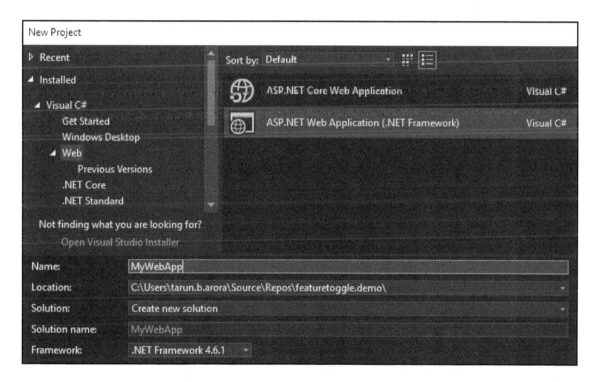

2. Simply build and run the website, then navigate to the **Contact** form:

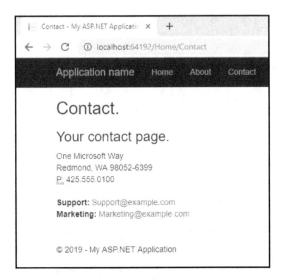

In the next section, we'll see how to use feature flags to deploy changes to the **Contact** form without releasing the changes to everyone.

How to do it...

1. In the MyWebApp project, add a reference to the FeatureToggle package:

2. Next, create a folder called `Toggle` and add a class called `NewContactForm.cs`. Copy the following code into this class file:

```
using FeatureToggle;
namespace MyWebApp.Toggle
{
    public class NewContactForm : SimpleFeatureToggle
    {
    }
}
```

3. Add a new app key in the `web.config` file; set the key name to `FeatureToggle.NewContactForm` and the value to `false`. This key will be used to control the feature flag:

```
<appSettings>
  <add key="webpages:Version" value="3.0.0.0" />
  <add key="webpages:Enabled" value="false" />
  <add key="ClientValidationEnabled" value="true" />
  <add key="UnobtrusiveJavaScriptEnabled" value="true" />
  <add key="FeatureToggle.NewContactForm" value="false"/>
</appSettings>
```

4. Next, modify the `Contact.cshtml` page under `Views\Home` to include the following code:

```
@{
var toggle = new MyWebApp.Toggle.NewContactForm();
    if (toggle.FeatureEnabled)
    {
      <img src="https://www.incimages.com/uploaded_files/image/970x450/getty_459885938_144096.jpg" />
    }
}
```

5. Build and run the project. Navigate to the **Contact** form page and you'll see that it's unchanged. Update the value of the `FeatureToggle.NewContactForm` key in the `web.config` file from `false` to `true`.

6. Now refresh the **Contact** form. You'll see the updated page with the image:

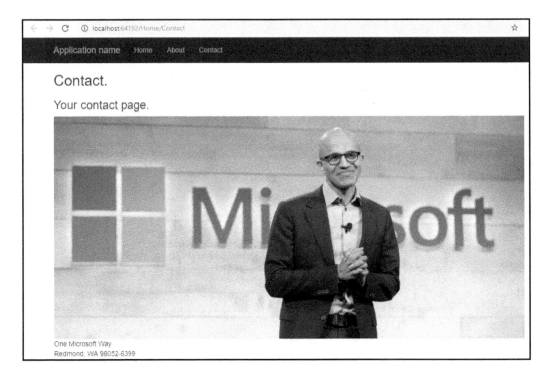

How it works...

The feature toggle package includes a series of providers that can be used to control the value of an object that can, in turn, be used to decide whether the feature is accessible. You may ask why we use feature toggle. Well, it is easy to construct a simple `if....else` condition using a config key to control when the page gets shown. While magic strings can be used, toggles should be real things (objects), not just a loosely typed string. This helps effectively manage the feature flags over time. When using real toggles, you can do the following:

- Find uses of the `Toggle` class to see where it's used
- Delete the `Toggle` class and see where a build fails

Feature flags allow you to decouple code deployments from feature releases. This simplifies testing code changes in production without impacting end users. By using feature flags, it's possible to control who can see a feature; it's also possible to phase in traffic to a new feature rather than opening up all users at once. You can read more about feature flags and their benefits here: `https://martinfowler.com/articles/feature-toggles.html`.

There's more...

The feature toggle package also provides the following feature toggle types:

- `AlwaysOffFeatureToggle`
- `AlwaysOnFeatureToggle`
- `EnabledOnOrAfterDateFeatureToggle`
- `EnabledOnOrBeforeDateFeatureToggle`
- `EnabledBetweenDatesFeatureToggle`
- `SimpleFeatureToggle`
- `RandomFeatureToggle`
- `EnabledOnDaysOfWeekFeatureToggle`
- `SqlFeatureToggle`
- `EnabledOnOrAfterAssemblyVersionWhereToggleIsDefinedToggle`

More details on these feature toggle types and their usage can be found at: `http://jason-roberts.github.io/FeatureToggle.Docs/pages/usage.html`.

Distributing multi-configuration tests against agents

Pipelines are a great way of running tests. The pipeline can be used to run unit tests, functional tests, and integration tests. If you have a large number of tests in your application, the verification process can slow down significantly. It can get even slower if you have a large matrix of configurations to run the tests against. For example, if you have a collection of selenium tests that perform UI-level verification, you may need to run these tests against Internet Explorer, Chrome, and Firefox and run the tests on Windows, macOS, and flavors of Linux.

In this recipe, we'll learn how easy it is to use a combination of a multi-configuration execution plan along with a pool of test agents to distribute the test execution.

How to do it...

In the **Variables** section in a build pipeline, define one or more variables that'll be used to describe the test matrix:

1. In our example, we need to test against multiple browsers on multiple platforms. So, I've created two variables, one for browsers and the other for platforms:

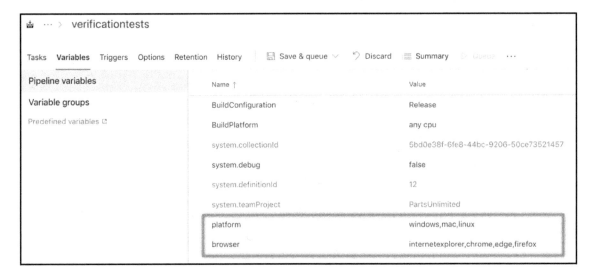

2. Next, create an agent pool with multiple agents. For the purposes of this recipe, I've created a build pool `buildgrid-01` with two agents:

3. In the **Agents** phase in the pipeline, change the **Execution plan** to **Multi-configuration** and set the **Multipliers** to the variables.

4. Set the **Maximum number of agents** to 2. The maximum agent count lets you specify the number of agents from your pool the job can distribute the tests on:

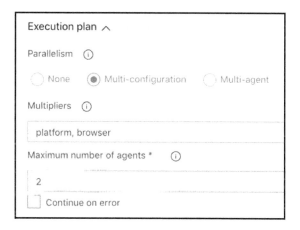

5. To pass the configuration value to your test, simply use the $(browser) and $(platform) variables in the test configuration:

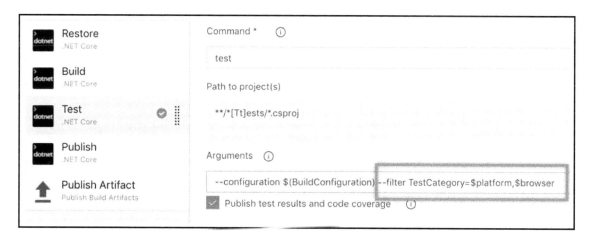

6. Save the changes and trigger the build. The build will distribute the matrix of execution across the pool of agents.

How it works...

The comma-separated values in the `platform` and `browser` variables are used to create the test matrix:

Browser	Internet Explorer	Chrome	Edge	Firefox
Platform	Windows	Windows	Windows	Windows
Platform	Mac	Mac	Mac	Mac
Platform	Linux	Linux	Linux	Linux

The multi-configuration test execution plan simply iterates through the comma-separated values one at a time and passes them to the $platform and $browser variables, which are then passed in to the test configuration. As you can see in the following screenshot, the test configuration is distributed across the two agents available in the pool:

There's more...

With multi-configuration you can run multiple jobs, each with a different value for one or more variables (multipliers). If you want to run the same job on multiple agents, then you can use the multi-agent option of parallelism. The preceding test slicing example can be accomplished through the multi-agent option.

Configuring parallel execution of tests using Azure Pipelines

Running tests to validate changes to the code is key to maintaining quality. For continuous integration practice to be successful, it is essential you have a good test suite that is run with every build. However, as the code base grows, the regression test suite tends to grow as well, and running a full regression test can take a long time. Sometimes, tests themselves may be long-running – this is typically the case if you write end-to-end tests. This reduces the speed with which customer value can be delivered, as pipelines cannot process builds quickly enough.

Being able to divide the test execution on multiple cores across a pool of agents can significantly reduce the time it takes to complete the test execution. While most build servers are multi-core, the agent orchestrating the pipelines doesn't always provide an easy way to distribute the test execution on multiple cores. In this recipe, we'll see how easy it is to enable parallel execution of tests using Azure Pipelines.

Getting ready

Create a new pipeline using the ASP.NET Core template. This will add the Visual Studio Test task to the pipeline.

Save the pipeline as `paralleltesting.demo`:

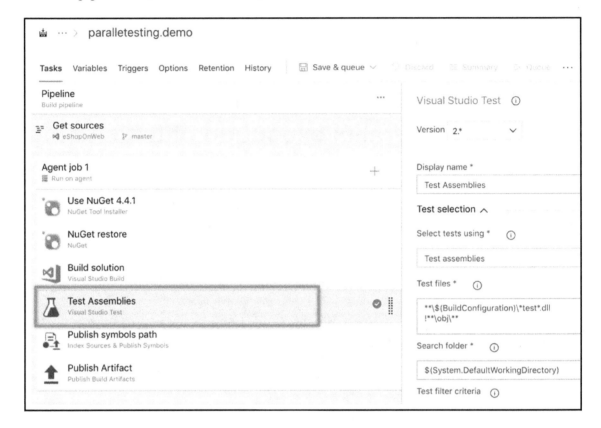

How to do it...

1. In the **Execution** section of the Visual Studio Test task, check the option to **Run tests in parallel on multi-core machines**:

2. In the **Advanced execution options** section, check the option to **Automatically determine the batch size** and set the batch size to be applied **Based on number of tests and agents**:

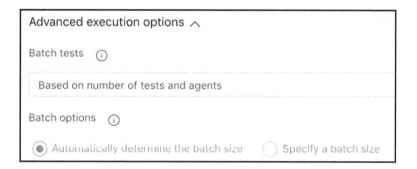

3. Save and trigger the build to execute the tests as per the settings in the Visual Studio Test task.

How it works...

The Visual Studio Test task (version 2) is designed to work seamlessly with parallel job settings. When a pipeline job that contains the Visual Studio Test task is configured to run on multiple agents in parallel, it automatically detects that multiple agents are involved and creates test slices that can be run in parallel across these agents. Furthermore, the task can be configured to create test slices to suit different requirements such as batching based on the number of tests and agents, the previous test running times, or the location of tests in assemblies:

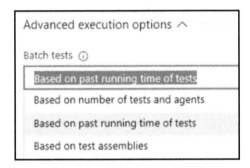

When the run parallel checkbox is checked, behind the scenes the `maxcpucount` value is set to 0, which internally configures the Visual Studio Test task to enforce that the test execution process isn't allocated affinity to just one CPU processor:

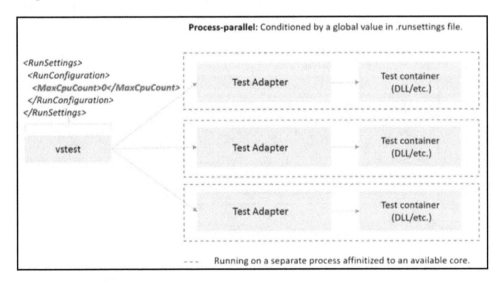

There's more...

The parallelism of test execution is offered by most test frameworks. All modern test frameworks, such as MSTest v2, NUnit, xUnit, and others, provide the ability to run tests in parallel. Typically, tests in an assembly are run in parallel. The Visual Studio test task already supports the previously listed testing frameworks, therefore the options of parallel execution and slicing based on the number of agents/tests and test assemblies is available to all supported testing frameworks.

Running SpecFlow tests using Azure Pipelines

SpecFlow is a testing framework that lets you define application behavior in plain, meaningful English text using a simple grammar defined by a language called **Gherkin**. SpecFlow is a very popular open source framework for **Behavior-Driven Development (BDD)**. SpecFlow democratizes testing to non-technical users by giving them a way of defining tests using the business domain and functional language, which can then be fleshed out as a functional test. In this recipe, we'll learn how SpecFlow tests can be integrated to run in Azure Pipelines.

Getting ready

Create a new pipeline using the ASP.NET Core template. In this recipe, we'll be mostly focusing on the Test task in this pipeline.

How to do it...

SpecFlow tests don't necessarily need the SpecRunner for execution: they can be run using MSTestv2 or any other compatible framework. However, using SpecRunner provides great benefits: for example, you can get some very useful analysis out of the tests that wouldn't necessarily be available if you used other test execution frameworks. Luckily, using SpecRunner for test execution doesn't require any installation on the agent!

The Visual Studio Test task supports triggering a test adapter as long as it can find the path to the custom test adapter:

1. To allow the test task to find the custom test adapter, it's best to include the test adapter as a NuGet package reference:

2. Since the custom test adapter is added as a NuGet package, it doesn't need to be called out as a specific path reference in the test task in the Azure Pipeline:

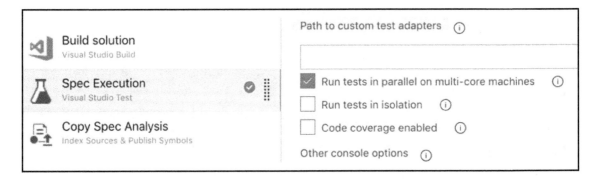

3. If the packages are added correctly, in the **Build** summary for this step you'll be able to see that the tests are executed using the **SpecFlow+ Runner** test adapter:

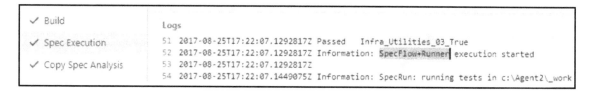

How it works...

When SpecFlow tests are executed in Visual Studio, an analysis report is generated by SpecFlow:

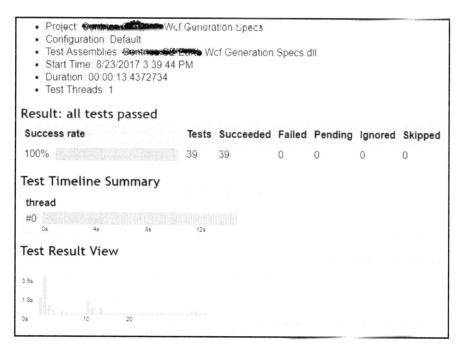

If the **Upload Attachment** option is checked in the test task, the SpecFlow test execution and analysis logs get attached to the test run results:

There's more...

By using the SpecFlow plus extension, available in the Azure DevOps Server marketplace you can easily publish your spec tests as living documentation within Azure DevOps Server. This can be achieved by using the SpecFlow+LivingDoc documentation (https://marketplace.visualstudio.com/items?itemName=techtalk.techtalk-specflow-plus) extension in your Azure Pipeline:

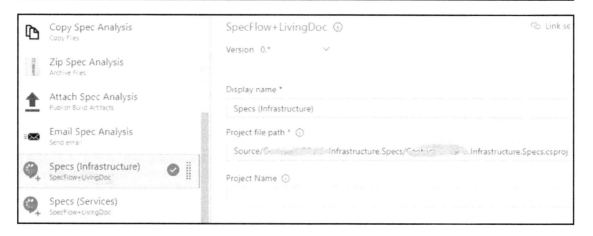

Personally, I think the SpecFlow+LivingDoc is pretty rough and needs some more work, but nonetheless, it provides great value even in its current state:

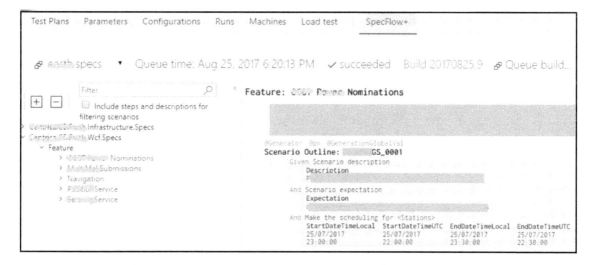

Analyzing test execution results from Runs view

In Azure DevOps Server 19, test execution results of both manual and automated testing are surfaced in the Runs page. The Runs page offers a unified experience for analyzing the results of tests executed using any framework. In this recipe, we'll learn how to analyze and action the test execution results in the Runs view in Team Web Portal.

Getting ready

Launch the Parts Unlimited team project, navigate to the **Test Hub**, and click on **Runs** to load the **Runs** page.

How to do it...

The **Runs** page displays the recent test runs. At first glance, you can see the test execution status, test configuration, build number, number of failed tests, and pass rate:

1. Navigate to the filters view by clicking the **Filters** tab. The query is defaulted to display the test runs from the last seven days.

2. Amend and add new clauses to show only the automated test runs for today:

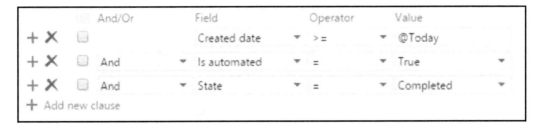

The query narrows down the test execution results to just one run:

3. Double-click on test run ID to open the test run for analysis. This view shows the run summary along with charts to visualize the test results by properties, traits, configuration, failures type, and resolution. Any attachments associated to the test run are also available in this view:

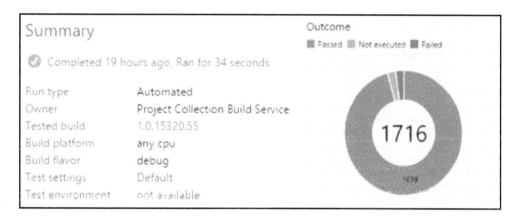

4. Navigate to the **Test results** tab to see the list of all tests executed as part of this test run. Prior to TFS 2015, you had to download the `trx` file and open it in Visual Studio to get to this information. This view provides the next level of detail; among other things, you can see the test execution duration and failure error messages:

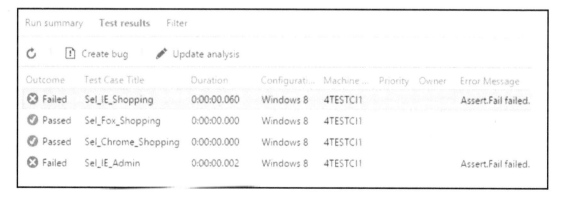

5. Select multiple tests and click on create a bug to create a bug type work item.

6. Click on **Update analysis** to add comments to the test results. You can also double-click a test to go to the next level of detail on its test execution:

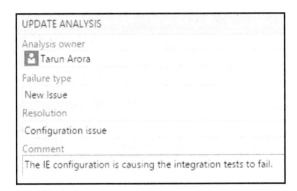

How it works...

This functionality gives you a unified test analysis experience irrespective of the framework on which you choose to execute your tests. In summary, you can query all test runs available in your Team Project, drill down into a specific test run to get a summary view of that run, visualize test runs using charts, query/filter the test results within a run, drill down to a specific test result, download attachments, and, last but not least, analyze test failures and file bugs.

Exporting test artifacts and test results from Test Hub

In Azure DevOps Server, test artifacts comprise test plans, test suites, test cases, and test results. It is common to have to export the test artifacts for the purposes of sharing and reporting. Back in the days of TFS 2013, Test Scribe delivered as a Visual Studio Extension was the only way to export these artifacts. Test Hub now boasts the email or print test artifacts functionality, which allows you to easily share test artifacts with stakeholders. The feature is simple to use and can be triggered from several places within the Test Hub.

Getting ready

Launch the Parts Unlimited team project and navigate to the Test Hub.

How to do it...

1. Select the **Test Plans** and click on **Email or print the test artifacts** from the toolbar:

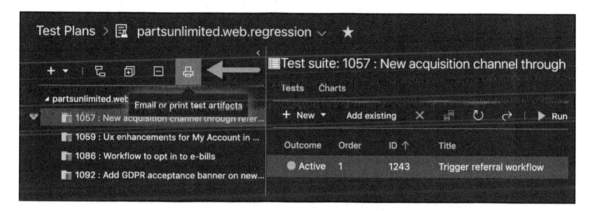

 You can export the artifacts from the root by selecting the top-level test suite.

Whether you chose to export from test plan or test suite in both the cases, you will get a new form to select 'what' and 'how', the 'what' in this case being the artifacts, and the how being email or print. A few items are worth highlighting in the following screenshot. The **Latest test outcome** option has been added in Update 1; selecting this option also exports the test results.

2. Choosing **Selected suite + children** recursively exports all children of the selected suite:

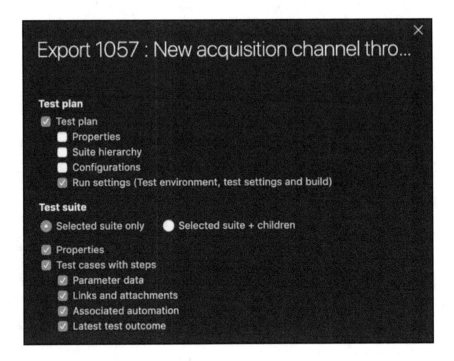

How it works...

Clicking on print or email starts the process of generating the extract. This may take up to a few seconds to complete, depending on the quantity and size of the artifacts being exported. Once the export has been completed, a form will pop up to show you the preview of the export. You can also edit and format the values from the preview form.

Since we had chosen the email option, the form has a field that allows us to choose the email address of the person we would like the export to be sent out to:

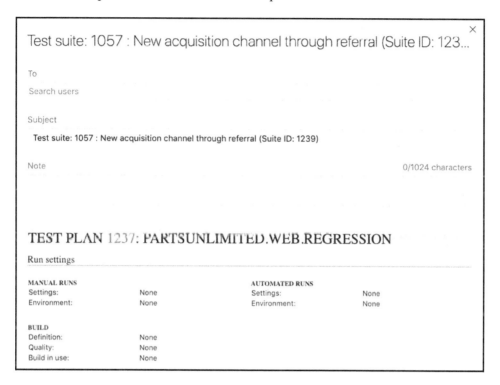

As illustrated in the following screenshot, the export also includes the test steps:

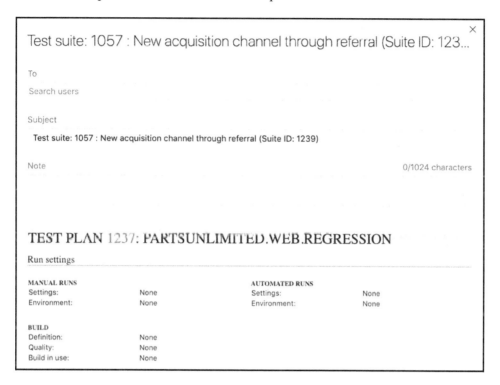

There's more...

It is possible to customize the format of the export by modifying the underlying template used by Azure DevOps Server during the export/print process. There are a few points to keep in mind before customizing the template.

You should create a backup of the original template; for example, copy it and rename it as `TestSuite-Original.xsl`. If not, when you upgrade Azure DevOps Server, the changes you made in the `TestSuite.xsl` file may get overwritten. The export does not support customization per project and the style changes will affect all projects in your Azure DevOps Server instance.

Follow the steps listed here to add your company logo to the export:

1. Log on to the Team Foundation Server application tier and navigate to the following path and add your company logo (`companylogo.png`) in this folder path: `C:\Program Files\Microsoft Team Foundation Server 14.0\Application Tier\Web Services\_tfs_resources\TestManagement\v1.0\Transforms\1033\TestSuite.xsl`.

2. Modify the `TestSuite.xsl` file in the `<installation path>\Application Tier\Web Services\_tfs_resources\TestManagement\v1.0\Transforms\<locale>\TestSuite.xsl` folder.

3. Open the `TestSuite.xsl` file in Notepad and add the following lines of code to include your company logo into the export template:

```
<div style="align:center;">
<img src="../../_static/tfs/18/_content/companylogo.png" />
</div>
```

The results of the customization can be tested by generating an export through the Test Hub.

Charting testing status on the dashboard in team portal

The charting tools in team portal provide a great way to analyze and visualize test case execution. The charts created through the charting tools can be pinned to custom dashboards. Both charts and dashboards are fantastic information radiators to share the test execution results with team members and stakeholders. In this recipe, we'll learn how to pin the test execution results on a custom dashboard in a team portal.

Getting ready

Follow the steps in the *Configuring dashboards in Team Project* recipe in `Chapter 1`, *Planning and Tracking Work*, to create a custom dashboard for testing.

How to do it...

1. Navigate to the Test Hub in the Parts Unlimited team project. The Test plan page gives you a list of test suites and a list of test cases for the selected suite. The **Charts** tab gives you a great way to visualize this information.
2. Click on the + icon and select **New test result charts**.
3. Select a bar chart and **Group by** as **Outcome**: this renders the test case outcome in the bar chart. Click **OK** to save the chart.
4. Right-click the newly created chart and pin the chart to the testing dashboard:

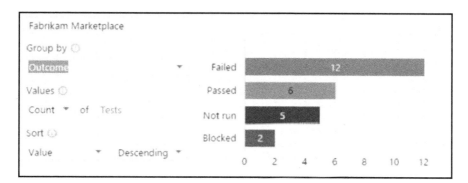

5. Now click on the + icon and select **New test case chart**. Test case chart types support trend charts; the supported trend period is from seven days to up to 12 months.

6. Select the stacked area chart type and choose to stack by State. This will allow you to visualize the state of the test cases over time.

7. Click **OK** to save the chart. Right-click the chart and pin to the dashboard:

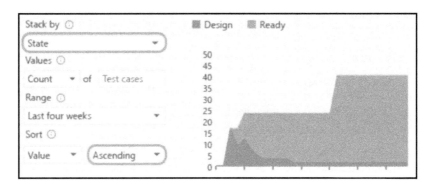

How it works...

The charts are calculated using the Work Item data. When Work Items are updated, the charts reflect the updates immediately. To learn more about the charting functionality in a team web portal, refer to the walk-through here: `http://bit.ly/1PGP8CU`.

6
Continuous Deployments

Continuous Deployment is the practice of teams to continuously deploy tested and working software to production. The release pipeline of Azure DevOps Server is just an orchestrator of the activities you do on an environment to get your software deployed and running. Another key technique of continuous deployments is the consistency of deployment steps - meaning you follow the same deployment steps across all your deployment environments. The advantage is repeatability, reliability - thus improving your overall delivery so that you release software to production sooner and consistently.

In this chapter, we will see different ways to deploy various types of resources using continuous deployment strategy. Not only will we see how to deploy applications, but will also see how to provision infrastructure so that we eventually achieve repeatable and reliable deployments of our software.

We will cover the following recipes:

- Deploying the database to Azure SQL using the release pipeline
- Consuming secrets from Azure Key Vault in your release pipeline
- Deploying the .NET Core web application to Azure App Service
- Deploying an Azure function to Azure
- Publishing secrets to Azure Key Vault
- Deploying a static website on Azure Storage
- Deploying a VM to Azure DevTest Labs

Deploying the database to Azure SQL using the release pipeline

Databases are an integral part of any application and should be part of your DevOps process, which means integrating changes continuously using source control and delivering every change to the environment.

However, most organizations still have a legacy way of deploying databases. Developers still have code stored procedures and commit to the source control, but when it comes to the deployment, a detailed release notes document is prepared on how the database has to be provisioned and handed over to the DBAs.

In this recipe, we will see how we can build a process to consistently develop and deploy the database to Azure SQLDB.

Getting ready

For this recipe, I am using a sample database called **AdventureWorks**, published by Microsoft. If you do not have this database already, Microsoft makes the backup file available for download on GitHub here: `http://bit.ly/2GNpvSo`. Go ahead and download the database as per your SQL Server version. Since I have SQL Server 2017 Express on my machine, I downloaded the `AdventureWorks2017.bak` file and then restored the database from the backup. Microsoft has instructions on restoring the database, which is documented here: `http://bit.ly/2GKK8hT`. Once you restore you should see the database in SQL Server Management Studio shown as follows:

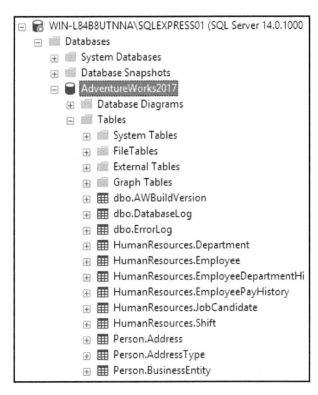

Creating a database project and importing the database

First, we need to ensure that we have **SQL Server Data Tools** (**SSDT**) installed with our Visual Studio version. This tool is available during Visual Studio installation with the data storage and processing workload. It is also available as a standalone installer for Visual Studio:

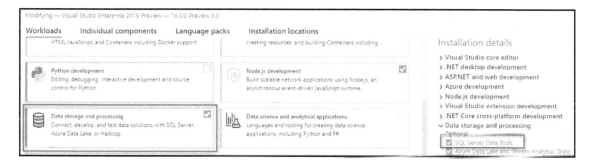

This development tool helps with database design, schema refactoring, and development of database using Visual Studio. Developers can benefit from familiar Visual Studio tools for database development with tools and assistance for code navigation, IntelliSense, debugging, and a rich editor. More information about SSDT can be found in the Microsoft documentation: `http://bit.ly/2tr5Bon`.

Create a new database project, import our existing AdventureWorks database, and commit it to the repository (for more information on how to do this, refer to `http://bit.ly/2tBia0j`):

Since we are going to be deploying to Azure SQL Database, I have changed the **Target platform** under **Project Settings**:

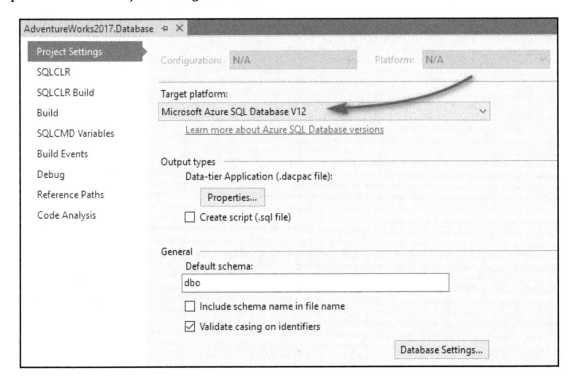

Right click on the project and then import the database. I have then committed the code (project) in my repository, as shown in the following screenshot:

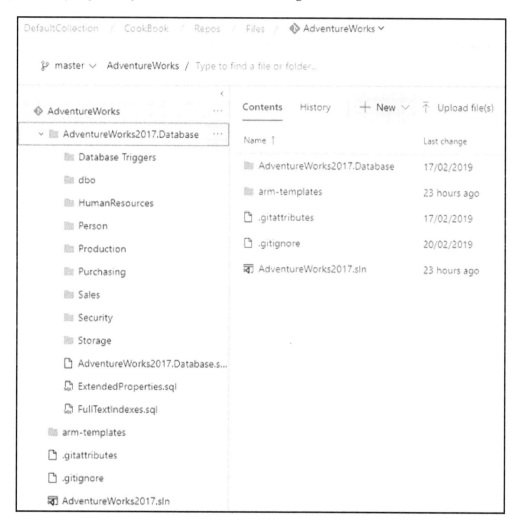

Creating a build definition

Next, we will create a quick build pipeline and produce a dacpac package for this database. A database package is a deployable package from your version-controlled database project. You can read more about it at http://bit.ly/2tr5Bon.

We will add the new YAML-based pipeline, so add a new file named `azure-pipelines.yml` in the repository and add the following content:

 The YAML file used in this recipe is available in the Chapter directory under *RCP01-Database-CD* folder

```
resources:
- repo: self
queue:
name: Default
demands:
- msbuild
- visualstudio

steps:
- task: VSBuild@1
displayName: 'Build solution AdventureWorks2017.sln'
inputs:
solution: AdventureWorks2017.sln
msbuildArgs: '/p:CmdLineInMemoryStorage=True'
platform: 'any cpu'
configuration: release

- task: CopyFiles@2
displayName: 'Copy Files to: $(Build.ArtifactStagingDirectory)'
inputs:
SourceFolder: '$(Agent.BuildDirectory)'
Contents: '**\*.dacpac'
TargetFolder: '$(Build.ArtifactStagingDirectory)'
flattenFolders: true

- task: PublishBuildArtifacts@1
displayName: 'Publish Artifact: databases'
inputs:
ArtifactName: databases
```

We have three simple tasks here under the `steps` element:

- We build `AdeventureWorks2017.sln`, which produces the `.dacpac` file, which is a packaged version of our database
- In the next task, we search for the `.dacpac` file in the build directory and copy only that file into our artifact-staging directory
- Lastly, we publish it as an artifact

Next, go to the **Builds** hub under the **Pipelines** service and click **New build pipeline**:

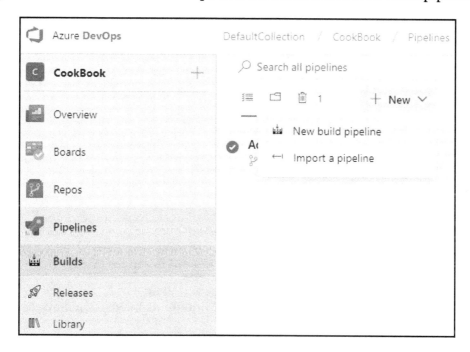

On the next screen, select the correct repository and branch and click **Continue**:

On the next screen, select the YAML template and click **Apply**:

You will be prompted to select the YAML file you committed earlier on the next screen. Select the file and under the **Triggers** tab, enable Continuous Integration. **Save & queue** the pipeline:

The build will run and produce the `.dacpac` file, which we will use as the artifact of this build. Now, you have a full continuous integration pipeline so that every time there are any commits in the database project, the build is triggered and the database project is compiled to check your SQL scripts for errors and also verify the schema changes:

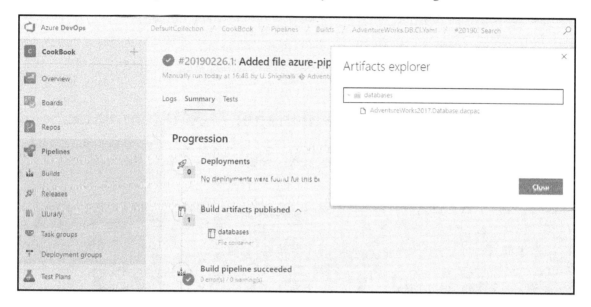

How to do it...

Now that we have our build pipeline producing the required artifact, it is time for us to start working on the deployment of this database in Azure. the time of writing, to deploy our existing database, we need to ensure that we have SQL Server provisioned. We could manually create the required SQL Server, but this means we have a manual activity during deployment. The correct solution would be to automate the provisioning of SQL Server as part of the pipeline. This means that even if the required resources are not present, our pipeline will ensure the integrity of the system and create the missing resources (in this case, SQL Server) and then deploy our database. We will be using **Azure Resource Manager** (**ARM**) templates to provision SQL Server in Azure. In simple terms, Azure Resource Manager templates can be used to consistently create/update resources in Azure.

For more information on Azure Resource Manager, visit `http://bit.ly/ 2FiNtn2`.

As part of the release pipeline, we would like to automate the following:

- The creation of Azure SQL server, if it doesn't exist
- The deployment of the database using the `dacpac` we produced

Creating Azure Resource Manager (ARM) templates

Azure Resource manager templates are simple JSON files that can be used to deploy one or many resources at once. A bare-minimum ARM template is made up of the following structure:

```
 Welcome          {} mywebapp.azuredeploy.json ●
1  {
2      "$schema": "https://schema.management.azure.com/schemas/2015-01-01/deploymentTemplate.json#",
3      "contentVersion": "1.0.0.0",
4      "parameters": {},
5      "variables": {},
6      "resources": [],
7      "outputs": {}
8  }
```

We will create an ARM template to provision the SQL Server on Azure:

1. Using your favorite editor, create a file named `sql.deploy.json`

The ARM templates used here are available under `RCP01-Database-CD` folder.

Let's quickly go through what we are doing in the `sql.deploy.json` ARM template. First, in the `parameters` section, we declared a few parameters:

```
{
    "$schema":
"https://schema.management.azure.com/schemas/2015-01-01/deploymentTempl
ate.json#",
    "contentVersion": "1.0.0.0",
```

```
    "parameters": {
        "environmentConfiguration": {
            "type": "object"
        },
        "sqlserverAdminLogin": {
            "type": "string"
        },
        "sqlServerAdminPassword": {
            "type": "securestring"
        },
    //rest of the ARM template is trimmed for the sake of brevity
}
```

The key parameters are `sqlserverAdminLogin` and the `sqlServerAdminPassword`. In the full ARM template, we also have a few generic parameters for environment-specific values, SKU, and the pricing tier. The values for these parameters can be passed during the deployment using a parameters JSON file.

Next, we use the `variables` section to declare a few variables. We use variables specifically to concatenate the server name with any prefixes. In this case, we would like to prefix `sqlserver-dev` in the DEV environment and `sqlserver-test` in the TEST environment, so that after variable processing our full SQL Server name will be `sqlserver-dev-1-<uniquestring>`.

```
    "variables": {
            "sqlServerName":
    "[toLower(concat(parameters('environmentConfiguration').prefix.
    sqlServer, '-1','-',uniqueString(resourceGroup().id)))]",
            "deployedAdventureWorksSqlDbName":
    "[toLower(concat(parameters('environmentConfiguration').prefix.
    sqlDb,'-', 'AdventureWorks'))]"
        },
```

The **resources** section defines SQL Server, which can be identified by the `Microsoft.Sql/servers` type, and the Azure SQL database, which is a child resource of the `databases` type.

```
        "resources": [
            {
                "name": "[variables('sqlServerName')]",
                "type": "Microsoft.Sql/servers",
                "location": "[resourceGroup().location]",
                "apiVersion": "2014-04-01-preview",
                "dependsOn": [],
                "properties": {
```

```
                              "administratorLogin":
        "[parameters('sqlserverAdminLogin')]",
                              "administratorLoginPassword":
        "[parameters('sqlServerAdminPassword')]"
                    },
                  //rest of the ARM template is trimmed for the sake of
        brevity
                  }
        ]
```

Lastly, the **outputs** section defines the output variables. The values for these variables are automatically set by the Azure Resource Manager and are available for us to consume soon after the deployment of the template. As you can see in the ARM template, we output the fully-qualified domain name of the SQL server (for example: databasename.database.windows.net), database name so that our pipeline can connect to the provisioned SQL Server and deploy the database. We will see how our pipeline makes use of these output variables soon.

```
"outputs": {
"sql.sqlserver.qualified.name": {
"type": "string",
"value":
"[reference(variables('sqlServerName')).fullyQualifiedDomainNam
e]"
 },
 "sql.sqlserver.name": {
 "type": "string",
 "value": "[variables('sqlServerName')]"
 },
 "sql.adventureworks.sqldb.name": {
 "type": "string",
 "value": "[variables('deployedAdventureWorksSqlDbName')]"
 }
 }
```

The next step is to create a parameters files so that we can supply values during deployment. You can also pass these parameters directly as arguments during deployment, but keeping them in a file and committed into source control ensures that we have a full audit history. Also, as you will see soon, it's easy to supply a path for these parameter files in the Azure DevOps Server pipeline.

Parameter files also allow us to define environment specific values. For example, assume we have a requirement to deploy this database package to environments named DEV first (with the requirement to suffix *dev* to our SQL Server), and then to TEST (suffix *test*). Since the suffix is changing between environments, we will be able to use two parameter files.

2. Create a file named `sql.deploy.param.dev.json` and paste in the following code. We will use this parameter file to deploy to the DEV stage:

```
{
    "$schema":
"https://schema.management.azure.com/schemas/2015-01-01/deploymentP
arameters.json#",
    "contentVersion": "1.0.0.0",
    "parameters": {
        "environmentConfiguration": {
            "value": {
                "prefix": {
                    "sqlDb": "sqldb",
                    "sqlServer": "sqlserver-dev"
                }
            }
        }
    }
}
```

3. Create a file named `sql.deploy.param.test.json` and paste in the following code. We will use this to provision our TEST stage. As you can see, our prefix for SQL Server is now `sqlserver-test`:

```
{
    "$schema":
"https://schema.management.azure.com/schemas/2015-01-01/deploymentP
arameters.json#",
    "contentVersion": "1.0.0.0",
    "parameters": {
        "environmentConfiguration": {
            "value": {
                "prefix": {
                    "sqlDb": "sqldb",
                    "sqlServer": "sqlserver-test"
                }
            }
        }
    }
}
```

4. Notice the change in sqlServer property. It has suffix *dev* in dev specific parameter file and *test* in test stage-specific parameter file. Commit the files into source control. I committed these to my repository on GitHub.

Creating the release pipeline

Now that we have the build pipeline ready and producing the database as an artifact, we are ready to consume it and deploy it to the environment.

1. Head over to the Release hub and create a new release pipeline. We will add two artifact sources to this pipeline. Add the artifact that was produced by our build pipeline:

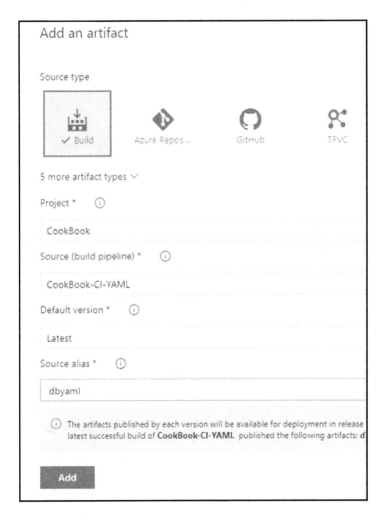

2. Add a second artifact, which will bring over our ARM templates from the GitHub repository:

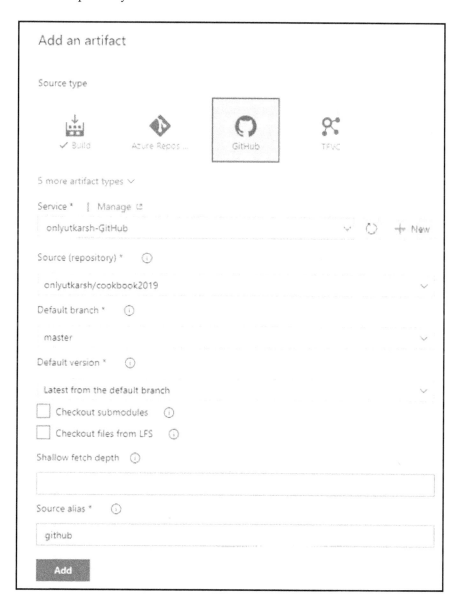

3. Click **+ Add** under the stages section and add a new stage; name it DEV:

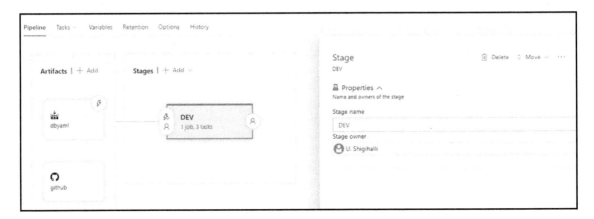

4. Create two variables, which we will use to pass the SQL admin username and password. Scope this variable to just the DEV stage so that we can use the different password for higher stages (for example, TEST). We also mark the variable password as secure (by clicking the lock icon) so that the password is not visible in the logs or by anyone editing the pipeline at a later date:

5. Under the **Pipelines** tab, click on the **1 job...** link and open the stage. We will now add tasks in this stage to use the artifacts.

    The first task we will add is the **Azure Resource Group Deployment** task and configure it as follows. Notice (marked in red) that we are passing the `sql` admin login and `sqlpassword` parameter values for ARM templates from the variables we just declared:

This step will just provision SQL Server and an empty database.

This task uses a service connection to securely connect to Azure. If you have not created a service connection before, please refer to the documentation.

1. Service connections for builds and releases: `http://bit.ly/2vcUCQe`
2. Granular deployment Privileges using Service Principals: `http://bit.ly/2vj0aZe`

6. Let's use an extension from the VS Marketplace (more on this in `Chapter 8`, *Azure DevOps Extensions*). This task is called **ARM Outputs** and it helps us create dynamic Azure DevOps variables from the ARM template output. If you remember, we have output variables defined in our ARM template to get SQL Server and Database names.

Once this task creates Azure DevOps pipeline variables, we will be able to use them in the pipeline for any other task. Let's add the ARM Outputs task and configure it as follows. Notice that we prefix our variables with the `arm.out.` string, and so our pipeline variables will be created in the following way: `arm.out.sql.server.qualified.name`:

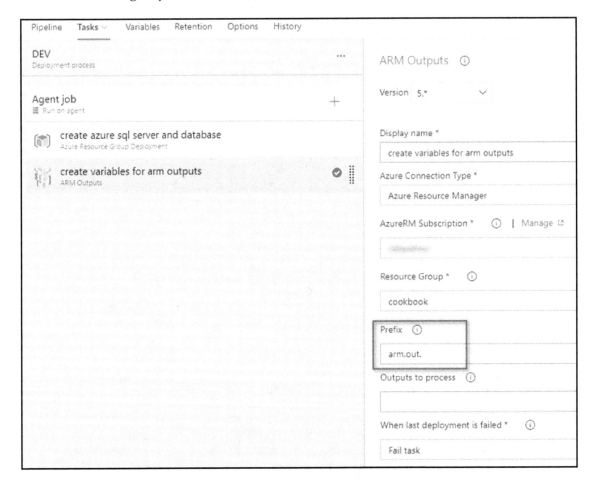

This task needs to be added just under the **Azure Resource Group Deployment** task.

 You can download and install the ARM Outputs extension from here: `http://bit.ly/2OBCTLh`.

7. Let's publish the database package (dacpac) to our provisioned SQL Server and Azure SQL Database. We will add the **Azure SQL Database Deployment task** and configure it as follows. For the SQL Server and Database name fields, we are passing the variables that were created by the ARM Outputs task:

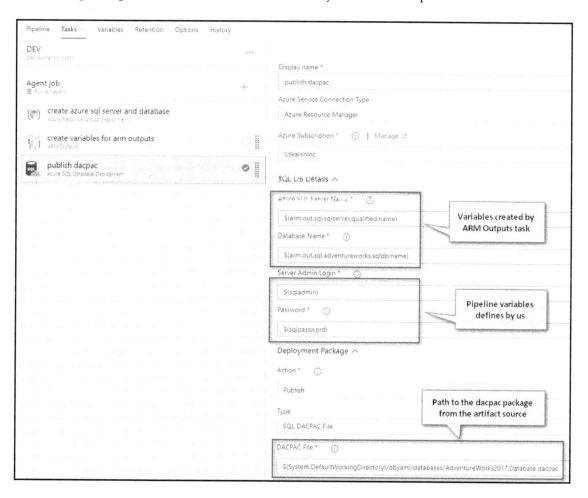

8. Save the pipeline and create a release. Your release pipeline will now create all the required resources and deploy the `.dacpac` file:

How it works...

In this recipe, we saw how easy it is to provision Azure resources (SQL Server and database) and deploy them using Azure DevOps Server pipelines. We created a database project using Visual Studio, which allows us to maintain our database (schema and scripts) as code. We then created a build pipeline, which ensures that we are not introducing any breaking changes by continuously building changes into our database code. Lastly, we created the release pipeline and, using build artifacts and ARM templates, we provisioned the necessary resources and deployed the database.

In the next recipe, we will extend this pipeline to deploy to a new stage, named TEST, and see how we can make use of variable groups to consume secrets from Azure Key Vault.

Consuming secrets from Azure Key Vault in your release pipeline

This recipe is an extension of the previous recipe; if you haven't already read the previous recipe, I recommend that you read it first.

In the previous recipe, we saw how to keep strings, such as passwords as pipeline variables and how to mark them as secure variables so that they are not visible in the logs or to anyone else editing the pipeline once saved. While it works really well, enterprises that are deploying to the cloud would love to centrally manage and maintain these secrets in Azure Key Vault.

 You can read more about Azure Key Vaults here: `http://bit.ly/2OAslff`.

Azure DevOps Server 2019 has native support for Azure Key Vault with variable groups. With variable groups in Azure DevOps Server, we can bring secrets from Azure Key Vault.

Getting ready

As a first step, we will manually create an Azure key vault and store the SQL Admin password as a single secret.

Creating a key vault in Azure

1. Go to `portal.azure.com` and then click on the **Create a resource** button. In the next blade, search for `Key Vault` and then click **Create**.

You will see **Create key vault** blade as in the following screenshot. Enter the details, such as key vault name, location, and pricing tier, and then click **Create**:

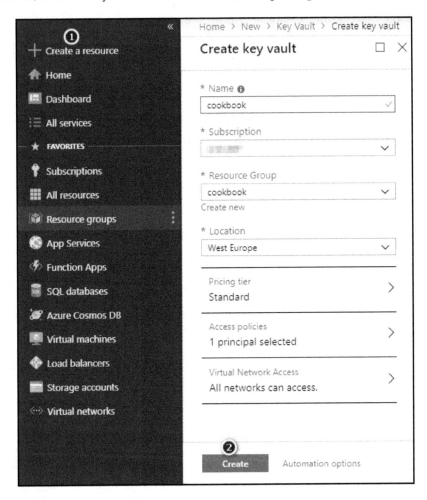

You will have a key vault created now.

2. Open the key vault, Click on + *Generate/Import.* Then provide a name for the secret and then SQL password you would like to use as a value for the secret

I have named the secret `sqlpassword`.

Creating a variable group and linking it to Azure Key Vault

Variable groups are defined and managed from the **Library** tab under the **Pipelines** tab. The advantage of a variable group is that you can make a set of variables available across the pipeline:

1. Click on the **+ Variable group** button; you will be presented with a screen asking for more information:

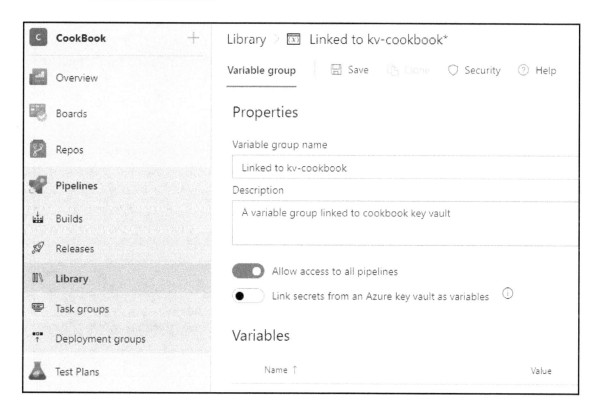

2. Give a name to the variable group, enable the **Link secrets from an Azure key vault as variables** flag option, and select the subscription and the key vault from the dropdown:

However, Azure DevOps will immediately give you an error. This is because the **service principal (SPN)** we are using from Azure DevOps to connect to Azure does not have permission to connect to the key vault. We will be able to solve this error by adding our SPN to the key vault's access policies.

3. Open the key vault to add the SPN that is used by Azure DevOps and click **OK**:

4. Go back to Azure DevOps Server and refresh the key vault name field; an error should appear. Click **+ Add** and a pop-up dialog will open to show all the available secrets. Select the secrets you would like to be available as part of the variable group and click **OK**:

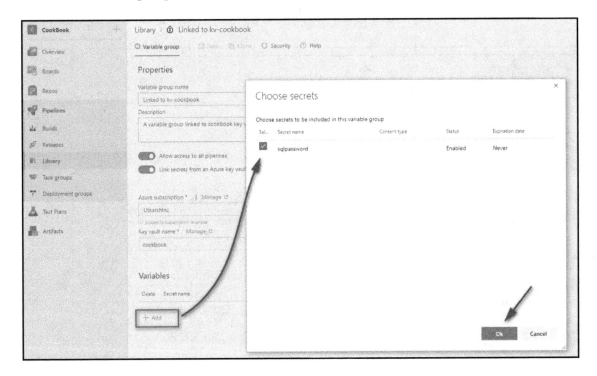

5. Click **Save** on the library:

Congratulations, you just created a variable group, which is now available to be consumed in the pipeline! In the next section, we will see how we can use this variable group in the release pipeline.

How to do it...

1. Go back to the release pipeline we created in the previous (*Deploying the database to Azure SQL using release pipeline*) recipe and enter the edit mode. Then, click the **Variables** tab. You might remember that we have a secret defined as a pipeline variable:

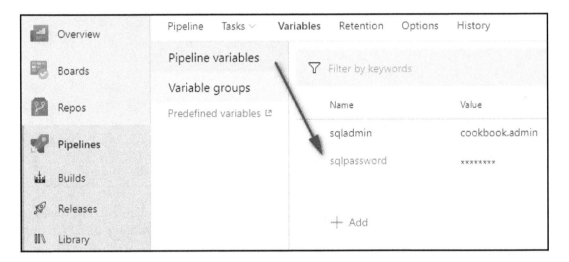

2. Because we will bring new value from the key vault via the variable group we defined earlier, we need to remove the pipeline variable, `sqlpassword`. Once done, click the **Variable groups** tab, then click the **Link variable group** button. You will see a new overlay window:

3. Select the variable group we defined and scope it to the DEV stage so that this variable is only allowed in the DEV stage, and then click the **Link** button.

Scoping the variable group to a particular stage has an advantage in that it allows us to use the secrets only for that particular stage. This allows us to define multiple variable groups (internally associated with different key vaults) and isolate the secrets to a particular stage. We can thus isolate secrets for different stages, such as PROD and DEV. This means that you will have granular control of your secrets – for example, you can allow your developers to read/modify secrets from the key vault that's used for the DEV stage, but limit access to the PROD key vault and the management of its secrets.

How it works...

Azure DevOps Server now intelligently brings in the latest values of the secret from the Azure key vault during runtime and passes them to the referenced task over the HTTPS channel. Each secret in the key vault is automatically created as a secret pipeline variable, which you can reference in our pipeline tasks like any other pipeline variables using the usual syntax (`%VARIABLE_NAME%` in a batch script, `$env:VARIABLE_NAME` in PowerShell, or `$VARIABLE_NAME` in bash scripts):

Pipeline variables	⌄	Name		Value
Variable groups	⌃	**Linked to kv-cookbook (1)**		Scopes: DEV
		A variable group linked to cookbook key vault		
Predefined variables ↗		sqlpassword		********

There's more...

Here are a few key facts about the variable group:

- Any changes to the secret values are automatically available during the run of the pipeline.
- Newly added secrets in the key vault are not automatically available in the pipeline. We will need to add them to the variable group.
- Deleting a variable group or removing the key-vault-linked secret from the variable will not remove the secret from the key vault.
- The variable group currently supports Azure key vault secrets only – cryptographic keys or the certificates are not supported.

See also

All the assets (variable groups and secure files) defined in the **Library** tab share the same security model. You can restrict who can create the variable group or the Library using permissions - For more on this is visit `http://bit.ly/2uPLWPp`.

Deploying the .NET Core web application to the Azure App Service

More and more users are switching to the .NET core framework these days. ASP.NET Core is a cross-platform framework for building modern applications. It offers many advantages over the traditional ASP.NET with many out-of-the-box features, such as dependency injection, which is suited for containers and those who want high performance.

 For more on ASP.NET Core and its benefits, visit `http://bit.ly/2P0vMfn`.

In this recipe, we will create a simple ASP.NET Core web app and deploy it into Azure App Service.

Getting ready

Here, we will just use the `dotnet` command to create the basic ASP.NET core application and commit it into the git repository. Then, we will create a new build pipeline to build the application and produce the artifact.

Creating the ASP.NET Core application

1. Ensure that you have the latest .NET Core SDK installed. If not, install the recommended version from `https://dotnet.microsoft.com/download/dotnet-core`.

   You can see the installed SDKs on your machine by using the following command.

   ```
   c:\aspnetcore-demo>dotnet --list-sdks
   2.1.202 [C:\Program Files\dotnet\sdk]
   2.1.505 [C:\Program Files\dotnet\sdk]
   2.1.602 [C:\Program Files\dotnet\sdk]
   2.2.105 [C:\Program Files\dotnet\sdk]
   ```

   For this demo, I am using 2.2 .NET Core.

2. Open the Command Prompt and run the following command to create an
    ASP.NET Core MVC application:

```
c:\aspnetcore-demo>dotnet new mvc --name MyWebsite --auth None
--no-https
The template "ASP.NET Core Web App (Model-View-Controller)" was
created successfully.
This template contains technologies from parties other than
Microsoft, see https://aka.ms/aspnetcore-template-3pn-210 for
details.

Processing post-creation actions...
Running 'dotnet restore' on MyWebsite\MyWebsite.csproj...
  Restoring packages for c:\aspnetcore-
demo\MyWebsite\MyWebsite.csproj...
  Generating MSBuild file c:\aspnetcore-
demo\MyWebsite\obj\MyWebsite.csproj.nuget.g.props.
  Generating MSBuild file c:\aspnetcore-
demo\MyWebsite\obj\MyWebsite.csproj.nuget.g.targets.
  Restore completed in 4.09 sec for c:\aspnetcore-
demo\MyWebsite\MyWebsite.csproj.

Restore succeeded.
```

We are supplying the name for our application as MyWebsite, using no
authentication with the --auth None argument. For simplicity we will not host
this website on https, hence pass the --no-https flag.

As you can see from the command output, the dotnet command creates an
ASP.NET Core MVC application and restores all the NuGet packages.

3. Run the website using the following command:

```
c:\aspnetcore-demo>dotnet run -p MyWebsite\MyWebsite.csproj
info:
Microsoft.AspNetCore.DataProtection.KeyManagement.XmlKeyManager
[0]
 User profile is available. Using
'C:\Users\utkarsh\AppData\Local\ASP.NET\DataProtection-Keys' as
key repository and Windows DPAPI to encrypt keys at rest.
Hosting environment: Development
Content root path: c:\aspnetcore-demo\MyWebsite
Now listening on: http://localhost:5000
Application started. Press Ctrl+C to shut down.
```

As you can see, our website is now running locally at `http://localhost:5000`:

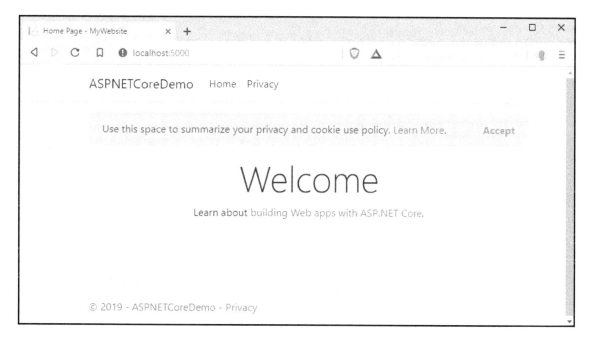

4. Creating the build pipeline and producing the artifact was covered in `Chapter 4`, *Continuous Integration and Build Automation*. If you have not checked it already, read the *Setting up a build pipeline for a .NET core application* recipe.

The YAML file for the build is in the relevant chapter folder under *RCP03-ASPNETCore-CD* directory. If you would like to know how to build using YAML file refer recipe *Deploying the database to Azure SQL using the release pipeline* in this chapter.

How to do it...

As we did in our first recipe, *Deploying the database to Azure SQL using the release pipeline*, we will also create the required infrastructure for our website using the release pipeline. To host our website in Azure, we need two things:

- **An app service plan**: Within Azure, an application runs inside the app service plan
- **An app service**: To host the website

- For more information on the app service plan, visit `http://bit.ly/2Pa9nwj`
- For more information on Azure App Service, visit `http://bit.ly/2PbfKzp`

Creating ARM templates

Let's create an ARM template that will create an app service plan and an empty app service:

1. Create a resource, `web.deploy.json`, and paste in the following content:

All the ARM templates referenced here are available under *RCP03-ASPNETCore-CD* folder

The important section is the `resources` array – you will see that in this ARM template, we are creating our app service plan and app service. We are also creating a slot named staging so that we can test our website before deploying it to the production slot (which is the default).

```
{
    "$schema":
"https://schema.management.azure.com/schemas/2015-01-01/deploymentTemplate.
json#",
    "contentVersion": "1.0.0.0",
    "parameters": {
        //code is trimmed for the sake of brevity
    },
    "variables": {
        "webAppServicePlanName":
"[concat(parameters('environmentConfiguration').prefix.appServiceWeb)]",
```

```
        "deployedWebAppName":
"[concat(parameters('environmentConfiguration').prefix.webApp, '-',
'mywebapp','-',uniqueString(resourceGroup().id))]",
        "myWebAppResourceId": "[resourceId('Microsoft.Web/Sites',
variables('deployedWebAppName'))]"
    },
    "resources": [
        //code is trimmed for the sake of brevity
        {
            "name": "[variables('deployedWebAppName')]",
            "apiVersion": "2016-08-01",
            "type": "Microsoft.Web/sites",
            "location": "[resourceGroup().location]",
            //code is trimmed for the sake of brevity
        },
        {
            "apiVersion": "2016-08-01",
            "type": "Microsoft.Web/sites/slots",
            "name": "[concat(variables('deployedWebAppName'), '/',
parameters('deploymentSlots')[copyIndex()])]",
            "kind": "app",
            //code is trimmed for the sake of brevity
        }
    ],
}
```

Finally, we are publishing the deployed web application name, and its URL as an output variable as you can see in the `outputs` object.

```
"outputs": {
        "my.webapp.name": {
            "type": "string",
            "value": "[variables('deployedWebAppName')]"
        },
        "my.webapp.uri": {
            "type": "string",
            "value":
"[concat('https://',reference(variables('myWebAppResourceId')).hostnames[0]
)]"
        }
    }
```

For more on deployment slots in Azure App Service, visit `http://bit.ly/2v4zhs0`.

We will also have a parameters file, which will allow us to override a few values, such as the web app prefix and SKU.

2. Create a parameter file named `web.deploy.parameters.json` and paste in the following content:

```json
{
    "$schema":
"https://schema.management.azure.com/schemas/2015-01-01/deploym
entParameters.json#",
    "contentVersion": "1.0.0.0",
    "parameters": {
        "environmentConfiguration": {
            "value": {
                "prefix": {
                    "appServiceWeb": "web-asp",
                    "webApp": "webapp"
                }
            }
        },
        "appServiceSkuName": {
            "value": "S1"
        },
        "appServiceSkuCapacity": {
            "value": 1
        }
    }
}
```

3. Commit the ARM templates and let's continue configuring the release pipeline.

Creating the release pipeline

Let's start building the release pipeline to deploy the application:

1. The first step is to create a new release pipeline and add the build artifact. To do that, Go to the *release* hub and create a New Release Pipeline and add the artifact.

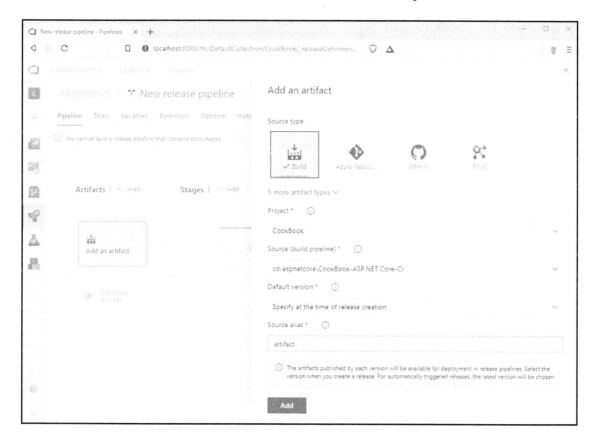

As you can see from the preceding screenshot, we are linking the build pipeline, which produces the deployable artifact for this release pipeline. Just for demonstration purposes, we are also setting the default version as **Specify at the time of release creation**, which means during the release creation, we will have to select the version of the artifact to be deployed we want to use.

2. Add both the web-deployable package and ARM templates as two artifacts to the release:

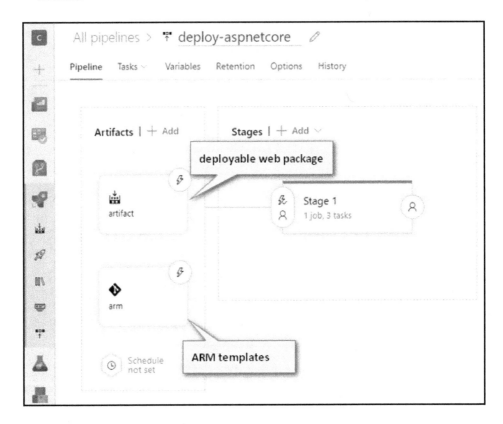

3. Click on the stage and add the following tasks:
    - **Azure resource group deployment task**: To deploy the ARM templates and create all the required Azure resources
    - **ARM outputs**: To get the output variables from the previous task and create the pipeline variables

- **Azure App Service Deploy**: This task will help us copy the deployable package to the app service we created in the first step:

For the first task, we are providing a path to our ARM template and parameters file:

4. Use the ARM Outputs task by Kees Schollart (`https://marketplace.visualstudio.com/items?itemName=keesschollaart.arm-outputs`) to create pipeline variables for each output variable from the ARM template. I am just prefixing our pipeline variables with the `arm.out.` string.

5. Add the Azure App Service Deployment task and configure it as follows:

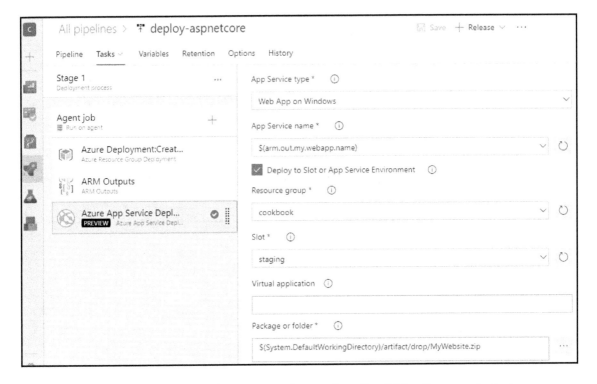

Notice that we are deploying it to the **staging** slot. This allows us to test our deployment in a different slot than the default *production* slot.

6. Save the release definition and trigger the release.

How it works...

Once you create the release, the deployment will start. The first step in the pipeline will first create an App Service Plan and other resources (slots for example) specified in the ARM template. The next step is to create the pipeline variables using the ARM Outputs task so that we can access the app service name we created in the previous task. Finally, we are using the **Azure App Service Deployment** task to deploy the application to the staging slot. We can then browse to the staging slot to see our website up and running:

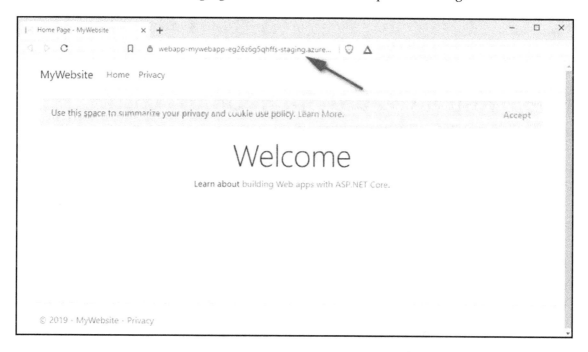

There's more...

In this recipe, we saw how we could deploy a web application from no infrastructure to a fully-hosted website in Azure using Azure DevOps Server 2019. We also saw how deployment slots allow us to isolate our deployments. We could extend this pipeline with more stages, such as DEV, TEST, and PROD. We can then use slots to isolate and open the new version of the website to only specific teams (say testing team) before swapping it with the production slot.

More information about deployment slots and management can be found at `https://docs.microsoft.com/en-us/azure/app-service/deploy-staging-slots`.

See also

Check out the following resources:

- Considerations on using Deployment Slots in your DevOps pipeline: `http://bit.ly/2P95vM5`
- App Service Plans: `http://bit.ly/2P905R1`

Deploying an Azure Function to Azure

Azure Functions are a new way to run your logic on a **serverless** technology in the cloud. Azure functions are hugely popular mainly because they can be cheaper compared to app service - as you have an option to pay only for the time spent running your code.

- Azure Functions documentation: `http://bit.ly/2Pb36jP`
- Serverless in Azure: `https://azure.microsoft.com/en-us/solutions/serverless/`

In this recipe, we will look at how to create an Azure Function in TypeScript and then we will look at how to deploy a sample Azure Function to Azure.

Getting ready

To create the Azure Function, you will need the following tools installed on your machine. Go ahead and install them all.

- VSCode: `https://code.visualstudio.com/`
- Azure Functions Extension for VS Code: `http://bit.ly/2Pd9OGk`
- NodeJS 8.0 and above: `https://nodejs.org/en/`
- PostMan: `https://www.getpostman.com/`

Creating a sample Azure Function

Once you install all the tools mentioned in the Getting ready section above,

1. Open Visual Studio Code, press *F1*, select **Azure Functions: Create New Project**, and then select **Browse** and select a folder to create the required files using the wizard:

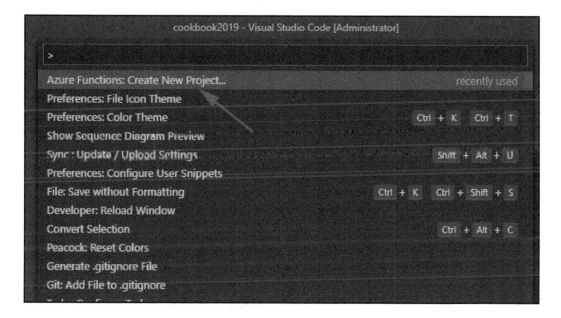

2. You will be prompted to select the language for the function. For this demo, we are going to select TypeScript:

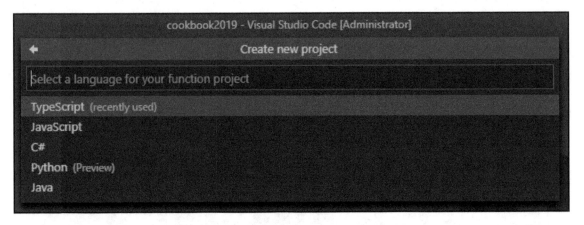

After that, you will be prompted to select the trigger for the Function. For more information on Azure Function triggers, check out `http://bit.ly/2Pi0Yal`.

3. For this demo, select **HTTP trigger**, which lets us invoke this function for an HTTP request (GET or POST):

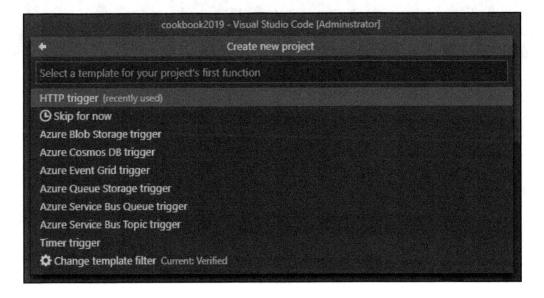

4. The wizard prompts us to give a name to the function. I named it `HelloWorld`:

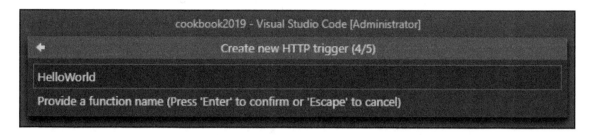

5. The wizard prompts us for the **Authorization** type; for demonstration purposes, we will select **Anonymous**:

You should now have the following folder structure:

6. Browse to this folder and run `npm install`. This will install all the required packages. Then, run `npm start` to build the function and run the function locally:

```
Hosting environment: Production
Content root path: C:\_Utkarsh\GitHub\cookbook2019\continuous-deployments\rcp-deploy-az-function
Now listening on: http://0.0.0.0:7071
Application started. Press Ctrl+C to shut down.

Http Functions:

        HelloWorld: [GET,POST] http://localhost:7071/api/HelloWorld
```

We can now open any REST client (I am using Postman) to check whether we get the right response:

As you can see, our function is running locally and we can make an HTTP request to get the desired response. Let's commit it to the source control and produce the output as an artifact.

The source code for Azure Function is in the GitHub repository under `RCP04-AzureFunction-CD` folder.

Creating the build pipeline

Creating the build pipeline is similar to what we did previously in *Deploying the database to Azure SQL using the release pipeline* recipe. This is a typescript project, and we have a few scripts in our scripts section in our `package.json`. The following is the YAML file for our build pipeline. As you can see, this is just made up of three tasks:

- Install the dependencies
- Build the project
- Publish the artifacts

These 3 steps are under *steps* section in the below YAML content.

 The YAML file is under relevant chapter folder under *RCP04-AzureFunctions-CD* directory in the code bundle.

```yaml
resources:
- repo: self
queue:
  name: Default
  demands: npm

trigger: none

steps:
- task: Npm@1
  displayName: 'npm install'
  inputs:
    workingDir: '$(build.sourcesdirectory)/continuous-deployments/rcp-
deploy-az-function/Function'
    verbose: false

- task: Npm@1
  displayName: 'install func cli'
  inputs:
    command: custom
    workingDir: '$(build.sourcesdirectory)/continuous-deployments/rcp-
```

```
deploy-az-function/Function'
    verbose: false
    customCommand: 'install -g azure-functions-core-tools --unsafe-perm
true'

- task: Npm@1
  displayName: 'npm build:production'
  inputs:
    command: custom
    workingDir: '$(build.sourcesdirectory)/continuous-deployments/rcp-
deploy-az-function/Function'
    verbose: false
    customCommand: 'run build:production'


- task: CopyFiles@2
  displayName: 'Copy Files to: $(Build.ArtifactStagingDirectory)'
  inputs:
    SourceFolder: '$(build.sourcesdirectory)/continuous-deployments/rcp-
deploy-az-function/Function'
    Contents: |
     dist/**
     HelloWorld/**
     node_modules/**
     bin/**
    TargetFolder: '$(Build.ArtifactStagingDirectory)'


- task: PublishBuildArtifacts@1
  displayName: 'Publish Artifact: drop'
```

Once the project has been built, we should see our Azure Function as a deployable artifact:

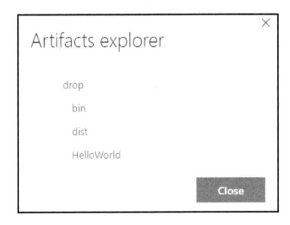

How to do it...

Now that our artifacts are all exactly how we want them to be, we can start building the release pipeline. Like we did in the previous recipes, we need to create the Azure Function app using ARM template and then deploy our function code in to the created Azure Function app. For this, we need to create an ARM template to provision the Azure Function app. As we mentioned previously, the Azure Functions provide cost benefits (you pay only for the time your code runs) over traditional websites, which require a full web server. For this purpose, Azure Functions has two kinds of pricing plans (which you can learn more about at https://docs.microsoft.com/en-us/azure/azure-functions/functions-overview):

- **Consumption plan**: When your function runs, Azure provides all of the necessary computational resources. You don't have to worry about resource management, and you only pay for the time that your code runs.
- **App Service plan**: Run your functions just like your web apps. When you are already using App Service for your other applications, you can run your functions on the same plan at no additional cost.

For this example, we are going to use the Consumption plan to ensure that we pay only for the time our function runs.

Creating the ARM template

1. Create a JSON file called `function.deploy.json` and copy the contents from the ARM template provided in the code bundle.

 The complete ARM template used in the recipe is available in the code bundle under *RCP04-AzureFunction-CD* folder with file named function.deploy.json

Notice the *resources* section. The first resource is the app service plan. We are setting `computeMode` as Dynamic, this ensures we are using the consumption plan. The second resource creates an Azure Function app resource.

```
"resources": [
    {
        "type": "Microsoft.Web/serverfarms",
        "apiVersion": "2015-04-01",
        "name": "[variables('appAppServicePlanName')]",
        "location": "[resourceGroup().location]",
```

```
        "properties": {
            "name": "[variables('appAppServicePlanName')]",
            "computeMode": "Dynamic",
            "sku": "Dynamic"
        }
    },
    {
        "name": "[variables('deployedFunctionAppName')]",
        "type": "Microsoft.Web/sites",
        "location": "[resourceGroup().location]",
        "kind": "functionapp",
        "apiVersion": "2016-08-01",
        "identity": {
            "type": "systemAssigned"
        },
        "dependsOn": [
            "[resourceId('Microsoft.Web/serverfarms',
variables('appAppServicePlanName'))]",
            "[resourceId('Microsoft.Storage/storageAccounts',
variables('storageAccountName'))]"
        ],
//code removed for the sake of brevity
```

As we create the resource, we are also setting a few necessary application settings. The last resource in the *resources* section creates a storage account, which is required for the function app.

Finally, we output the function app name after deployment is successful so that we can deploy the function code into this application.

```
"outputs": {
        "helloworld.fnc.name": {
            "type": "string",
            "value": "[variables('deployedFunctionAppName')]"
        }
    }
```

2. Create the parameter file and save it as `function.deploy.parameters.json`:

```
{
    "$schema":
"https://schema.management.azure.com/schemas/2015-01-01/deploym
entParameters.json#",
    "contentVersion": "1.0.0.0",
    "parameters": {
        "environmentConfiguration": {
            "value": {
                "prefix": {
```

```
                        "functionApp": "helloworld-fnc",
                        "appServiceApp": "helloworld-fnc-asp",
                        "storageAccount": "helloworld",
                        "storageAccountconnection": ""
                },
                "appTierSettings": {
                        "storageAccountTypeForFunctionApp":
        "Standard_LRS"
                }
            }
        }
    }
}
```

3. Commit both of the files to the source control.

To create the release pipeline, we follow the same steps that are followed in the previous recipes in this chapter. Go to the **Release** page and create a new release pipeline. Add the arm template as an artifact. Add tasks to the pipeline to deploy the ARM templates, as we did in previous *Deploying .NET Core web application* recipe. These steps create the Azure Function application and then output the function name.

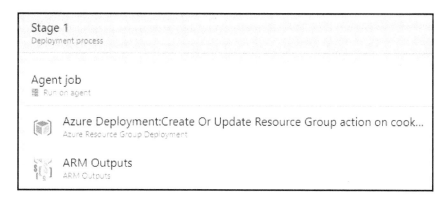

4. Publish the function package to the created Azure Function application:

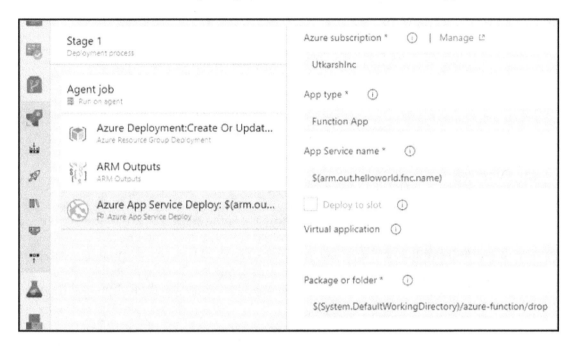

How it works...

In this recipe, we saw how to build a simple Azure Function and produce the artifacts in the build pipeline. We then saw how to create the Azure Function application using ARM templates. The release pipeline creates the required resources in Azure and then deploys our function into the provisioned function app. If you go to the portal and browse the resource group, you will see three resources created:

Open the function app and you should see our `HelloWorld` function:

Click on the **Get function URL** and you should be able to get the complete URL of the function. Make the REST call to the function to verify that it works:

See also

Here are some helpful links regarding what we covered in this recipe:

- Automating resource deployment for your function app in Azure Functions: http://bit.ly/2v93DcU
- Durable functions: http://bit.ly/2vakoo1
- Provisioning a function app on a Consumption plan (ARM templates): http://bit.ly/2v7f1pN
- Creating serverless applications: http://bit.ly/2v5wD5t

Publishing secrets to Azure Key Vault

Applications contain many secrets, such as connection strings, passwords, certificates, and tokens, which, if leaked to unauthorized users, can lead to a severe security breach. This can also result in serious damage to the reputation of the organization and can cause compliance issues.

Azure Key Vault allows you to manage your organization's secrets and certificates in a centralized repository. The secrets and keys are further protected by **Hardware Security Modules (HSMs)**. It also provides versioning of secrets, full traceability, and efficient permission management with access policies.

For more information on Azure Key Vault, visit https://docs.microsoft.com/en-us/azure/key-vault/key-vault-overview.

In this recipe, we will see how we can automatically publish secrets in our pipeline so that secret management is automated.

Getting ready

For this recipe, we are assuming you already have a key vault in the Azure portal. If you don't, please refer to the *Creating a key vault in Azure* section in the *Consuming secrets from Azure Key Vault in your release pipeline* recipe.

Next, install a marketplace extension named Azure Utility Tasks (`http://bit.ly/2PiPQtJ`). This extension provides a few utility tasks, and one of them publishes secrets to Azure Key Vault. We will see how we can use this task shortly:

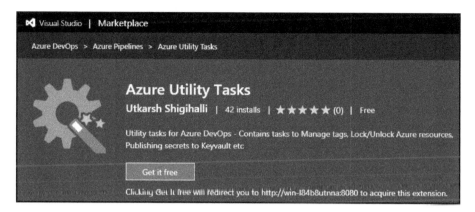

How to do it...

1. Let's create the release pipeline, add a stage, and save it. This is similar to what we have done in other recipes in this chapter. Assuming you have a stage with no artifacts, your release pipeline will look as follows:

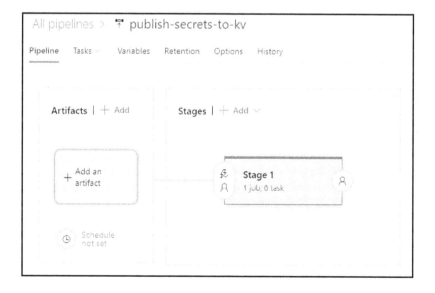

Next, let's see how we can add secrets using PowerShell.

2. To add secrets using the Azure CLI, simply set the secret in the existing Azure Key Vault task using the Azure CLI task as follows, with just one line. Notice that we have added a secret variable named `secretValue`:

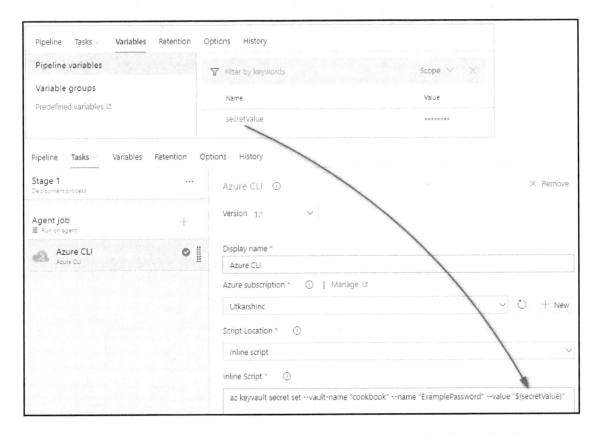

 To use the Azure CLI task, your agent machine needs to have the Azure CLI installed. Read more about it at `http://bit.ly/2Pjv9h4`.

3. In the Azure CLI task, you probably noticed that you had to write the Key Vault name. If we have to publish/add multiple secrets to the key vault, we would have to repeat this line multiple times for each secret. This is where custom tasks, which are available in the Visual Studio Marketplace, help. The **Publish secrets to Azure Key vault** task from *Azue Utility Tasks* extension allows you to publish multiple secrets at once:

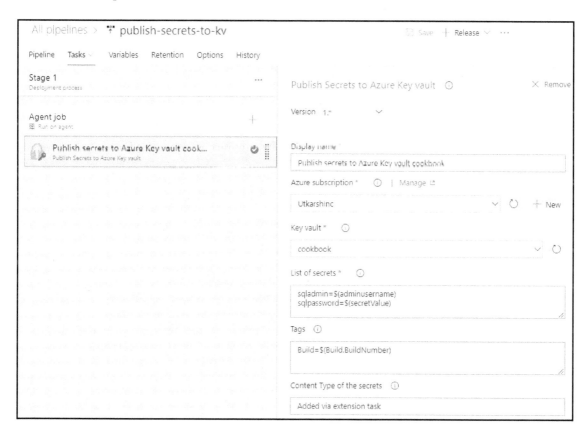

As you can see from the preceding screenshot, the task also allows you to select the Key Vault from the dropdown, and each secret is separated by a new line. Run the release and you will see all your secrets in the key vault being added:

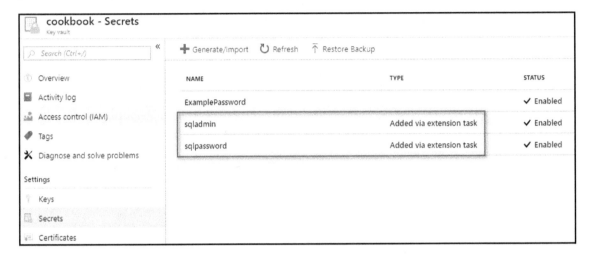

How it works...

The automation of publishing secrets to the key vault greatly reduces your dependency on manual scripts and also any errors in doing so. In this recipe, you saw how easy it was to insert secrets into the azure key vault, which is a central repository to manage all your secrets, keys, and certificates. The recipe showed you two ways that you can automate inserting secrets into the key vault via the Azure DevOps Server release pipeline.

There's more...

We could extend this pipeline to provision the key vault itself. The steps would be similar to what we have done in the previous recipes. A step to deploy the ARM template which will use a Resource Group Deployment task to provision the key vault and a step to get the provisioned key vault name as an output parameter and eventually using it to add secrets to the provisioned key vault.

In doing so, we can extend this pipeline to automate end-to-end key-vault provisioning and also inserting secrets after creation.

See also

Check out the following resources to learn more about what was covered in this recipe:

- **Azure Key Vault ARM templates:** `https://docs.microsoft.com/en-gb/azure/templates/microsoft.keyvault/allversions`
- **Azure Key Vault best practices:** `https://docs.microsoft.com/en-gb/azure/key-vault/key-vault-best-practices`

Deploying a static website on Azure Storage

Static websites have become very popular in the last few years and are based on the JAMstack (JavaScript, APIs, and Markup) architecture. The generated websites are super lightweight, fast, and easier to develop. As of December 2018, you can host static websites on Azure Storage accounts of the **General Purpose v2 (GPv2)** type.

In this recipe, we will see how we can configure a storage account to host a static website. We will then deploy a simple static website to this storage account so that we can browse our website.

- For more information on what JAMStack architecture - `https://jamstack.org/`
- More information on Static website hosting on Azure Storage: `http://bit.ly/2P1Ytne`

Getting ready

To host the website, we will first need to have a static website. Creating a static website using JAMStack architecure is outside the scope of this recipe, but you can check out this post on how to build and automate publishing a Jekyll website: `http://bit.ly/2PlRcDU`.

I am assuming you already have a static website and published artifact, as follows:

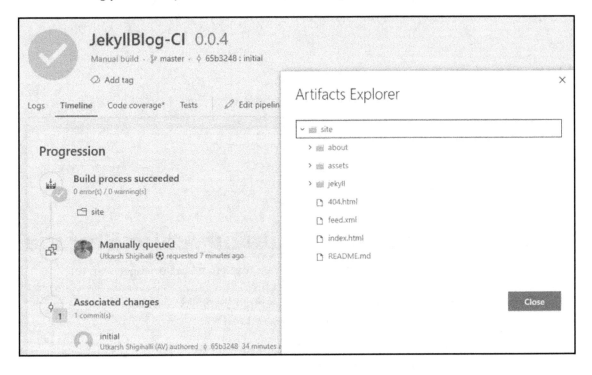

Creating a storage account from the Azure portal

From the Azure portal, it is to create a storage account of the **General Purpose v2 (GPv2)** type. You will see a **Static website** setting - Enable the setting and optionally set the index document name and error document name. Once static website hosting is enabled, a container named $web will be created, if it doesn't already exist. Any content copied to the $web container will automatically be served on the primary endpoint:

Files on the $web container are served through **anonymous** access requests and will only have read permissions.

Creating an Azure Storage Account ARM templates

Automating the creation of the GPv2 storage account and enabling this setting will require a bit more work. Let's start by creating an ARM template.

Create a JSON file named `storageaccount.deploy.json` and paste in the following content:

The source code is available under Chapter folder inside RCP06-StaticWebsite-CD directory.

```
{
    "$schema":
"http://schema.management.azure.com/schemas/2015-01-01/deploymentTemplate.j
```

```
son#",
    "contentVersion": "1.0.0.0",
    "parameters": {
        //code is trimmed for the sake of brevity
    },
    "variables": {
        "storageAccountUniqueName":
"[take(toLower(concat(parameters('storageAccountName'),
uniqueString(resourceGroup().id))),24)]"
    },
    "resources": [
        {
            "name": "[variables('storageAccountUniqueName')]",
            "type": "Microsoft.Storage/storageAccounts",
            "apiVersion": "2018-07-01",
            "location": "[parameters('location')]",
            "properties": {
                "accessTier": "[parameters('accessTier')]",
                "supportsHttpsTrafficOnly":
"[parameters('supportsHttpsTrafficOnly')]"
            },
            "dependsOn": [],
            "sku": {
                "name": "[parameters('accountType')]"
            },
            "kind": "[parameters('kind')]"
        }
    ],
    "outputs": {
        "storageaccount.unique.name": {
            "type": "string",
            "value": "[variables('storageAccountUniqueName')]"
        },
        "storageaccount.url": {
            "type": "string",
            "value":
"[reference(variables('storageAccountUniqueName')).primaryEndpoints.web]"
        }
    }
}
```

This ARM template just has one resource, of
the `Microsoft.Storage/storageAccounts` type. The template accepts a couple of
parameters, such as `accountType` and `storageAccountName`. We will create a parameter
file named `storageaccount.deploy.parameters.json` and paste in the following
content. The parameter file provides default values for the ARM template:

```
{
    "$schema":
"https://schema.management.azure.com/schemas/2015-01-01/deploymentParameter
s.json#",
    "contentVersion": "1.0.0.0",
    "parameters": {
        "location": {
            "value": "westeurope"
        },
        "storageAccountName": {
            "value". "staticwebsitedemo"
        },
        "accountType": {
            "value": "Standard_LRS"
        },
        "kind": {
            "value": "StorageV2"
        },
        //code is trimmed for the sake of brevity
    }
}
```

Notice that in the parameter file above, we provide a value as `StorageV2`, for the
parameter *kind* which requests Azure Resource Manager to provision the Azure Storage
GPv2 storage account.

Commit the ARM template into the source control and optionally create the build pipeline
produce ARM templates as artifacts. You could include simple tests to test the ARM
templates as part of the build pipeline as well.

How to do it...

1. Create a new release pipeline and add both the static website and ARM templates as artifacts:

The first steps will just deploy our storage account ARM template. These steps are similar to what we have done in other recipes. The first task deploys the ARM template and the next task produces the pipeline variables for our ARM template output variables. In our case, we will output the storage account name and the storage account primary endpoint from our ARM template:

2. Run the release. We see that our storage account has been created, but that the static website setting is still disabled:

At the time of writing, this Disbaled/Enabled Static website setting is not available via the ARM template. Instead, we have to use the Azure CLI to enable this setting.

3. We update the pipeline to install the `storage-preview` extension for Azure CLI. Add an *Azure CLI* task and execute the `az extension add --name storage-preview` command to add the extension:

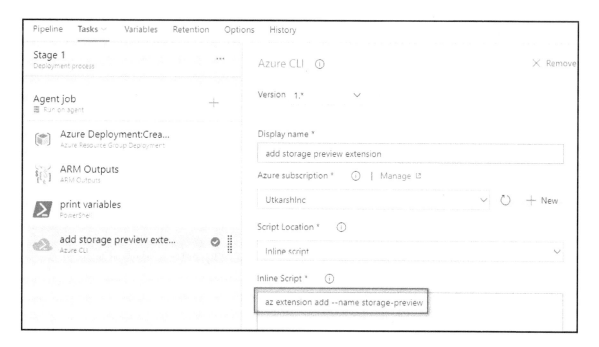

4. Using the Azure CLI, enable the **Static website** feature for our storage account. To do that, we execute the following command, again using Azure CLI task:

```
az storage blob service-properties update --account-name
<ACCOUNT_NAME> --static-website --404-document
<ERROR_DOCUMENT_NAME> --index-document <INDEX_DOCUMENT_NAME>
```

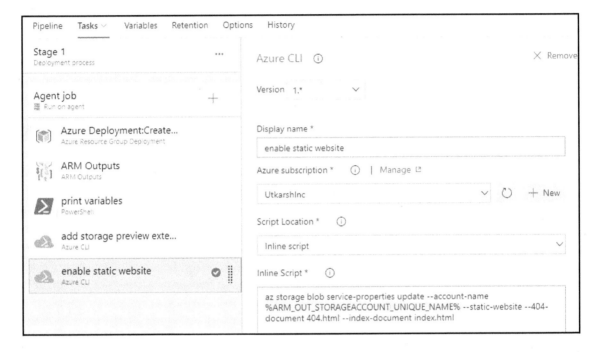

Notice that we are using our ARM template output variable, `storageaccount.unique.name`, to pass the storage account name to this Azure CLI command. Running our pipeline now, we can see that the storage account is created and also that the static website feature is enabled. The only remaining step is to copy the contents of our static website to the `$web` container:

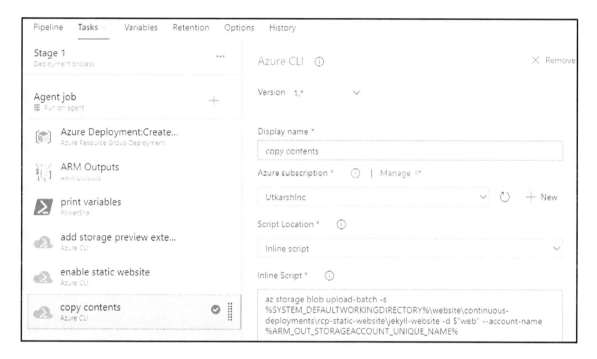

The command we are using to copy the contents is as follows:

```
az storage blob upload-batch -s <SOURCE_PATH> -d \"$web" --
account-name <ACCOUNT_NAME>
```

We are using a variable to pass the source path for our website contents and account name.

5. Run the release pipeline. You should have your static website ready and available on your primary endpoint:

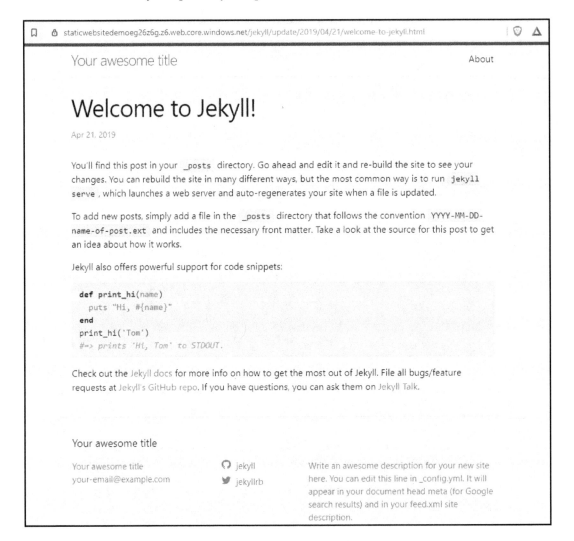

How it works...

The pipeline we created in this recipe shows how we can use ARM templates and Azure CLI commands to easily automate the creation of required storage account to deploy a static website. We saw how, even when the ARM template does not provide full capabilities to automate the *Static Website* feature, the Azure DevOps server helps us to integrate any tool available into the pipeline—in this case, we used the Azure CLI to enable the static website feature and copy its contents.

There's more...

Hosting a static website on Azure Storage makes your site available on the primary endpoint. However, in most scenarios, you would like to host your website on your custom domain, such as `https://www.myorganization.com/blog` You could do that using the Azure **Content Delivery Network (CDN)**. Azure CDN also allows you to use custom SSL certificates, rewrite rules, and more.

For more on how to use Azure CDN and enabling custom domains for your static website, visit `http://bit.ly/2vgXvQ8`.

See also

Check out these resources for more information:

- We used Jekyll to generate a static website, but it is just one of the many static generators that's available. There is a full list of static site generators here: `https://www.staticgen.com/`.
- You can configure a custom domain name for your Azure storage account at `http://bit.ly/2venQ1b`.

Deploying an Azure Virtual Machine to Azure Dev Test Lab (DTL)

Development teams are often limited by the infrastructure that is available to them to deploy and test their changes. The cloud promises to address this by giving you an infinite resource capacity that you can consume in a pay-as-you-go subscription model. Enterprises making their first foray into the cloud are keen to test the waters by moving development and test workloads to the cloud. However, the biggest apprehension when moving to the cloud for Development and Testing teams is repeatability, security, and governance. Microsoft understands the trend, so to help customers make the move, it has introduced a new service called Azure Dev Test Lab.

Azure DTL is a service that helps development teams quickly create heterogeneous environments in Azure while minimizing waste and controlling cost. The biggest unique selling proposition for Azure DTL is the ability to lock down the lab by securing the network to a private subnet, applying governance policies at the lab level, and giving the development teams autonomy within the lab. The ability to create and repeat helps scale the solutions and the integration with the existing toolchain helps reusability.

You can learn more about Azure DTL by watching this introductory video: `https://azure.microsoft.com/en-gb/resources/videos/index/?services=devtest-lab`.

If you don't already have an Azure DTL in your Azure subscription, you can create one by following this walkthrough: `https://docs.microsoft.com/en-gb/azure/lab-services/tutorial-create-custom-lab`.

In this recipe, we'll learn how to securely connect our Azure DevOps server to an Azure subscription. We will then use Azure DevOps Server to provision virtual machines using an ARM template into the newly created Azure Dev Test Lab.

Getting ready

The Azure Dev Test Labs team provides a free Visual Studio marketplace extension. This free extension provided by Microsoft delivers multiple builds and release pipeline tasks that allow you to create machines, delete machines, and create custom images from existing machines in Azure DTL:

For simplicity, we also have an Azure DTL ready that was manually created using the portal:

How to do it...

1. Create a release pipeline and add the Azure DevTest Labs create VM task. Select the subscription and provide the ARM template:

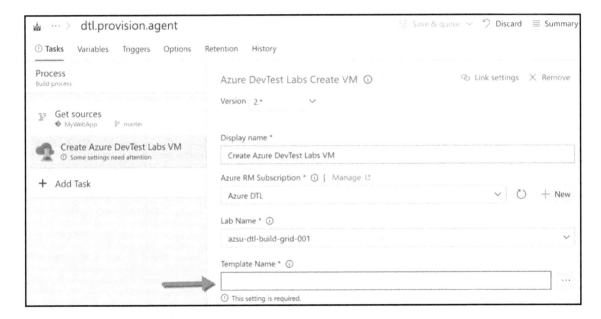

For the template field, you could provide the ARM template for the custom VM image according to your needs. You'll be delighted to know that it's possible to generate an ARM template for provisioning right from within the Azure portal.

2. In order to generate the ARM template for the VM, we would like to provision in Azure DTL; head over to the DTL in Azure Portal and click through to create the desired VM. You can choose from a range of preconfigured base images, but I recommend opting for the latest Visual Studio Enterprise image:

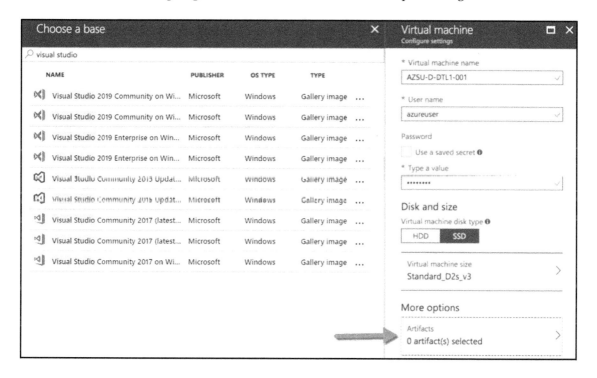

3. Click the **Automation options** link to get the complete ARM template for the VM:

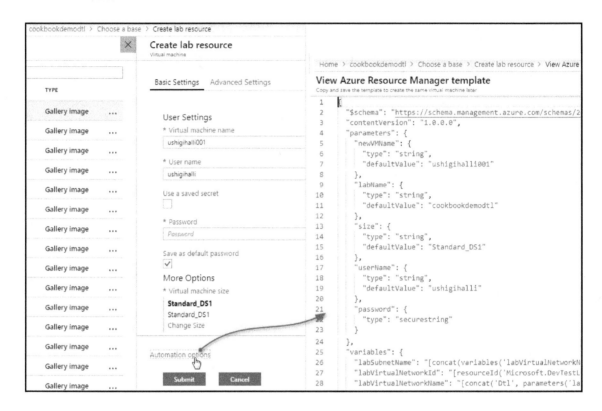

Notice I have also set an expiration date for this VM in the *Advanced Settings* so that the VM gets automatically deleted on the set date and time.

4. Copy the JSON contents in to file and commit it into source control. Create a release pipeline, add the **Azure DevTest Labs Create VM** task, and provide the required input, specifically the VM name, username, and password, for the VM. We will also pass the expiration date for the VM so that the VM gets deleted automatically:

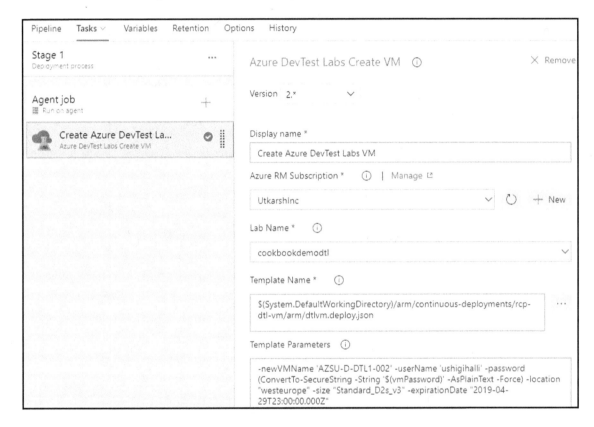

5. Run the release pipeline and you should soon see a new VM spun up based on the ARM template and added to the DevTest labs:

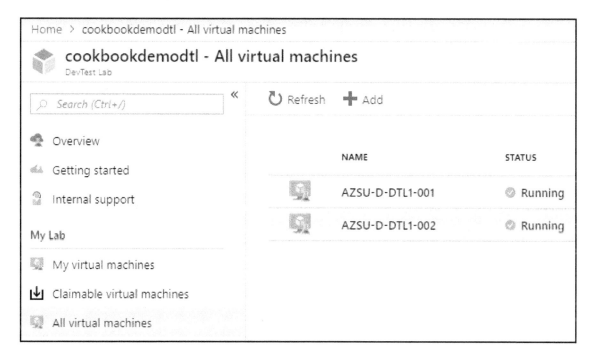

How it works...

Thanks to the power of Azure DevOps Server and ARM templates, we saw how we can generate ARM templates for our custom DevTest Labs VM images. We then used the generated ARM templates to spin new VMs in our Azure DevTest Labs lab.

There's more...

We could extend this recipe, for example, to build an Azure DevOps Server build agent grid. An automated process to add and remove build agents allows you to scale up and scale down on demand. There will always be periods when the build infrastructure is in high demand and periods when it's underutilized. By using virtual infrastructure to host your agents, you could save significant money by decommissioning the agents when they are not in use. This recipe showed you a quick way to spin the VMs on demand. We could add artifacts that are available for DTL VMs (the Azure Pipelines Agent artifact, for example) and generate an ARM template with it to automatically create a VM and add an artifact:

See also

DevTestLabs Artifacts allow you to add the custom software/tools you need to your Azure DTL VMs as you provide them. You are not limited to using just the available artifacts. You could build your own custom artifacts, which is very easy to do. Check out these resources for more information:

- Create custom artifacts for your DevTest Labs virtual machine: `http://bit.ly/2vi2akG`
- All of the Azure DTL artifacts are open source on GitHub, which you could use as references: `https://github.com/Azure/azure-devtestlab/tree/master/Artifacts`

7
Azure Artifacts and Dependency Management

In order to release software often and consistently, it is essential that software dependencies are managed using a good package management solution. Managing dependencies, if not thought through, can over a period of time become extremely difficult to maintain especially due to managing versions, testing of the packages and nested dependencies.

Azure Artifacts is Microsoft's solution to package management. Originally available as a separate extension on Visual Studio Marketplace, it is now pre-installed in Azure DevOps Services and Azure DevOps Server 2019, TFS 2018, and 2017. In this chapter, we will explore a few recipes on how to use Azure Artifacts to host your NuGet and npm packages. We will also see how to deploy packages to Azure Artifacts using build and release pipelines.

Later, we will see how we can incrementally make our packages available to consumers using artifact views and finally we will utilize third-party extension to scan security vulnerabilities in our application dependencies. Azure Artifacts is available as a separate hub in Azure DevOps Server.

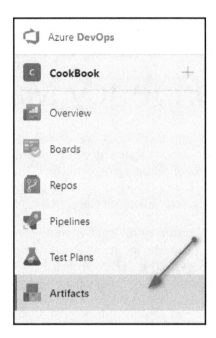

In this chapter, we will cover the following recipes:

- Publishing a NuGet package to Artifacts
- Consuming a NuGet package in Visual Studio from the Artifacts feed
- Testing a NuGet package using Artifact views
- Publishing an NPM package to Artifacts
- Consuming an NPM package from the Artifacts feed
- Scanning for vulnerabilities in your package using WhiteSource

Publishing a NuGet package to Artifacts

NuGet packages are ZIP files containing the `.nupkg` extension, where the common code is packaged and shared with others. In this recipe, we will explore how to create a sample NuGet package and set up a build pipeline that will continuously deliver new versions of the package.

 An introduction to NuGet can be found at `https://docs.microsoft.com/en-us/nuget/what-is-nuget`.

Azure Artifacts introduces the concept of feeds. A feed is a container for your package; you can consume and publish packages to and from a feed. Azure Artifacts allows you to create multiple feeds; however, planning the name and number of feeds for your collection beforehand will help improve the management of permissions for your feeds and NuGet packages.

Another key aspect of Azure Artifacts is known as upstream sources. Upstream sources allow a single feed to store the packages you produce along with the packages that you consume from the remote feed. Each dependent remote package will be cached and made available through the Azure Artifacts feed. The benefit of this is that even when the remote feed is down or the package on the remote feed is removed, you will still be able to continue using the feed from the cached version, thus causing no disruption.

 You can find out more information about upstream sources at `http://bit.ly/2vg8byj`.

Getting ready

For this recipe, we will use a sample NuGet package. You can find the code for this sample NuGet package in the source code bundle under *Chapter07* folder.

Creating an Artifact feed in Azure Artifacts

1. Let's create a feed for publishing our NuGet package. To do this, first, head to the **Artifacts** hub and click on the **+ New Feed** button:

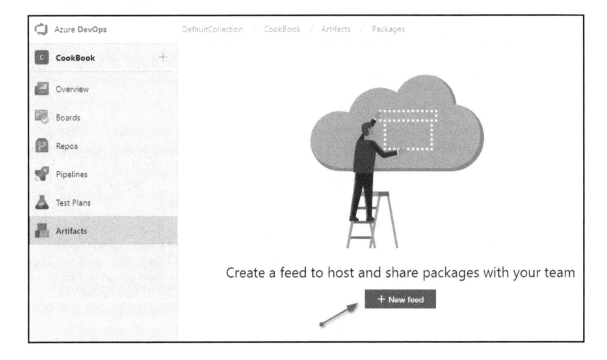

2. Next, provide a name for the feed and select the visibility. Keep the default settings as they are, so that our feed is visible to everyone in the collection:

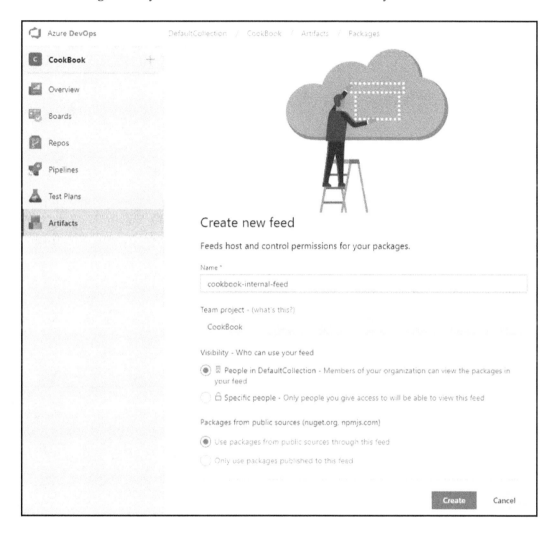

3. Finally, allow the feed to cache the upstream (or remote) packages into this feed so that any external dependent NuGet packages are cached and served from our Artifacts feed. Once you click on **Create**, the feed will be created and made visible, as shown in the following screenshot:

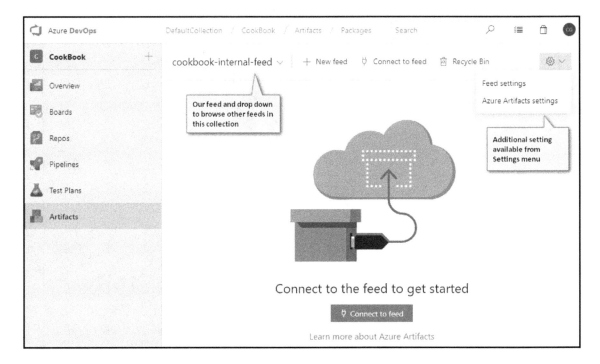

You can also set additional settings for the feed, such as retention policies for the packages, views, and other permissions, from the **Settings** menu - we are also covering this in the *How to do it* section below.

 More information on securing and sharing packages using feed permissions can be found at `http://bit.ly/2Pt30Er`.

How to do it...

Our sample NuGet package is a .NET Core 2 NuGet package. To start with we will set up **Continuous Integration** (**CI**) so that we produce the NUPKG file every time the package is built.

Creating a build definition to produce the NuGet package

1. Create a new file called `azure-pipelines.yml` and paste in the following code:

 The source code for NuGet package and YAML file for the build used in this recipe is in this Chapter's code pack under *RCP01-NuGet-Artifact* folder

```yaml
resources:
- repo: self
queue:
  name: Default

name: $(major).$(minor).$(rev:r)
variables:
  major: 1
  minor: 0
  buildconfiguration: release

steps:
- task: DotNetCoreInstaller@0
  displayName: 'Use .NET Core sdk 2.2.104'
  inputs:
    version: 2.2.104

- task: DotNetCoreCLI@2
  displayName: 'dotnet build'
  inputs:
    projects: '$(build.sourcesdirectory)/artifacts/dotnetcore-nuget/MyClassLib/MyClassLib.csproj'
    arguments: '--configuration $(BuildConfiguration) /p:Version=$(build.buildnumber)'

- task: DotNetCoreCLI@2
  displayName: 'dotnet pack'
  inputs:
    command: pack
    packagesToPack: 'artifacts/dotnetcore-nuget/MyClassLib/MyClassLib.csproj'
    nobuild: true
    versioningScheme: byBuildNumber

- task: PublishBuildArtifacts@1
  displayName: 'Publish Artifact: drop'
```

Notice that we set a build name that is in the format of
`$(major).$(minor).$(rev:r)`. We are creating variables *major*, *minor* and
patch in the variables section. We are using this build name to set the version for
our NuGet package so that it gets versioned as `1.0.4`. We are also building our
project using the `dotnet build` command, which is again using
the `buildconfiguration` variable. The value release for `buildconfiguration`
variable tells the dotnet command to optimize the code during compilation. We
have defined these variables in YAML file format, as well under the `variables`
section. Lastly, we are using `dotnet pack` command to package this library in to
a NuGet package.

More on *dotnet* commands - `https://docs.microsoft.com/en-us/`
`dotnet/core/tools/dotnet?tabs=netcore21`

2. Run the build and you should see that our NuGet package is created and made
   available as an artifact:

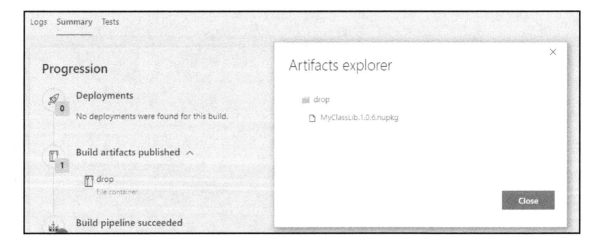

Creating a release pipeline to publish a NuGet package to the feed

Next, we will need to create a release pipeline in order to publish the artifact to the feed that we previously created. Azure Artifacts has a concept called **views**, which are unique to Azure Artifacts. You can refer to the *Testing NuGet packages using Artifact views* recipe in this chapter for more details.

In this recipe, we will publish to the default @local view using our release pipeline:

1. Create a new release pipeline and add a stage and link to the build pipeline that we created earlier:

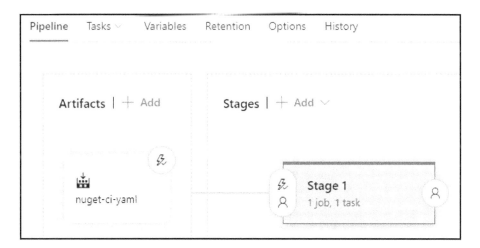

2. Go to **Tasks** and add the **.NET Core** task.

3. Select the `nuget push` command, and then select our feed from the **Target feed** drop-down menu:

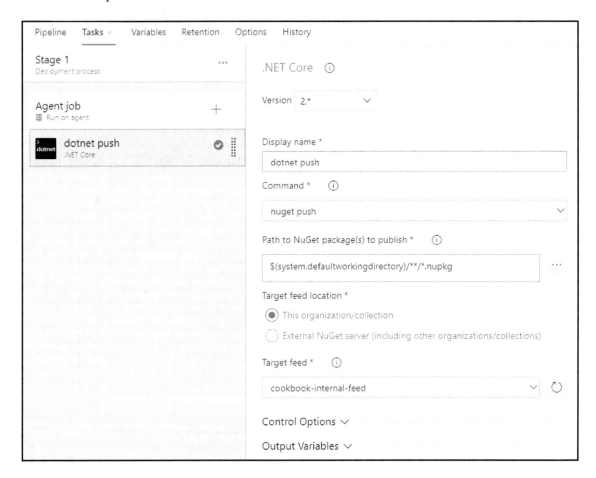

4. Create the release and you should see your NuGet package published to the feed:

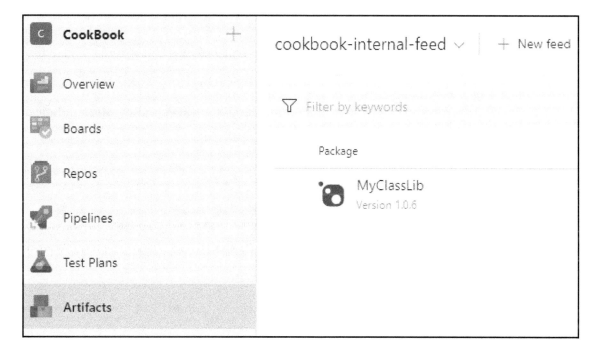

Granular feed permissions in feed settings

Packages are immutable, meaning that once you publish a particular version of the package, you cannot publish the same version again. The version number is permanently reserved. Additionally, Azure Artifacts shows deleted package versions by default:

1. You can change this setting in the **Feed settings** page. You can also enable package badges to use them in to your markdown files, and also set the maximum number of versions that you would like to keep in **Retention policies**:

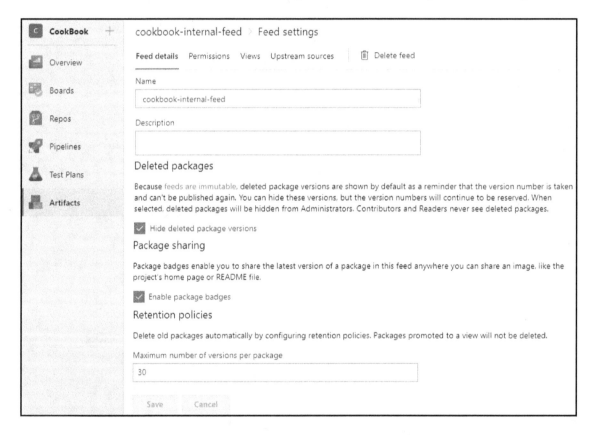

 For better performance, it is recommended that you set the limit for the maximum number of versions per package that you would like to retain.

How it works...

We created a simple NuGet package using .NET Core and set up the build pipeline for our NuGet package. The build pipeline was then added as an artifact to our release pipeline, which we published to the created feed. We then explored how the *feed* permissions can be controlled using the feed settings. In the next recipe, we will look at how we can connect to our feed and consume the NuGet package in Visual Studio.

There's more...

Azure Artifacts can also be used as a symbol server for your organization. Symbol servers enable your developers to connect and debug the applications.

 More information on how you can publish symbols for debugging applications can be found at `http://bit.ly/2PpxkQi`.

See also

- **Package versioning**: `http://bit.ly/2vlw07G`
- **Best practices for using Azure Artifacts**: `http://bit.ly/2vhGqp5`

Consuming a NuGet package in Visual Studio from the Artifacts feed

In the previous recipe, we learned how to create a NuGet package and publish it to Artifacts in Azure DevOps Server. In this recipe, we will look at how we can consume the NuGet package in Visual Studio.

Getting ready

The recipe is a continuation of the previous *Publishing a NuGet package to Artifacts* recipe. If you have not read it, then we recommend that you go through it before continuing.

How to do it...

Let's examine how we can consume the NuGet package in Visual Studio by performing the following steps.

Connecting to the feed in Artifacts

1. Go to **Artifacts** and select the correct feed (if you have multiple feeds); then, copy the package source URL, as follows:

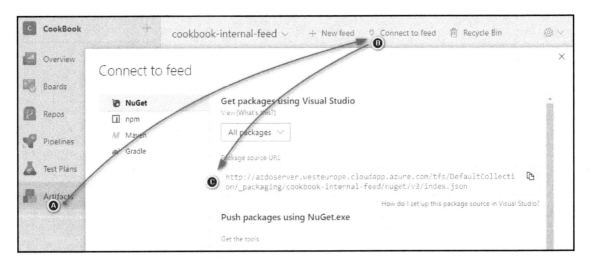

2. Open Visual Studio, go to the **Tools** menu, and then select **Options**:

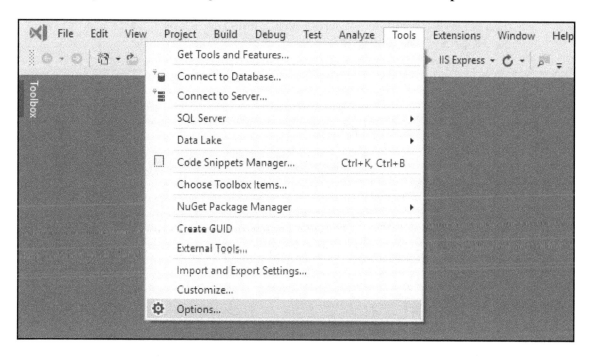

3. In the **Options** window, go to **Package Sources** and click on the + icon in the top-right corner to add a new package source. Provide a name for the source and then paste in the copied URL from *Step 1*. Finally, click on **Update** and then click on **OK** to close the dialog:

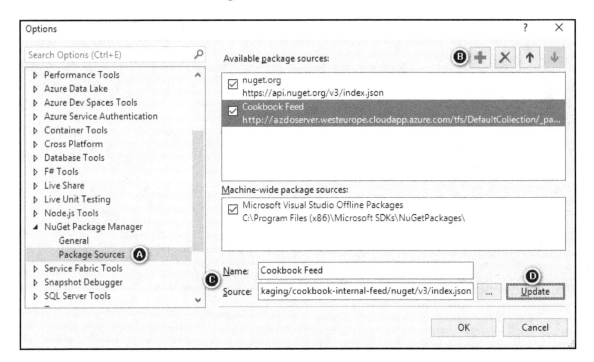

If you have enabled upstream sources (such as NuGet or npm) for your feed, then uncheck the `https://www.nuget.org/` feed in the preceding window, so that you only fetch feeds from our Artifacts feed and not from public feeds such as `https://www.npmjs.com/` or `https://www.nuget.org/`.

4. Open the solution that you would like to reference packages from this feed to, right-click on **Dependencies**, and then select the **Manage NuGet Packages...** option:

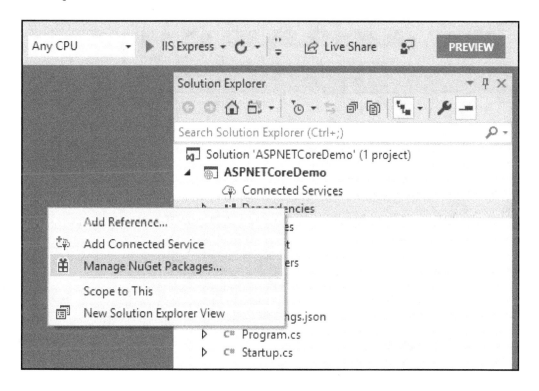

5. Next, you might be prompted to provide credentials in order to authenticate the feed. Enter these as requested and then click on **OK**:

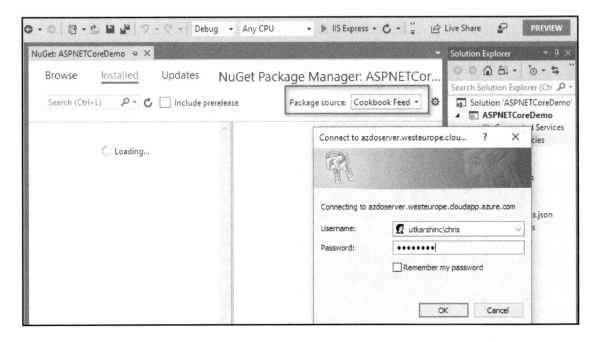

6. Now if you go to the **Browse** tab, you will see your published NuGet package:

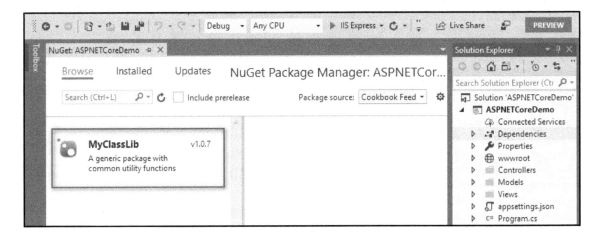

7. Select the package and click on **Install**. Since our package internally depends on Newtonsoft.json, Artifacts also downloads the dependent NuGet package from our feed using the upstream sources:

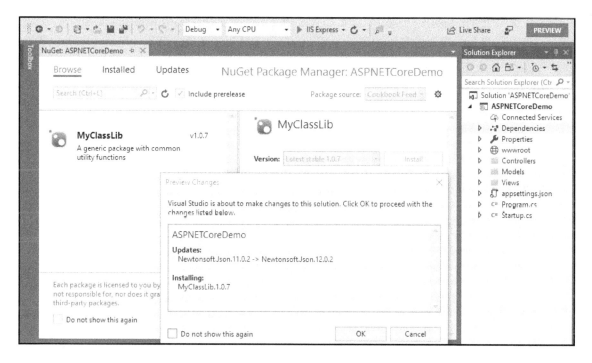

You have now referenced the NuGet package (along with its dependencies) from the Artifacts feed directly.

How it works...

As you saw in this recipe, Azure DevOps Server Artifacts makes it very convenient for you to consume the packages from your internal feeds. Once you add a feed source in Visual Studio, developers will be able to refer to any package that is available in the feed.

There's more...

Adding the feed to Visual Studio with upstream sources enabled and all other external sources disabled ensures that we only consume packages from our feed – without having to worry if the external source is available or not. Azure Artifacts seamlessly caches the dependent packages when the reference in your NuGet package and makes them available.

 If any dependent package has not yet been saved in your feed, then they will not be available through your feed.

See also

- **Dependency management**: `http://bit.ly/2PrcOd5`
- **The benefits of upstream sources**: `http://bit.ly/2Prb4FO`
- **Best practices for feed owners**: `http://bit.ly/2PovcIs`

Testing a NuGet package using Artifact views

As mentioned in the previous recipe, packages are immutable. This means that package versions are reserved as soon as you publish them to the feed. You cannot publish the same version of the package again.

Semantic versioning ensures that versions correctly convey the change. The version numbers are in `Major.Minor.Patch` format and, optionally, can contain additional labels such as **1.0.0-alpha** or **1.0.0-beta**:

- The `MAJOR` version is used when you make incompatible API changes
- The `MINOR` version when you add functionality in a backward-compatible manner
- The `PATCH` version is used when you make backward-compatible bug fixes

Additional labels for prerelease and build metadata are available as extensions to the MAJOR.MINOR.PATCH format.

However, with the NuGet package, proper testing can be done only after it has been packaged and versioned.

In this recipe, we will see how we can use artifact views to consume prerelease packages and eventually promote them after testing.

Getting ready

By default, come with three views. The @local view is the default view when you create a feed that contains all the packages published to the feed, and also all the packages from an upstream source. The next two views are @prerelease and @release. The latter two views can be renamed or deleted if required.

Go to **Feed settings** and verify that you see three views; then, ensure your default view is set to @local:

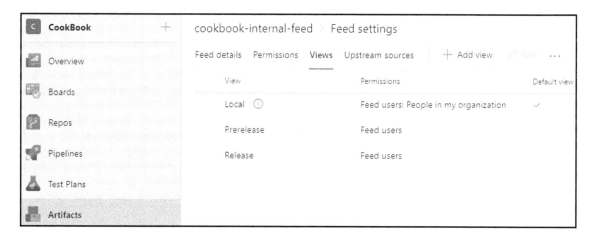

How to do it...

Currently, we have `v1.0.7` installed from the `@local` view in our solution. The feed shows that there is a new `v1.0.9` version that is available for us to test:

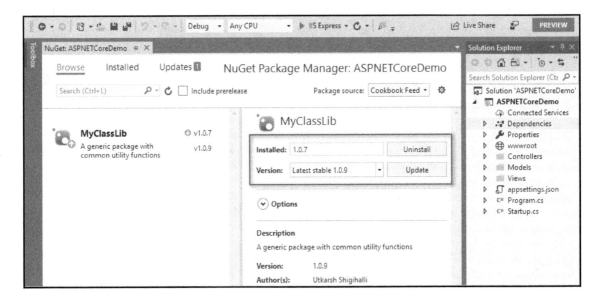

As the developers of this NuGet package, we will install the new 1.0.9 version and test that it is working as expected. Once we are happy with the changes, we can make it available to our testers:

1. Go to the feed and open the NuGet package; then, click on **Promote**:

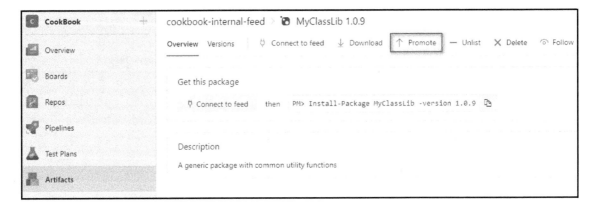

2. In the dialog that appears, select `@prerelease`:

This promotes the package to the `@prerelease` view. This package is now available to anyone who has access to the `@prerelease` view. You can also control the permission for each view; we have made the `@prerelease` view available for members of our *developers* and the *architecture* group.

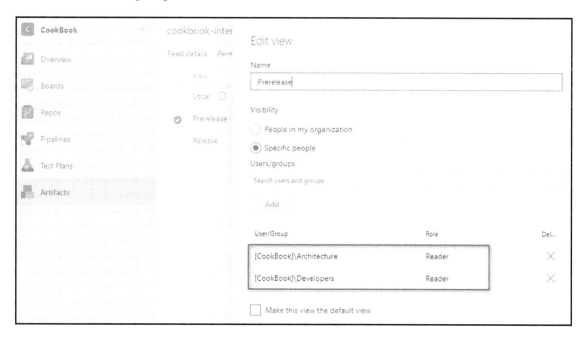

Developers and members of the architecture group can connect to this view directly in the same way that we can - select *Connect to feed* and select the correct view to get the correct package source URL:

We covered connecting to the feed and consuming the feed in the previous *Consuming NuGet package in Visual Studio from Artifacts feed* recipe:

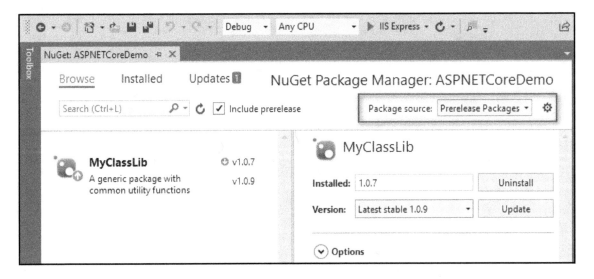

How it works...

In traditional NuGet package repositories (such as `https://www.nuget.org/`), after publishing the NuGet package, it is made immediately available to all of your consumers. The only way to fix this defect is to release a new version of the package.

However, with views, you are able to promote your releases slowly – one view at a time – and so, control who has access to the package. Once the NuGet package is properly tested by users of the `@local` and `@prerelease` views, you can make it available to all your consumers from the `@release` view.

There's more...

Package versioning is a big problem to solve and there are various ways to tackle it. However, there is no one-size-fits-all solution. After implementing the semantic versioning for the packages, we recommend that you discuss with your team and finalize the solution and workflow of how the packages will be moved. If you are using Git version control, there are tools available, such as GitVersion (`https://gitversion.readthedocs.io/en/latest`), which can help you to implement semantic versioning based on the Git commit history, which might be useful in better conveying the changes.

See also

- **Determine and communicate quality**: `http://bit.ly/2ProdyG`
- **The metadata cache**: `http://bit.ly/2PrRyZH`

Publishing NPM packages to Artifacts

npm is the package manager. The npm packages are cross-platform packages developed using JavaScript. `npmjs.com` is the popular public registry hosting these node packages.

However, many organizations develop custom node modules or in-house UI frameworks, which they prefer keeping on-premises rather than on public repository at `https://www.npmjs.com/`.

In this recipe, we will create a sample npm module and set up a build pipeline so that its version is updated with each build. We will then create a release pipeline to publish the package to our Artifacts feed.

Getting ready

Our sample npm module allows any user to consume the module by using the `require` statement. Calling the function will just print the demo statement to the console. For this recipe, you need to have NodeJS installed in your machine. If you don't have it already, download and install it from `https://nodejs.org/en/download`.

To check the version of the node on your machine, after installing node, run the following command and it should print version of the node installed.

```
C:\Users\utkarsh>node -v
v10.15.3
```

Creating NPM package

1. Create a folder, then create a file named `package.json` using the `npm init` command. For simplicity, the following code is the `package.json` file that I have created after completing the `npm init` prompts. You can copy and paste if you would like to use it as is:

```
{
  "name": "print-azure-devops",
  "version": "1.0.0",
  "description": "A demo npm package which just prints Azure DevOps
Server 2019",
  "main": "index.js",
  "scripts": {
    "test": "echo \"Error: no test specified\" && exit 1"
  },
  "keywords": [
    "demo"
  ],
  "author": "Utkarsh Shigihalli (www.visualstudiogeeks.com)",
  "license": "ISC"
}
```

2. Next, add a `readme.md` file and add content explaining the node module – this appears on the package page.

3. Our `package.json` file states that the main executable for our module is the `index.js` file. So, let's create that now; create a `index.js` file and paste in the following code:

```
exports.printAzureDevOps = function () {
    console.log("Azure DevOps Server 2019")
}
```

As you can see, this npm package exposes a simple function named `printAzureDevOps()`, which, when used, will just print `Azure DevOps Server 2019` to the console.

Later on in this chapter, we will look at how to connect to this feed and consume it in a client application.

How to do it...

As you saw previously, our npm package is a simple node module, which users can use to print sample text. In this section, we will set up the CI so that we produce the new version of our npm package for every build; then, we will publish it as a build artifact. We will then consume this artifact in the release pipeline and publish the npm package to our feed.

Creating the build pipeline to update the package version

1. Create the `azure-pipelines.yml` file and paste in the following code:

 The sample node module and YAML file are in the code bundle under *RCP04-NPM-Artifact* folder.

```
resources:
- repo: self
queue:
  name: Default
  demands: npm
name: 1.0.$(rev:r)

steps:
- task: Npm@1
  displayName: 'npm version'
  inputs:
```

```
command: custom
workingDir: 'artifacts/npm-print-azure-devops'
verbose: false
customCommand: 'version $(build.buildnumber)'

- task: PublishBuildArtifacts@1
displayName: 'publish npm package as artifact'
inputs:
PathtoPublish: '$(build.sourcesdirectory)/artifacts/npm-print-
azure-devops'
ArtifactName: 'npm-package'
```

As you can see, our build pipeline is made up of just two steps. The first step uses the npm task to run the `npm version` command and supply the build number. So, the actual command becomes `npm version <new version>`. This step updates the version of the node module and sets it to build number. The last step just publishes the full contents of the directory after the module version is updated.

Creating the release pipeline to publish the npm package

1. Create a new release pipeline and add the build artifact of the build pipeline that we created in the preceding *Creating the build pipeline* section:

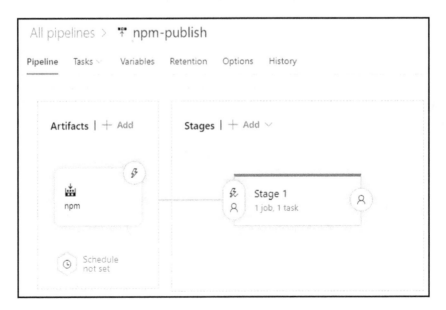

2. Next, add an npm task and select the **publish** command.

3. Select the correct working folder containing your `package.json` file and select our **Artifacts** feed as the target feed:

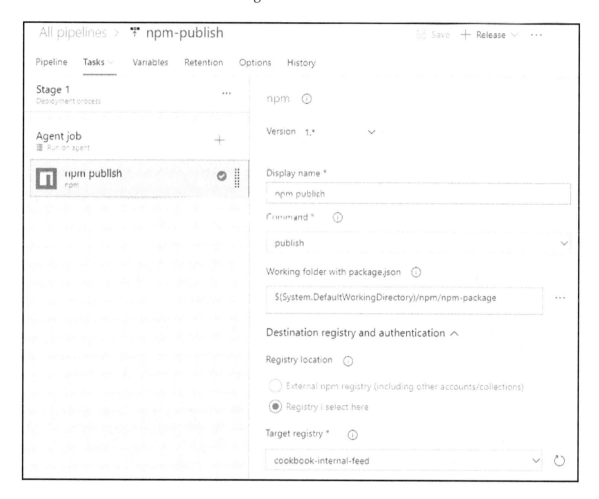

4. Save the release pipeline and create the release. The npm package should be published to our **Artifacts** feed:

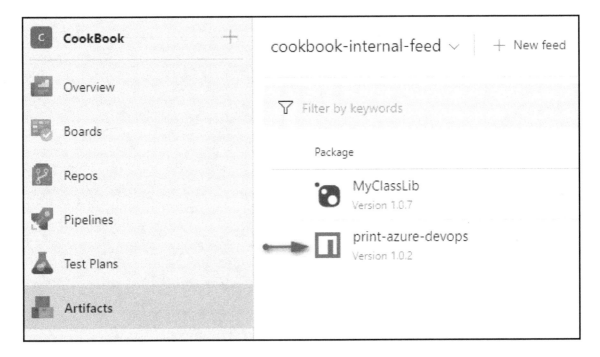

How it works...

In this recipe, we learned how to create a sample npm package and a build pipeline. The build pipeline works by simply updating the version for every build (npm recommends the semantic versioning of packages). We then created a release pipeline and consumed our build artifact, and then published the npm package to the Artifacts feed.

There's more...

Azure Artifacts fetches most of the metadata in the npm package from the package.json file, and displays them on the package page under **Artifacts**. Keeping the metadata accurate and clean ensures that the package can be easily discovered. From the following screenshot, you can see where each piece of data is coming from. Keeping this information accurate within your organization ensures that your packages convey useful information to consumers and also helps them getting discovered easily:

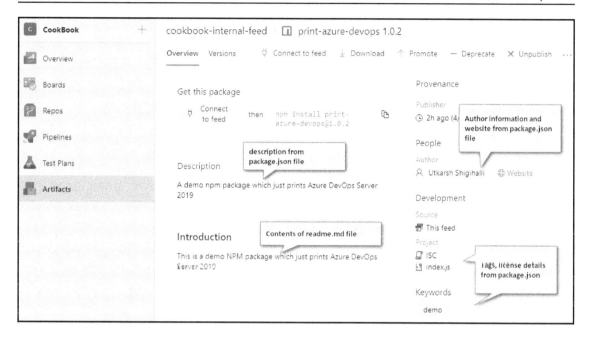

See also

- Although in this recipe, we are updating the version number for each build, it is not advised. The npm recommends semantic versioning for reliable packages. This is explained in more detail at `https://docs.npmjs.com/about-semantic-versioning`.

- The consumption of the npm package by the developer machine requires a few additional steps. You can learn more about this at `https://docs.microsoft.com/en-us/azure/devops/artifacts/get-started-npm?view=azure-devopstabs=windows#set-up-authentication-on-your-development-machine`.

Consuming NPM package from the Artifacts feed

In the previous recipe, we published our sample npm package to Azure Artifacts. In this recipe, we will explore how we can consume the artifact that we published and make use of it. Since we have already enabled upstream sources for our repository, we can also fetch all the dependent packages from our feed.

Getting ready

This recipe is a continuation of the previous *Publishing NPM package to Artifacts* recipe. I recommend that you read it before continuing if you have not already done so.

To demonstrate the upstream npm package, I installed the `colors` package into our original module using the `npm install colors --save` command. This created an external dependency in our node module so the Artifacts would cache this external package into our feed.

I also changed the code in our `index.js` file so that we can use the `colors` module and print the console text in blue:

```
var colors = require("colors")
exports.printAzureDevOps = function () {
    console.log("Azure DevOps Server 2019".blue)
}
```

I have highlighted the changed text in **bold**.

Commit the changes and publish the package using the build and release pipelines, as discussed in the previous recipe. You should be able to see the dependencies if you browse the package in our feed:

How to do it...

Let's perform the following steps:

1. Go to **Artifacts** and click on **Connect to feed**; then, click on the **npm** link and copy the text (as indicated by **D** in the following screenshot):

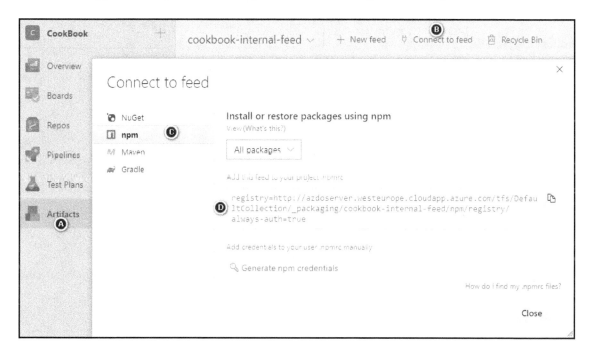

2. Create a `.npmrc` file in your HOME directory (`C:\Users\<username> \.npmrc` in Windows or `$home/.npmrc` in Linux or Mac systems) and paste in the content. Since Artifacts requires authentication, you also want to click on **Generate npm credential** and then add the contents to the `npmrc` file. This generates a 90-day token.

> If you have included the credentials, then it is not advised to commit the file into the source control.

3. Create a simple client node application in a new folder and use the `npm init` command. We then install our npm package using the `npm install print-azure-devops --save-dev` command. For simplicity, the following is my `package.json` file. Notice that our npm module is referenced in the `devDependencies` section:

> The source code for this sample client application is included in the code bundle under *RCP04-NPM-Artifact* folder.

```
{
  "name": "temp",
  "version": "1.0.0",
  "description": "",
  "main": "index.js",
  "scripts": {
    "test": "echo \"Error: no test specified\" && exit 1"
  },
  "keywords": [],
  "author": "",
  "license": "ISC",
  "devDependencies": {
    "print-azure-devops": "~1.0.0"
  }
}
```

4. Create a new file called `print.js` and paste in the following code:

```
var printaz = require("print-azure-devops")
printaz.printAzureDevOps();
```

As you can see in the preceding block, we are referencing our npm package by using the require statement and then making use of the function. To test the function, run the `node print.js` command and you should see `Azure DevOps Server 2019` printed to the console:

```
c:\_Utkarsh\GitHub\cookbook2019\artifacts\printTest>node print.js
Azure DevOps Server 2019
```

How it works...

We connect to the Azure DevOps Server Artifacts feed using the `.npmrc` file, which maintains the registry and authentication tokens. Once connected, we can use the usual npm commands to get any npm packages. As with NuGet, Artifacts brings any dependent npm packages (in our case, the `colors` package) and caches them in our feed. We then consumed the npm package from the Artifacts feed in our demo application and explored how to use it.

There's more...

Azure Artifact feeds require authentication. So, you will need to store the credentials in the `.npmrc` file along with the registry URL. Microsoft recommends keeping two `.npmrc` files: first, the `.npmrc` file at the root of the repository with just the registry URL, which you can commit into the source control so that team members can share and connect to the same feed; and second, the `.npmrc` file in your HOME directory, which includes the generated credentials. This approach enables you to share the project's `.npmrc` file with the whole team while keeping your credentials secure.

Generate npm credentials on the **Connect to feed** dialog generates a 90-day token, which you can use in your `.npmrc` file. If you would like the token to be valid for longer than 90 days, then you will need to generate a **personal access token** (**PAT**) token with limited scope packaging (read and write). You can find out more information about this at `http://bit.ly/2vkp5fm`.

See also

- **The npm config files**: `https://docs.npmjs.com/files/npmrc`

Scanning for vulnerabilities in your package using WhiteSource

Today, developers don't hesitate to use components that are available in public package sources (such as npm or NuGet). With the aim of faster delivery and better productivity, using open source software (OSS) components is encouraged across many organizations. However, as the dependency on these third-party OSS components increases, the risk of security vulnerabilities or hidden license requirements also increases compliance issues.

For a business, this is critical, as issues related to compliance, liabilities, and customer **personally identifiable information** (**PII**) can cause massive privacy and security concerns. Identifying such issues early on in the release cycle gives you an advanced warning and allows you enough time to fix the issues. There are many tools such as WhiteSource, Veracode, and Checkmarx that are available, can scan for these vulnerabilities for us within the build and release pipelines.

In this recipe, we will explore how we can make use of these tools to scan vulnerabilities in our dependent NuGet packages. We will be using the free WhiteSource Bolt extension to scan our dependencies during our CI build.

Getting ready

The first step is to install the WhiteSource Bolt extension from the Visual Studio Marketplace:

1. Go to `https://marketplace.visualstudio.com/items?itemName=whitesource.ws-bolt` and install the extension:

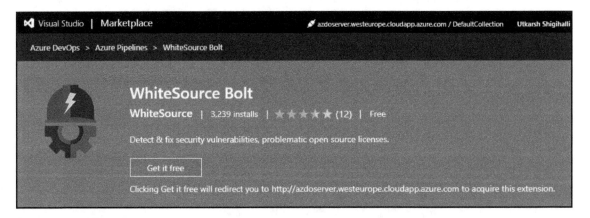

You can find out more information about how to install the extension at `http://bit.ly/2viImh3`.

2. After you install the extension, you should see a new **WhiteSource Bolt** hub under **Pipelines**. Click on it, and fill in your email address and name, and then click on **Save**:

How to do it...

We will use the existing build pipeline that we built in the first *Publishing a NuGet package to Artifacts* recipe of this chapter:

1. Open the `azure-pipelines.yml` file and add the following code under `steps` after the `dotnet build` task:

```
- task: whitesource.ws-bolt.bolt.wss.WhiteSource Bolt@19
  displayName: 'WhiteSource Bolt'
  inputs:
    cwd: '$(build.sourcesdirectory)'
```

2. Commit the changes and trigger the build. The **WhiteSource Bolt** task now automatically scans all the dependencies and generates a report of vulnerabilities and any other issues (such as outdated libraries, for example). The report is available in the **Whitesource Bolt** hub under **Pipelines**.

3. Click on the hub and you will see a report as follows:

How it works...

The WhiteSource Bolt free extension provides a pipeline task named WhiteSource Bolt. This task can be used to build or release the pipeline, and it helps us to automatically scan for any security vulnerabilities or compliance issues with dependencies and then generate a report.

> The free version only allows you to scan the project up to 5 times a day. For enterprise level scenarios, you should consider the commercial offering by WhiteSource.

There's more...

As conveyed in this section's introduction, scanning for security vulnerabilities ensures that you can catch issues early on in the delivery lifecycle. This shift-left approach of ensuring that the code is secure at all stages of the software development life cycle offers many benefits. By having a repeatable, efficient early warning system for security vulnerabilities in your pipeline, you can limit the number of unwanted vulnerabilities being introduced to the system.

See also

- **Fortify extension**: https://marketplace.visualstudio.com/items?itemName=fortifyvsts.hpe-security-fortify-vsts
- **Checkmarx extension**: https://marketplace.visualstudio.com/items?itemName=checkmarx.cxsast
- **Veracode**: https://marketplace.visualstudio.com/items?itemName=Veracode.veracode-vsts-build-extension
- **Secure DevOps Kit**: https://marketplace.visualstudio.com/items?itemName=azsdktm.AzSDK-task

8
Azure DevOps Extensions

Visual Studio Marketplace serves as a marketplace for Azure DevOps, Visual Studio, Visual Studio Code extensions, as well as pay-for-usage extensions such as the Artifacts extension, and Test Manager extension. It also sells subscriptions for Microsoft products (HockeyApp, Xamarin University, and so on). According to Microsoft, at the time of writing, VS Marketplace has more than 8,000 extensions and close to six thousand publishers. What's more, 130,000+ users and developers have been visiting the marketplace in search of extensions.

As you will see from a few of the following recipes, writing extensions is effortless. All you need is a basic knowledge of web development using HTML, CSS, and JavaScript. If you are interested in writing just build and release pipeline tasks, even knowledge of PowerShell is enough. If you have a lot of your useful utility PowerShell scripts hidden in your organization and want to make it useful for the rest of the world, now is the time to expose them as extensions and join this million developer ecosystem.

In this chapter, we will go in depth into knowing more about extensions and also see a few recipes that will show you how easy it is to develop and extend the Azure DevOps server.

Extensions and extensible points: So, what are **extensions**? Extensions are installable units for Azure DevOps Server and add additional capabilities, for example:

- Build and release tools
- UI enhancements for BuildHub
- Work item forms
- Dashboard widgets
- Custom utility tasks such as managing tags, publishing secrets to Azure Key Vault, and so on

These additional integrations provide a simple and effective way to reach new users by helping them get the most out of their DevOps environment. With extensions, you also have an option to integrate external services with Azure DevOps Server. Most extensions can be installed on both Azure DevOps Services (formally known as **VSTS**) and also on Azure DevOps Server (TFS). At the time of writing, there are close to a thousand extensions (paid and free included) on the market of different types.

 Extensions are always installed at the collection level and can only be installed by the **collection administrator** with **edit collection level information**. The rest of the users can only request an extension to be installed.

Extension structure: Azure DevOps extensions are made up of mainly three types. They are as follows:

- **Manifest.json file**: A simple JSON file that contains the metadata (name, ID, version, scopes, the category of the extension, and so on) for the extension. It is useful for packaging into the VSIX file.
- **Scripts**: These files contain the logic of the extension and also any dependencies. They are either PS1 or JS files.
- **Assets**: Any images, screenshots, or text files used to display information about your extension in the marketplace:

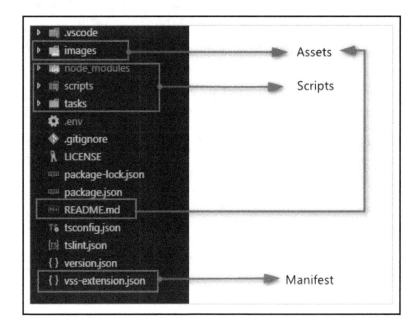

The extension can be of different types and can be categorized as follows:

- **Pipeline (build/release) task extensions**: These can be consumed in pipelines (build and release) and are available as tasks for the Azure DevOps agent.
- **UI extensions**: UI extensions, as the name suggests, use different extension points within Azure DevOps and enhance the usability of the Azure DevOps Server. There can be many types of UI extensions:
  - Hub/hub groups
  - Add menus/toolbars
  - Extend work item form
  - Add new service connections to connect to other systems
  - Add new artifact types
  - Add custom release gates
  - Add dashboard widgets

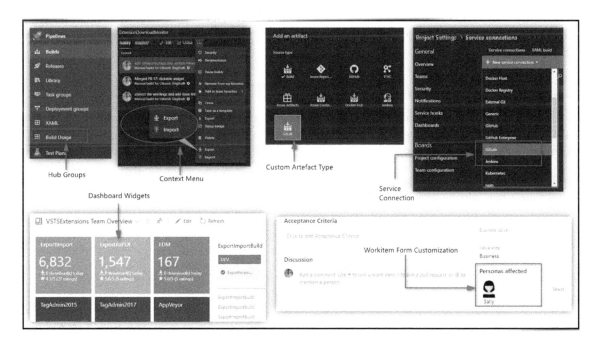

The pipeline tasks can be written in either PowerShell or JavaScript. UI extensions, on the other hand, will need to be created in JavaScript only. At the moment of writing this, tasks written in PowerShell can only be run on Windows-based build agents. JavaScript-based extensions are cross-platform and hence can be run on either Windows or Linux-based agents. With PowerShell Core being generally available, this might change, but at the moment, the choice of language (PowerShell or JavaScript) needs to be decided based on the platform you would like to support.

In this chapter, we will cover the following recipes:

- Creating the VS Marketplace publisher
- Creating a simple task to clean folders
- Creating a UI extension
- Creating a service connection extension to connect to GitLab
- Creating a pipeline task to consume a custom service connection
- Publishing extensions to marketplace through CI/CD

Creating the VS Marketplace publisher

Every extension that needs to be published to the marketplace needs to be published from a publisher. All extensions live under that publisher. Anyone can create the publisher by going to VS Marketplace management portal.

In this recipe, we will see how we can create a VS Marketplace publisher. In the next recipe, we will use this publisher while creating the task and also while publishing the task.

Getting ready

Creating the publisher is easy and to create one, you should have Microsoft account email address (@outlook.com/@hotmail.com for example).

Let's start creating a publisher:

1. Navigate to the VS Marketplace management portal by going to this
   URL: `https://aka.ms/vsmarketplace-manage`.

2. If you have not already signed in, you will get a prompt when using your
   Microsoft account:

3. Sign in using your Microsoft account. If you do not have a Microsoft account
   already, create one. You can also use your **Azure Active Directory** (**AAD**)-linked
   corporate account if you would like to create the publisher using your corporate
   account.

How to do it...

1. Go to VS Marketplace management portal (`https://marketplace.visualstudio.com/manage`). You might get presented with the following screen:

2. Clicking **Create publisher** button, you will be presented with the form with all the input fields to create the required publisher:

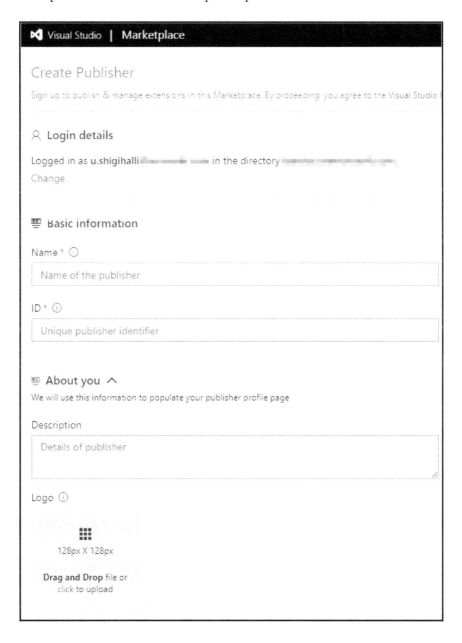

3. Enter all the required information and click **Create**. Ensure you have checked the **Send publisher verification request in order to publish extensions publicly for Azure DevOps Services** option. Publisher verification will be conducted by Microsoft and it is mandatory if you would like your extensions to be made public:

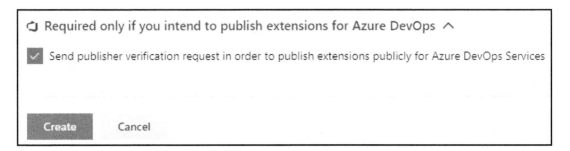

4. The publisher will be created and you will be ready to publish the extension.

If the publisher is unverified, you will be able to publish the extension as a private extension only. The average time is two to three working days for Microsoft to verify the publisher. Once the publisher is verified, you are free to make your extension public, which will allow others to find and install your extension.

You will be able to provide access to this publisher to additional users within your organization. This allows organizations to enable multiple users to author an extension under one publisher account.

Creating a simple task to clean folders

To get comfortable with creating extensions, in this recipe, we will create a simple pipeline extension. This extension will contain a single task to take a `minmatch` search pattern (`https://aka.ms/minimatchexamples`) and delete files and/or folders in a specified directory. The task can be used in the build or release pipeline to clean build artifacts, and eventually you will publish the cleaned directory.

Getting ready

We are going to develop this extension using **TypeScript**, which automatically gets transpiled into JavaScript. Writing in JavaScript ensures that this extension is automatically cross-platform and hence a task, or tasks, can run on Windows, Mac, or Linux-based agents. Our development environment will be as follows:

- **Editor – VSCode**: Free developer-friendly editor. However, you are free to use any editor with which you are comfortable.
- **Language – Typescript**: Provides type checking and other benefits (more info can be found here: `https://www.typescriptlang.org`). Install it using the `npm install -g typescript` command.
- **NPM packages for the task**:
    - **Azure Pipelines Task Lib**: Contains utility functions and required dependencies to be recognized by Azure Pipelines agents (`https://www.npmjs.com/package/azure-pipelines-task-lib`).
    - **del package**: A utility node package to delete the folders (`https://www.npmjs.com/package/del`).
- **Node CLI for Azure DevOps (tfx-cli package)**: Command-line utility to package and publish the extensions for Azure DevOps (`https://www.npmjs.com/package/tfx-cli`).

How to do it...

Let us first start by creating the manifest file.

Creating manifest

We will start by creating the `manifest` file, which contains the metadata about our extension:

1. To do that, open Visual Studio and right-click and create a new file and name it `vss-extension.json`.
2. Copy the complete code from the `vss-extension.json` file provided in the code bundle and paste it in the file you have created in *step 1*:

```
{
    "manifestVersion": 1,
    "id": "cookbook-clean-folder",
```

```
"name": "Clean Folder",
"publisher": "onlyutkarsh",
"version": "0.0.6",
"public": false,
"description": "A simple utility extension to delete
files/folders based on glob pattern specified",
"categories": [
    "Azure Pipelines",
    "Azure Repos"
],
//code is trimmed for brevity
```

 For more information about each element of the manifest file, click here: http://bit.ly/2R0mvIA.

Key elements to note in the file are `version`, `id`, `contributions`, `publisher`, and `files`. Here is an explanation of each:

- `version`: Version of the extension.
- `id`: The unique identifier for the extension.
- `contributions`: Various contributions this extension will contain. Our extension is going to contain only a pipelines task, so the contribution will be of `ms.vss-distributed-task.task` type.
- `publisher`: A unique publisher ID of the author of the extension. You need a publisher to be created if the extension needs to be published to the marketplace. We have already seen how we can create the publisher in the *Creating the VS Marketplace publisher* recipe.

Installing dependencies

1. We will now need to initialize and install the NPM dependencies. To do that, first we will need to initialize `package.json`.
2. In Visual Studio Code, click **View** | **Terminal** and type `npm init -y`. This will create `package.json` with the basic elements already filled.
3. Next, let's install the required packages, in our case, those are the `azure-pipelines-task-lib` and `del` packages. So, in the terminal, execute the following command:

```
npm install azure-pipelines-task-lib del --save
```

4. Next, we will need to install a few `dev` dependencies. These dependencies provide us type definitions and help TypeScript to perform type checking. Since these are development-time dependencies only, we are going to use the `--save-dev` flag.

```
npm install @types/del @types/node @types/q --save-dev
```

So, our final `package.json` file looks as follows:

```
{
    "name": "clean-folder",
    "version": "1.0.0",
    "description": "",
    "main": "index.js",
    "scripts": {
        "test": "echo \"Error: no test specified\" && exit 1"
    },
    "author": "",
    "license": "ISC",
    "dependencies": {
    "azure-pipelines-task-lib": "~2.7.7",
    "del": "~3.0.0"
    },
    "devDependencies": {
        "@types/del": "~3.0.1",
        "@types/node": "~10.12.15",
        "@types/q": "~1.5.1"
    }
}
```

Creating the task.json file

Each task has to have the JSON file describing the inputs for the task:

1. Let's create a JSON file. Create a new file and save it as `task.json`. The complete code can be found in the `Chapter08` folder of the code bundle.

2. Notice the `inputs` element. We have two elements for two inputs we will need—first, for the directory to clean and second, for the search pattern.

 `id` and `name` are unique identifiers for the task and `version` and need to be incremented every time we upload the task.

```
{
    "id": "20a947f2-c251-42e8-8376-5d7c5c1f8e71",
    "name": "cleanfolder",
    "friendlyName": "Clean Folder",
    "description": "Clean folder using the glob pattern",
    "helpMarkDown": "[More
Information](https://marketplace.visualstudio.com/items?itemNam
e=onlyutkarsh.utkarsh-utility-tasks) -
v#{GitVersion.MajorMinorPatch}#",
    "category": "Utility",
    "visibility": [
        "Build",
        "Release"
    ],
    //code is trimmed for the sake of brevity
```

Finally, notice the **execution** element of the `task.json`.

```
"execution": {
        "Node10": {
            "target": "index.js"
        },
        "Node": {
            "target": "index.js"
        }
    }
```

This is telling the pipeline agent that our execution handler is `Node` (for both Node v10 and older Node versions) and that the agent should look for a file named `index.js` in the task to start the execution. The agent passes the inputs filled by the user to `index.js`.

Creating the script (index.js) file

1. The next step is to create the script file that will have logic to clean the directory given the path and the search pattern.
2. Right-click on the explorer and create a new file and name it `index.ts`, paste the following code, and save it. When built, the file automatically gets transpiled into an `index.js` file:

```
import * as tl from "azure-pipelines-task-lib";
import * as del from "del";

async function main() {
  try {
      let sourceDir = tl.getInput("rootDirectory", false) ||
      tl.getVariable("System.DefaultWorkingDirectory");
      let globPattern = tl.getDelimitedInput("qlobPattern",
"\n");

      console.info(`Deleting contents from '${sourceDir}'`);
      console.info(`Glob pattern:`);
      console.info(`${globPattern.join("\n")}`);
      let paths = del.sync(globPattern, {
          cwd: sourceDir,
          root: sourceDir
      });

      console.info(`Deleted content:`);
      console.info(`********************`);
      console.info(`${paths.join("\n")}`);
      console.info(`********************`);
      console.info("All Done");
  }
  catch (error) {
      console.error("Error occurred", error);
      tl.error(error);
      tl.setResult(tl.TaskResult.Failed, error);
  }
}

main()
    .then(() => {  })
    .catch(reason => {
    console.error(reason);
});
```

How it works...

In the first two lines of the `index.ts` file we created in *Creating the script file section* above , we are importing the modules we need so that we get the necessary functions to use in the task. The task library import lets us read the inputs and also set the result to success or failure. Next, we create a simple `main()` function that is automatically called when the task is executed. Within the `main` method, we first read the inputs, specifically directory path, and the search pattern. Note that we are letting users specify multiple glob patterns separated by a new line that we read using `tl.getDelimitedInput("globPattern", "\n")`. The `del` package understands the glob pattern by default, and hence we just need to set the directory passed as a working directory and cleaning is automatically handled by the package.

See also

- Microsoft has open sourced most of the tasks on GitHub (`https://github.com/Microsoft/azure-pipelines-tasks`); all the tasks are good candidates to reference and learn writing tasks.
- Different extension points are maintained here: `https://docs.microsoft.com/en-us/azure/devops/extend/reference/targets/overview?view=vsts`.
- The `task.json` schema is maintained on GitHub here: `https://github.com/Microsoft/azure-pipelines-task-lib/blob/master/tasks.schema.json`.
- Microsoft Contribution Guide Extension: `https://marketplace.visualstudio.com/items?itemName=ms-samples.samples-contributions-guide`.

Creating a UI extension

In the previous recipe, we saw how to create a build and release pipeline task to clean the directory. Pipeline tasks help you to use them in your build and release pipeline and assist you in automating the activities as per your task's logic.

In this topic, we will see how to create UI extensions that integrate and extend the user interface of the Azure DevOps Server. The UI extensions internal structure is similar to pipeline tasks—containing a manifest file, assets, and code files.

Because UI extensions integrate and run on the server (which is a web interface), you will always use JavaScript to write your core logic. Some of the popular UI extensions are as follows:

- **Azure Artifacts:** `https://marketplace.visualstudio.com/items?itemName=ms.feed`
- **Delivery Plans:** `https://marketplace.visualstudio.com/items?itemName=ms.vss-plans`
- **Test Manager:** `https://marketplace.visualstudio.com/items?itemName=ms.vss-testmanager-web`

In this recipe, we will build a UI extension that will customize the work item form so that we get a new context menu. The idea is to help testers so that they can automatically generate test cases for well-written user acceptance criteria. The user will be able to click our menu item and generate the manual test cases.

Getting ready

To show you the outcome of our working extension, please see the following screenshot:

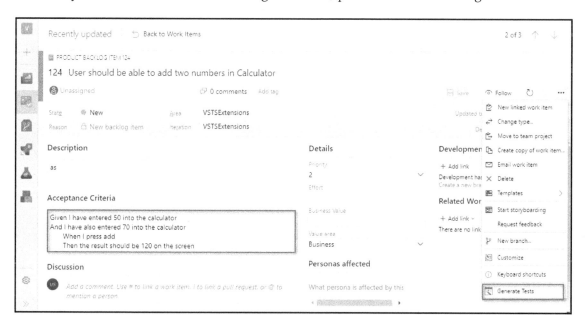

We will be adding a context menu named **Generate Tests** and clicking that the extension will parse the acceptance criteria and do simple parsing of the acceptance criteria written in Gherkin statements (`https://docs.cucumber.io/gherkin/reference`) and generate manual test cases and assign it to the first available test plan.

We will again write this using TypeScript language. We will use the following:

- **Editor – VSCode**: Free developer-friendly editor. However, you are free to use any editor you are comfortable with.
- **Language – TypeScript**: Provides type checking and other benefits (`https://www.typescriptlang.org`). Install it using `npm install -g typescript`.
- **NPM packages for the task**:
    - **Microsoft VSS Web Extension SDK**: An SDK to communicate with Azure DevOps UI (`https://www.npmjs.com/package/vss-web-extension-sdk`).
    - `html-parse-stringify`: A utility node package to parse the acceptance criteria HTML (`https://www.npmjs.com/package/del`).
    - `sanitize-html`: A utility node package to clean the HTML from the acceptance criteria field (`https://www.npmjs.com/package/sanitize-html`).
    - **Node CLI for Azure DevOps (tfx-cli package)**: Command-line utility to package and publish the extensions for Azure DevOps (`https://www.npmjs.com/package/tfx-cli`).

How to do it...

As in the previous recipe, we will again start by creating a manifest file. We will then add the script file (`.js` file) and a few assets to finally use it in the marketplace.

Creating manifest.json

As discussed in the introduction to this chapter, manifest (`vss-extension.json`) file contains the metadata for the extension.

1. Create a new file in VS code and name it `vss-extension.json`. The complete code can be found in the code bundle under `RCP03-UIExtension-Extensions` folder. Paste the complete code in the `vss-extension.json` file:

```
{
    "manifestVersion": 1,
    "id": "acceptance-demo",
    "version": "0.0.8",
    "name": "Acceptance Criteria to Test Case",
    "description": "Convert acceptance criteria written in
Gherkin to Test cases.",
    "publisher": "onlyutkarsh",
    "public": false,
    "targets": [
        {
        "id": "Microsoft.VisualStudio.Services"
        }
    ],
//code is trimmed for the sake of brevity
```

2. Now install the dependencies:
   1. As in the pipeline extension, we need to initialize NPM and install all the required node packages. As before, do that by running the `npm -y` command.
   2. Next, run following command to install the required dependencies:

      ```
      npm install vss-web-extension-sdk sanitize-html html-
      parse-stringify
      ```

   3. To provide the required types, add additional `dev` dependencies using the following command:

      ```
      npm install @types/jquery @types/node --save-dev
      ```

Your `package.json` should now look as follows:

```
{
    "name": "demo1",
    "version": "1.0.0",
    "description": "Utility extension",
    "main": "index.js",
    "author": "Utkarsh Shigihalli",
    "license": "MIT",
    "scripts": {},
    "devDependencies": {
        "@types/jquery": "^3.3.21",
        "@types/node": "^10.12.9",
        "typescript": "^2.9.2"
    },
    "dependencies": {
        "html-parse-stringify": "^1.0.3",
        "sanitize-html": "^1.19.1",
        "vss-web-extension-sdk": "^5.141.0"
    }
}
```

3. Finally, we need the `VSS.SDK.min.js` file from `vss-web-extension-sdk` to be referenced in our files so that we can consume utility functions from it. Thus, we need to copy this file from the `<root folder>\node_modules\vss-web-extension-sdk\lib\` folder. I have copied this file into a separate directory called `lib` as shown here:

Creating the HTML page to host initialization code

Now we will start creating the HTML page we defined in the contribution section of our manifest file. The HTML page acts as a host page for our JavaScript action handler and initialization code. Azure DevOps Extension SDK loads this file dynamically when we click on the menu item we defined in the manifest file:

1. Create a file named `generateTestCase.html` and paste the following code:

 The file name is case sensitive and the name you declare in the `vss-extension.json` manifest file should match the file you create here.

```html
<!DOCTYPE html>
<html lang="en">
    <head>
        <script src="../lib/VSS.SDK.min.js"></script>
        <script>
                VSS.init({
                explicitNotifyLoaded: true,
                usePlatformScripts: true,
          });
        VSS.ready(function () {
        console.log("VSS Ready ");
        VSS.require(["src/generateTestCase"], function (generate) {
        console.log("Initialization complete...")
          });
      });
        </script>
    </head>
    <body style="overflow:auto;">
    </body>
</html>
```

We are doing a couple of key things here in the `head` tags of this file:

1. First, we reference the `VSS.SDK.min.js` file we copied in the previous step. This file contained all the required modules for working with Azure DevOps extensions. Specifically, VSS SDK ships its own version of the `require` module.

2. In the first part of the `script` section, we initiate the handshake with the host window and specify that we will explicitly let Azure DevOps know when the extension is loaded by setting `explicitNotifyLoaded: true`. We will also notify from our script file when the loading is complete as you will see next. Now we will specify that we require the platform scripts (controls, REST clients, and so on) from the SDK, thus making Azure DevOps load any inbuilt scripts before loading our extension.

3. In the next step, with `VSS.ready()`, we are registering a callback that gets called once the initial handshake is completed with the host window. Within this callback function, we load our `generateTestCase` module, which we are going to write next.

 For more information on the all available methods with the VSS SDK, please visit `http://bit.ly/2GZiVtp`.

Creating the script file

At this point, we have created the `vss-extension.json`, initialized NPM and installed the dependencies using `package.json`, and also created an HTML page to host the initialization code for our extension.

In this step, we will write the code to read the acceptance criteria written in Gherkin format, parse the text, and finally create the test cases:

1. Create a file name, `generateTestCase.ts`, and paste the following text.

```
/// <reference types="vss-web-extension-sdk" />
import { WorkItemFormService } from
"TFS/WorkItemTracking/Services";
import * as TestClient from "TFS/TestManagement/RestClient";
import * as WitClient from "TFS/WorkItemTracking/RestClient";
//code is trimmed for the sake of brevity

export class GenerateTestCase {
    public async execute(actionContext) {
        try {
            let work = await WorkItemFormService.getService();
            let availableFields = await work.getFields();
            let values = await
work.getFieldValues(["System.Id",
"Microsoft.VSTS.Common.AcceptanceCriteria"]);
```

```
//some of the code is trimmed for the sake of brevity

        let testClient = TestClient.getClient();
        let plans = await
testClient.getPlans(webContext.project.id);
        console.log("plans", plans);

        let selectedPlan = plans[0];
        let suite = await
testClient.getTestSuitesForPlan(webContext.project.id,
selectedPlan.id);
        console.log("suite", suite);

        //some of the code is trimmed for the sake of
brevity
                witDoc =
testBaseHelper.saveActions(witDoc);
                let witClient = WitClient.getClient();
                let workitem = await
witClient.createWorkItem(witDoc, webContext.project.id, "Test
Case", false, false, true);
                alert(`Workitem ${workitem.id} is
created`);
                await
testClient.addTestCasesToSuite(webContext.project.id,
selectedPlan.id, suite[0].id, `${workitem.id}`);
                console.log(workitem);
            });
        });
    }
    catch (err) {
        alert(err);
    }
    }
}
let content = "";
function getAcceptanceCriteria(ast) {
    //code is trimmed for the sake of brevity
}
VSS.register(VSS.getContribution().id, context => {
    let action = new GenerateTestCase();
    return action;
});
VSS.notifyLoadSucceeded();
```

Full source is available in the code bundle under `RCP03-UIExtension-Extensions` folder.

2. Create another file named `GherkinParser.ts` and paste the code from `GherkinParser.ts` file from the code bundle. This exposes a function to parse the gherkin text and give a tree of scenarios and features:

```
export function parseGherkin(text: string) {
    //code is trimmed for the sake of brevity
    return features;
}
```

How it works...

Let's first decipher the `generateTestCase.ts` file. Notice at the bottom of the `generateTestCase.ts` file we have the following:

```
VSS.register(VSS.getContribution().id, context => {
    let action = new GenerateTestCase();
    return action;
});
VSS.notifyLoadSucceeded();
```

The first thing we do here is to register an object that this extension exposes to the host frame. We do that using the `VSS.register()` function. This takes two parameters:

- The first is the `instanceId`, which is the menu `id` we registered in the manifest. This should be a fully qualified name in the `<publisherid>.<menu-id>` format. We could hardcode the menu ID as `onlyutkarsh.sample-work-item-menu.`, but using `VSS.getContribution().id` makes it simpler and automatically gets the right ID.
- The second parameter is an object and we are passing a function that returns the object instance. Within this function, we instantiate and return the object of our class. The class should have a public function named `execute`. VSS SDK automatically invokes this method to be called when our context menu is clicked.

Finally, remember how we specified `explicitNotifyLoaded: true` in the preceding HTML file? The last line, `VSS.notifyLoadSucceeded()`, in `generateTestCase.ts`, notifies that the extension has been loaded successfully.

Let's understand `GenerateTestCase.ts`. As you might have seen, the core logic of parsing the acceptance criteria and generating a test case lies in our `GenerateTestCase` class.

First, we have a couple of `import` statements. Most of them are from `RestClient` classes from VSS SDK, which allow us to query `WorkItem`, `TestPlans`, and `TestSuites`. The rest of the import statements provide utility methods (`SanitizeHtml`, `html`, and `parser`) to clean the acceptance criteria text.

At the start of the `try` block, we first get the web context from the SDK, and this returns an object containing collection and project information:

```
let webContext = VSS.getWebContext(); // contains collection, project and
user details.
```

To read the acceptance criteria from the work item form, we need to consume `WorkItemFormService` from the VSS SDK. We do that using the following code:

```
// get acceptance criteria
let work = await WorkItemFormService.getService();
let values = await work.getFieldValues(["System.Id",
"Microsoft.VSTS.Common.AcceptanceCriteria"]);
let rawAcceptanceCriteria =
values["Microsoft.VSTS.Common.AcceptanceCriteria"];
```

The acceptance criteria returned by the preceding call is in the raw form including the HTML tags. But we are interested only in the text form. So, we remove the HTML tags using `html-parse-stringify` and the `sanitize-html` utility NPM packages. Note that `getAcceptanceCriteria` is a utility function that recursively scans for elements which has text tag with the help of `html-parse-stringify`

Finally, we are are using our `parseAsGherkin()` utility function from `parser.ts` to get the list of features and scenarios and each line under scenario becomes a step:

```
// parse acceptance criteria to gherkin syntax tree
let ast = html.parse(rawAcceptanceCriteria);
getAcceptanceCriteria(ast);
let sanitizedAcceptanceCriteria = SanitizeHtml(content, {
    allowedTags: [],
    allowedAttributes: []
});
let parsedResponse = parser.parseAsGherkin(sanitizedAcceptanceCriteria);
```

Now that we have the acceptance criteria in a usable format, we will get the `TestPlan` and `TestSuite` so that we can create `TestCase` for each scenario and add `TestStep` to each line of the scenario. To query `Test` objects, we will need to use `TestClient`. We do that as follows:

```
let testClient = TestClient.getClient();
let plans = await testClient.getPlans(webContext.project.id);
let selectedPlan = plans[0]; //for demo purpose we are selecting the first
available test plan
let suite = await testClient.getTestSuitesForPlan(webContext.project.id,
selectedPlan.id);
```

Next, we traverse through each scenario and for each line item, we create `TestStep` using the following code. The following code is using the `scenario` title for the `TestCase` title. Finally, once the test case is created, we add that to the first `TestSuite` in the selected `TestPlan`:

```
//code is trimmed for the sake of brevity
let helper = new TestBaseHelper();
let testBaseHelper = helper.create();

        parsedResponse.forEach(feature => {
            feature.Scenarios.forEach(async scenario => {
                let witDoc: JsonPatchDocument =
                    [
                        {
                            "op": "add",
                            "path": "/fields/System.Title",
                            "value": scenario.Text
                        },
                        {
                            "op": "add",
                            "path": "/fields/System.Description",
                            "from": null,
                            "value": feature.Desire
                        }
                    ];
                scenario.Steps.forEach(step => {
                    let testStep = testBaseHelper.createTestStep();
                    testStep.setTitle(step);
                    testBaseHelper.actions.push(testStep);
                });
                witDoc = testBaseHelper.saveActions(witDoc);
                let witClient = WitClient.getClient();
                let workitem = await witClient.createWorkItem(witDoc,
webContext.project.id, "Test Case", false, false, true);
                alert(`Workitem ${workitem.id} is created`);
```

```
                    await
testClient.addTestCasesToSuite(webContext.project.id, selectedPlan.id,
suite[0].id, `${workitem.id}`);
                console.log(workitem);

            });
    });
```

How it works...

Apart from `id`, `version`, and `publisher`, the important sections in the manifest file above are as follows:

- **Scopes**: This element defines the authorization scopes required for this extension. Because our extension needs to needs to create a test case, which is a work item as well, our extension will request for `vso.work_write` and `vso.test_write`. For a full list of scopes click here: `http://bit.ly/2RfhiwJ`.

- **Demands**: Demands let your extension declare capabilities that are necessary for your extension to work. For example, if you would like this extension to be dependent on another extension installed, say the Test Manager extension, we could write a demand using `extension/{id}` syntax as follows—where `ms.vss-testmanager-web` is the `id` of the extension from the marketplace URL for the Test Manager extension—`https://marketplace.visualstudio.com/items?itemName` `=ms.vss-testmanager-web`:

    ```
    "demands": [
        "extension/ms.vss-testmanager-web"
    ],
    ```

    For a full list of available demands, click here: `http://bit.ly/2scMspr`.

- **Contributions**: This section defines the contributions. Because we are extending a work item form's context menu, we add a contribution of the `ms.vss-web.action` type and target `ms.vss-work-web.work-item-context-menu` so that when clicked on, the context menu action is triggered.

The `properties` section under contribution defines additional menu item properties; `text` defines the menu text, and the value for `title` is displayed as a tooltip when hovered over the menu item; `toolbarText` is shown when the cursor is on the menu item; `icon` is for the menu item; and finally `uri` is the URI of the HTML page, which has the action handler for the registered menu item.

- **Files**: This element defines the assets and script that need to the part of the extension. Please note, we are setting `"addressable": true` for all the assets that need to be accessible via a URL by Azure DevOps. We also include the `src`, `lib`, and `images` directories, as they contain our necessary files for the marketplace.
- **Public**: This controls whether the extension is visible to everyone on the VS marketplace. It is a good idea to keep this to `false` during development.

There's more...

- Although we used VSS Web Extension SDK in this recipe, Microsoft is developing a react based SDK called **Azure DevOps Web Extension SDK**, which will replace the VSS Web Extension SDK we used.
- For more information on Azure Dev Web Extension SDK - https://github.com/Microsoft/azure-devops-extension-sdk
- Sample extension using Azure DevOps Web Extension SDK - https://github.com/Microsoft/azure-devops-extension-sample

Creating a service connection extension to connect to GitLab

Service connections in Azure DevOps Server (and Services) lets you connect to external services. Service connections once created can be used in your build or release pipelines.

Service connections are created at the project level. This means a service connection created for one project is not available in another project.

GitLab, if you don't know already, is another cloud Git service provider. Azure DevOps Server, by default, provides a service connection to connect to GitHub and lets you connect to an external Git repository using an **External Git** connection. Unfortunately, the External Git service connection lets you connect to one repository (or project if you are a GitLab user):

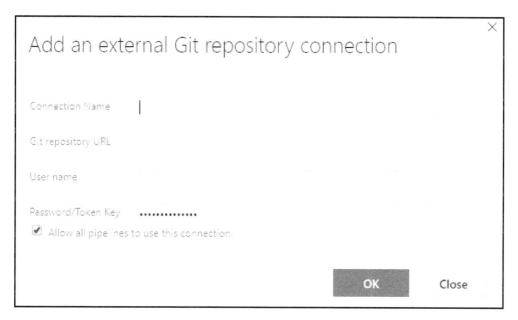

If you need to connect to another repository, you need to create another service connection with a different Git repository URL and save it as a different service connection.

We can solve this problem by creating a custom service connection that lets us connect to GitLab. In this recipe, we will see how to create custom service connections.

We can then use this new service connection to connect to other GitLab repositories in our pipeline. At the end of the recipe, a new service connection dialog will show a new custom GitLab connection type:

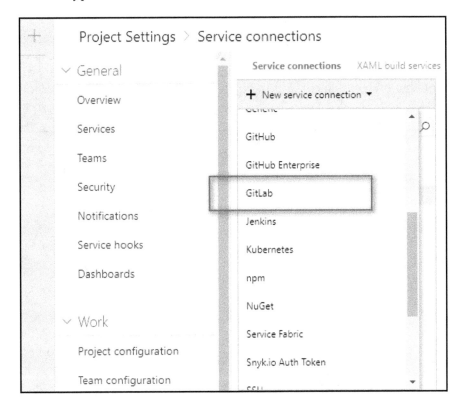

Selecting this service connection type will prompt users' GitLab credentials and save it so that this connection can be used in the pipeline:

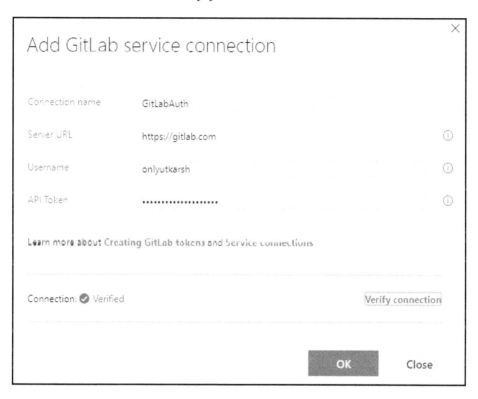

To authenticate with GitLab, you have three options as follows. In this recipe, we will allow users to authenticate with GitLab using personal access tokens:

- Oauth2 tokens
- Personal access tokens
- Session cookies

 More information about supported authentication types for GitLab can be found here: `http://bit.ly/2VKQiUr`.

Getting ready

The first step is to create the manifest file (`vss-extension.json`) with our extension metadata. As in other recipes, Azure DevOps exposes a service connection as a contribution in the manifest, thus allowing us to add our custom service connection contribution.

The steps we will have to get this working are as follows:

1. Create a manifest file and define service connection contribution.
2. Define input fields for the contribution to accept **Connection name**, **Server URL**, **Username**, and **API Token**.
3. Provide help links.
4. Provide a **Verify connection** link, as shown in the following screenshot:

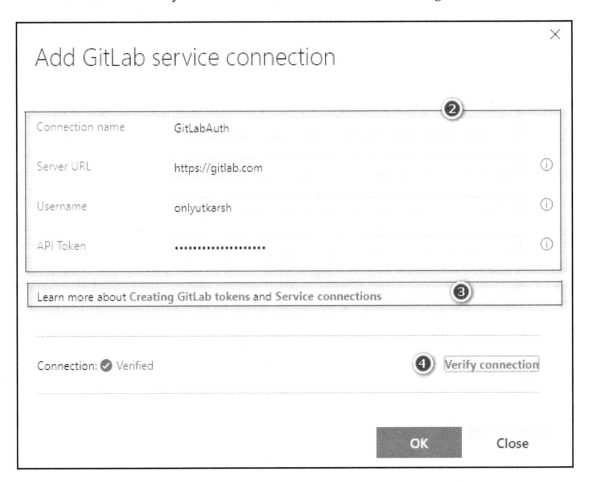

How to do it...

1. Open Visual Studio Code, and create a new file and call it `vss-extension.json`. Add the contribution of type `ms.vss-endpoint.service-endpoint-type`. For rest of the content in the `vss-extension.json`, take a look at the file in `RCP04-GitLab-Extensions` folder.

 Please note we are extending the same extension in the next few recipes. You might see more information in the source code. I am highlighting the content relevant to this recipe below.

```
{
//some of the code is trimmed for the sake of brevity
    "manifestVersion": 1,
    "contributions": [
    {
      "id": "gitlab-downloadrepo-task",
      "type": "ms.vss-distributed-task.task",
      "targets": [
        "ms.vss-distributed-task.tasks"
      ],
      "properties": {
       ....
       ....
       },
       "inputDescriptors": [
         {
       ....
       ....
       ],
       "dataSources": [
         ....
         ....
       ],
       "authenticationSchemes": [
         {
           "type": "ms.vss-endpoint.endpoint-auth-scheme-token",
           "inputDescriptors": [
             {
               "id": "apitoken",
               "name": "API Token",
               "description": "GitLab API Token",
               "inputMode": "passwordbox",
               "isConfidential": true,
```

```
                    "validation": {
                      "isRequired": true,
                      "dataType": "string"
                    },
                    "helpMarkDown": "<a
href=\"https://docs.gitlab.com/ee/user/profile/personal_access_tokens.html\
" target=\"_blank\"><b>Creating a personal access token</b></a>"
                  }
                ],
              "headers": [
                 ....

                 ....
              ],
              "helpMarkDown": "Learn more about <a
href=\"https://docs.gitlab.com/ee/user/profile/personal_access_tokens.html\
" target=\"_blank\"><b>Creating GitLab tokens</b></a> and <a
href=\"https://docs.microsoft.com/en-us/vsts/pipelines/library/service-endp
oints?view=vsts\" target=\"_blank\"><b>Service connections</b></a> "
            }
          },
      ....
```

For defining a custom service connection, adding a contribution to a manifest file is enough. We will see how it works in the next section.

How it works...

As we have seen in other recipes, a few of the fields such as `name`, `id`, `publisher`, and so on, are critical for defining the extension. We have covered these in the previous recipes. Let's dig deeper.

The key piece of information is in the contributions array. For defining a custom service endpoint, we add a contribution of the `ms.vss-endpoint.service-endpoint-type` type that targets `ms.vss-endpoint.endpoint-types`.

Next, under the properties element, we have name, icon, and **Display name** fields that uniquely identify this custom endpoint. These are used to select this service connection in the pipeline task:

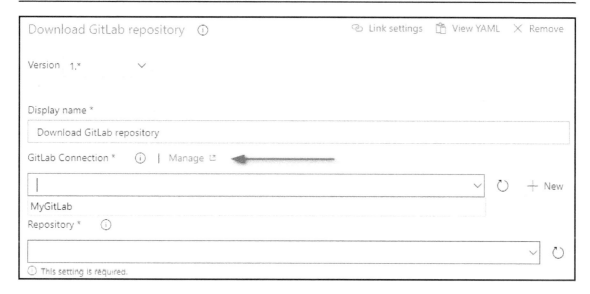

 Tasks using a custom service connection need to provide input for the service connection they support. We will see how we can write a task to make use of this service connection in our next recipe.

Next, our custom service connection has input fields to accept values from the user. Specifically, for accepting the name for the service connection, API URI (this can be custom URL for GitLab Enterprise edition) for authenticating with GitLab, username and finally private access token. We did that by adding a properties section for our contribution.

So let's look into these, one by one:

- `url`: URL is a mandatory field that every custom service connection needs to provide. In our case, we know that the default value will be `https://gitlab.com`. So, we define it as follows:

```
"url": {
    "displayName": "Server URL",
    "value": "https://gitlab.com",
    "helpText": "Client service connection for GitLab. You
don't need to change this unless you are using self hosted
GitLab instance, in which case you may need to point to your
instance URL. ",
    "isVisible": true
},
```

- `helpText`: This provides tooltip information. If you want this field not to be invisible (and not editable) for the user, use the `isVisible` property. For more details, see `http://bit.ly/2RGtbew`.

- `inputDescriptors`: Input fields are defined under `inputDescriptors` array. We create an input field for the username. Using the username, we will validate the PAT token by making a REST call to an authenticated API: `https://<endpointurl>/api/v4/users?username=<username>`. We define the inputs as follows:

```
{
    "id": "username",
    "name": "Username",
    "description": "Username you use to login to GitLab. This
is required only to validate your PAT token using 'Verify
connection' link below.",
    "inputMode": "textbox",
    "isConfidential": false,
    "validation": {
    "isRequired": true,
    "dataType": "string"
    }
}
```

As you can see in the preceding code snippet, we make it a text field using `isConfidential` and make sure the user enters their string value here. We also set `inputMode` as `textbox`, but `text area` and `combo box` are also supported.

 Although GitLab only needs a personal access token for API calls, our intention is to authenticate a PAT token using a **Verify connection** link when a user is creating the service connection. We do that using the `dataSources` field as you will see in a moment.

- `dataSources`: Service endpoints support querying data from external services through REST API. In our contribution, we are utilizing the well-known `TestConnection` data source. Adding this to our contribution automatically provides us with the **Validate connection** hyperlink. Clicking on that automatically calls the REST URL defined for `endpointUrl` under `TestConnection`. We validate the response using `resultSelector`, which is a `jsonpath` expression. In our case, we are just validating whether we received a valid 200 HTTP response using `jsonpath:$[*]`.

For more information on data sources, please see `http://bit.ly/2HgLpzk`.

Another thing you might have noticed is that we did not define an input field for a **Personal Access Token** (**PAT**). This is because Azure DevOps automatically provides a mechanism to handle authentication schemes. You will see it as follows.

- `authenticationSchemes`: This element defines how our custom service connection handles the authentication. This is a critical field for any API endpoints that need authentication, as successful authentication will enable dropdowns in task inputs to populate the values:

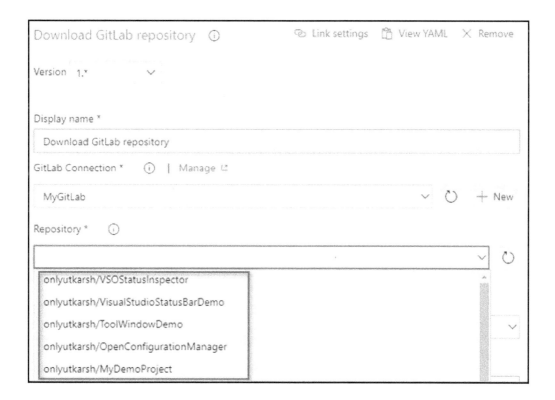

The Azure DevOps support service connection contribution endpoint supports many different types of authentication schemes. For more information, see `http://bit.ly/2M3L3um`.

In our custom service endpoint for GitLab, we are authenticating with PAT, so we use `ms.vss-endpoint.endpoint-auth-scheme-token`. We then define an input to store our PAT. Notice we make `isConfidential: true` and `inputmode: passwordbox` so that PAT is masked when entering. We have also made it mandatory by defining `isRequired: true`.

Finally, we have also defined a headers array. This allows us to send any required additional data to the REST API calls in the header. This is required because the GitLab API expects us to send the PAT for each request in the header as `Private-Token: <PAT>`.

See also

Many of the inbuilt tasks in Azure DevOps that connect to external services such as GitHub, Bitbucket, and Azure make use of data sources and authentication schemes. Microsoft has published many of the extensions on GitHub at `http://bit.ly/2McbE8V`.

Creating a pipeline task to consume a custom service connection

In the previous recipe, we created a custom service connection to connect to GitLab. However, service connections on their own are not useful unless they are used to connect to a third-party service in the pipeline task. In this recipe, we will create a custom pipeline task to download the source code from GitLab using the custom service connection we created in the preceding section. We will also extend the manifest file created and add a few additional data sources so that they can be used in the task to show available repositories (projects), branches, and so on:

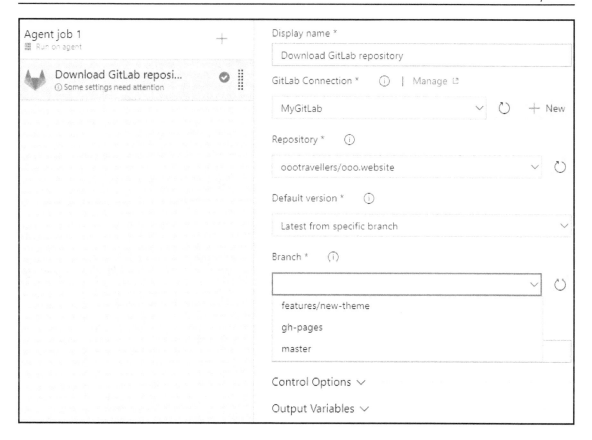

Getting ready

In this recipe, we will do the following:

1. Install dependencies
2. Add task.json
3. Use a custom service connection for GitLab as input
4. Allow users to select a repository and branch using data sources and bindings
5. Write a script to download the source from GitLab
6. All the files used in this task are in the code bundle

By the end of this recipe, the extension will allow us to connect to GitLab using the custom service connection we built in the *Creating a service connection to connect to GitLab* recipe. We'll also be able to download the source using the task we create in this recipe.

How to do it...

Let's look at the three tasks that we need to perform.

Installing dependencies

Because we will be writing this in TypeScript, we will use a few NPM packages that will help us in making GitLab REST calls and also interact with the Azure Pipelines task library:

1. Create a `package.json` and paste the following text. Alternatively, you can run `npm init -y` and then install all the packages one by one, as we did in the previous recipes:

```json
{
    "name": "onlyutkarsh-gitlab-dev",
    "version": "0.0.0",
    "description": "download artifact task",
    "main": "index.js",
    "scripts":{},
    "author": "Utkarsh",
    "license": "ISC",
    "dependencies": {
    "axios": "^0.18.0",
    "events": "^3.0.0",
    "fs-extra": "^7.0.0",
    "path": "^0.12.7",
    "azure-pipelines-task-lib": "^2.7.7"
    }
}
```

Adding task.json

As you have seen in the previous recipes, we need to add the `task.json` for our Download GitLab Repository task. As you might remember, `task.json` defines the structure of the inputs for the pipeline task:

1. Create a `task.json` file in Visual Studio Code and paste text from the code bundle from `RCP04-GitLab-Extensions` folder:

```json
{
  "id": "ca83284d-c3f5-46a5-ba52-dacd68ea6747",
  "name": "downloadgitlabrepositorycookbook",
```

```
        "friendlyName": "Download GitLab repository",

        "minimumAgentVersion": "2.115.0",
        "instanceNameFormat": "Download GitLab repository",
        "inputs": [
            {
                "name": "connection",
                "type": "connectedService:GitLab",
                "label": "GitLab Connection",
                "defaultValue": "",
                "required": true,
                "helpMarkDown": "GitLab service connection"
            },
            //code is trimmed for the sake of brevity
        ],
        "dataSourceBindings": [
            {
                "target": "definition",
                "endpointId": "$(connection)",
                "dataSourceName": "Repositories",
                "parameters": {},
                "resultTemplate": "{ \"Value\" : \"{{id}}\",
\"DisplayValue\" : \"{{{path_with_namespace}}}\" }"
            }
    //code is trimmed for the sake of brevity
        ],
        "execution": {
            "Node": {
                "target": "index.js",
                "argumentFormat": ""
            }
        }
    }
}
```

As you saw in *Creating a simple task to clean folders* recipe this task.json again has an execution section with target file for execution which we will create next.

Creating a core script to download a source from GitLab

1. Create a file called `index.ts` (remember a TypeScript file when built gets transpiled into a JavaScript file with the same name as `index.js`) and paste as per the `index.ts` file in this repository:

```
//some of the code is trimmed for the sake of brevity. refer
the code bundle.
import * as tl from "azure-pipelines-task-lib";
import * as url from "url";
import * as path from "path";
import { GitWrapper, IGitExecOptions } from "./gitwrapper";
import * as fse from "fs-extra";
import { GitApi } from "./gitapi";

async function main() {
    try {
        let _this = this;

        // get the task vars
        let debugOutput = tl.getVariable("system.debug");
        debugOutput = debugOutput || "false";
        let isDebugOutput: boolean = debugOutput.toLowerCase()
=== "true";

        tl.debug("Finding repository url");
        let gitApi = new GitApi();
        let repoUrl = await gitApi.getRepoUrl(endpointUrl,
definition, token);
        console.info(`Repo Url: ${url.format(repoUrl)}`);

        //code is trimmed for the sake of brevity
            if (versionSelector === "latestDefaultBranch") {
                tl.debug("Finding commit for default branch");
                commitId = await
gitApi.getLatestCommitIdFromBranch(endpointUrl, definition,
token);
            }
            else if (versionSelector ===
"latestSpecificBranch") {
                tl.debug(`Finding commit for '${branch}'
branch`);
                commitId = await
gitApi.getLatestCommitIdFromBranch(definition, token, branch);
```

```
            }
            console.info("Cloning repository...");
            let gitWrapper = new GitWrapper();
            gitWrapper.username = username;
            gitWrapper.password = token;

            // Git clone
            await gitWrapper.clone(formattedRepoUrl, false,
        downloadPath, options);
            // Checkout branch
            await gitWrapper.checkout(branch, options);
            // Checkout commit
            await gitWrapper.checkout(commitId, options);

            console.info("Done");
            tl.setResult(tl.TaskResult.Succeeded, "");
        }
        catch (error) {
            console.error("Error occurred", error);
            tl.error(error);
            tl.setResult(tl.TaskResult.Failed, error);
        }
    }

    main()
        .then(() => console.info("All Done!"))
        .catch(reason => console.error(reason));
```

From the `imports` section of this file, you might have noticed that we are referencing two utility files named `gitapi.ts` and `gitwrapper.ts`. Both files are available in the code bundle.

How it works...

In the `task.json` file, we first set `id`, `name`, and friendly name, which uniquely identifies this task name when installed. Next, under the inputs array, we start adding inputs. Let's analyze them one by one.

The first input is a prompt for the GitLab service connection, which we have declared as follows:

```
    {
        "name": "connection",
        "type": "connectedService:GitLab",
        "label": "GitLab Connection",
```

```
            "defaultValue": "",
            "required": true,
            "helpMarkDown": "GitLab service connection"
    }
```

Notice that the type of this input is `connectedService:GitLab`—`connectionService` signals that this is a service connection type and GitLab is a service connection type. This allows Azure DevOps to display only GitLab service connections in the dropdown. We also mark it as mandatory.

Once the service connection is selected by the user, we then ask the user for the repository, and we display a picklist with all the user repositories in the drop-down. To do that, we add the input as a picklist:

```
    {
        "name": "definition",
        "type": "pickList",
        "label": "Repository",
        "defaultValue": "",
        "required": true,
        "properties": {
        "EditableOptions": "True"
        },
        "helpMarkDown": "GitLab repository id"
    }
```

We want this input to show a dropdown of repositories. To do that, we need to make a REST API call to GitLab (`https://gitlab.com/api/v4/projects?owned=true`) to fetch the repositories using the token provided in the service connection.

First, we define a `dataSource` under the `dataSources` section in the `vss-extension.json` file:

```
"dataSources": [
    {
    "name": "Repositories",
    "endpointUrl": "{{{endpoint.url}}}api/v4/projects?owned=true",
    "resultSelector": "jsonpath:$[*]"
    }
    . . .
]
```

The `resultSelector` field allows you to filter the JSON response using a `jsonpath` expression. In this case, we are selecting the full HTTP response using the expression `jsonpath:$[*]`.

The sample JSON response from the GitLab will be in this form:

```
{
    "id":4,
    "description":null,
    "default_branch":"master",
    "ssh_url_to_repo":"git@example.com:diaspora/diaspora-client.git",
    "http_url_to_repo":"http://example.com/diaspora/diaspora-client.git",
    "web_url":"http://example.com/diaspora/diaspora-client",
"readme_url":"http://example.com/diaspora/diaspora-client/blob/master/README.md",
    "tag_list":[],
    "name":"Diaspora Client",
    "name_with_namespace":"Diaspora / Diaspora Client",
    "path":"diaspora-client",
    "path_with_namespace":"diaspora/diaspora-client",
    "created_at":"2013-09-30T13:46:02Z",
    "last_activity_at":"2013-09-30T13:46:02Z",
    "forks_count":0,
"avatar_url":"http://example.com/uploads/project/avatar/4/uploads/avatar.png",
    "star_count":0
  }
```

 You can test your JSON path expression using this free online tool: `http://jsonpath.com/`.

Next, in the `task.json` file, we define a `dataSourceBinding` under `dataSourceBindings` as follows:

```
"dataSourceBindings": [
    {
        "target": "definition",
        "endpointId": "$(connection)",
        "dataSourceName": "Repositories",
        "parameters": {},
        "resultTemplate": "{ \"Value\" : \"{{id}}\", \"DisplayValue\" : \"{{{path_with_namespace}}}\" }"
    }
    ...
]
```

This is to bind the `dataSourceName` named `Repositories` (defined in the preceding code snippet) to our input named `definition` so that repositories can be shown for that input. Notice the `"dataSourceName": "Repositories"` field; this is how we bind the data source to the input fields, in this case to an input field named `definition` using `"target": "definition"`. Another key aspect is the `resultTemplate` field.

This field defines a template of how data needs to be transformed to be displayed in the input field named `definition`. The template is defined as a mustache template expression.

 To find more information about the mustache template, read `https://mustache.github.io/`.

We would like to display repositories in the format of `<username>/<project name>` (for example: `onlyutkarsh/bio`). Hence, we use the mustache template as defined previously. Notice we are setting `Value` as `id` from the JSON response from GitLab (to uniquely identify the selected repository) and we use the `path_with_namespace` field from the JSON response as `DisplayValue`.

We do a similar data source binding to our other input fields' branch and version, which is visible when the user selects `Latest from specific branch` for the `Default version` field.

In the manifest file of the extension, we define data sources to make REST calls to GitLab:

```
"dataSources": [
        ...
        {
          "name": "Branches",
          "endpointUrl":
"{{{endpoint.url}}}api/v4/projects/{{{definition}}}/repository/branches",
          "resultSelector": "jsonpath:$[*]"
        },
        {
          "name": "CommitsFromSelectedBranch",
          "endpointUrl":
"{{{endpoint.url}}}api/v4/projects/{{{definition}}}/repository/commits{{#if
branch}}?ref_name={{{branch}}}",
          "resultSelector": "jsonpath:$[*]"
        },
        ...
    ]
```

In task.json, we then define bind data sources to inputs:

```
"inputs": [
    ...
    {
      "name": "definition",
      "type": "pickList",
      "label": "Repository",
      "defaultValue": "",
      "required": true,
      "properties": {
        "EditableOptions": "True"
      },
      "helpMarkDown": "GitLab repository id"
    },
    {
      "name": "versionSelector",
      "type": "pickList",
      "label": "Default version",
      "required": true,
      "helpMarkDown": "Version of artifact",
      "defaultValue": "latestDefaultBranch",
      "options": {
        "latestDefaultBranch": "Latest from default branch",
        "latestSpecificBranch": "Latest from specific branch",
        "specificVersion": "Specific version"
      }
    }
    ...
  ],
"dataSourceBindings": [
    {
      "target": "definition",
      "endpointId": "$(connection)",
      "dataSourceName": "Repositories",
      "parameters": {},
      "resultTemplate": "{ \"Value\" : \"{{id}}\", \"DisplayValue\" :
\"{{{path_with_namespace}}}\" }"
    },
    {
      "target": "branch",
      "endpointId": "$(connection)",
      "dataSourceName": "Branches",
      "parameters": {
        "definition": "$(definition)"
      },
      "resultTemplate": "{ \"Value\" : \"{{{name}}}\", \"DisplayValue\" :
\"{{{name}}}\" }"
```

```
    },
    ...
  ]
```

Notice how `dataSourceBindings` array sets the target (which has the input field name `inputs[]`) and uses data source (using `dataSourceName` property).

See also

- The extension is public `https://marketplace.visualstudio.com/items?itemName=onlyutkarsh.gitlab-integration`
- For an up to date extension refer the code `https://github.com/onlyutkarsh/gitlab-integration`.
- More information on data source and data binding can be found here: `http://bit.ly/2HgLpzk`.
- More information on authentication schemes can be found here: `http://bit.ly/2D7mASa`.

Publishing extensions to the marketplace

For extensions to be used in the Azure DevOps Server/Service, extensions need to be published to the VS Marketplace. As highlighted at the beginning of this chapter, VS Marketplace is the one-stop shop for extensions - tools that extend Azure DevOps.

In all the recipes we worked through in this chapter, we created various types of extensions. However, one thing we have not done is to publish the extensions we created to the marketplace.

Extensions can be published in either public or private visibility modes. Extension visibility is controlled via a public flag in the manifest file. To make an extension usable and visible to the public, you need to mark the extension as public by setting the flag in the manifest as shown:

```
{
  "public": true
}
```

The default visibility, if you do not specify in the manifest file, is private. This means the published private extension is visible to the publisher and the publisher of the collection has access too. Similarly, in Azure DevOps Services, an extension with `public: false` is visible only to the publisher and to other organizations that the user has given access to.

Microsoft provides a cross-platform tool named `tfx-cli` that we can use to publish an extension. More information on this is well documented at `http://bit.ly/2MrScoq`.

However, in this recipe, we will see how we can publish an extension in a consistent manner by using the Azure DevOps pipeline. We will gain some immediate benefits by automating extension publication:

- By automating our deployment in the pipeline, we will have the ability to push our changes quickly and with confidence.
- We will be able to test our Azure DevOps extension in our own private account before releasing it to a wider audience.
- The marketplace requires us to update the extension version each time we publish. Manually changing this is a hassle and we will be able to automate this easily using the pipeline.

Getting ready

There are a few prerequisites for publishing extensions to the marketplace:

- A publisher account. We have seen how to do this in the *Creating the VS Marketplace publisher* recipe of this chapter.
- A proper icon for your extension of at least 128 x 128 pixels in size.
- A good description of the extension in the `overview.md` or `readme.md` files that appears on the extension page on the marketplace.
- Finally, to make your extension public, the publisher needs to be verified. If the publisher is not verified, the extension can only be published as a private extension.

The following steps will help you to get started with this recipe:

1. Browse to Visual Studio Marketplace at `https://marketplace.visualstudio.com` and install the Azure DevOps Extension Tasks extension. You will be required to connect to Visual Studio Marketplace in the Azure DevOps Server context.

   To do that, from the header, click on the icon next to your profile link `Browse Marketplace`:

   Visual Studio Marketplace will highlight Azure DevOps Server context by showing the collection name.

2. Search for `azure devops extension tasks` and you will see the extension, as shown in the following screenshot:

3. Click on the extension and then click the `Get free` button. Then click on the `Install` button to install the extension on to your Azure DevOps Server collection. Now if you go to **Manage Extensions** page, you should see the extension installed.

That is all we need for now in order to work on this recipe.

How to do it...

To start, we will publish the **Clean Folder** task we created in the *Creating a simple task to clean folders* recipe in this chapter. To follow true DevOps practice, we will build once and deploy multiple times.

1. Create a build pipeline, which will transpile our code and publish it as an artifact.
2. Create a release pipeline with two stages to deploy the VSIX file (a packaged extension for Azure DevOps).
3. In the first stage, we will deploy it privately to our local Azure DevOps Server. This will allow us to test our task on our local Azure DevOps Server.
4. The next stage is to publish the extension to Visual Studio Marketplace and make it available to the general public.

Creating the build pipeline

Our `build` definition is comprised of the following steps:

- **Install all the npm dependencies**: Our dependencies are referenced in `package.json`. Note that, we have two `package.json` files, one at the `vss-extension.json` level and another one at the task level under task folder. For simplicity, I have defined a couple of scripts under the scripts section. The `initdev` runs `npm install` command for the `package.json` file and installs all the dependencies.
- **Compile and lint the scripts**: Our script is written using TypeScript, but we need to transpile them to `.js` using the `tsc` command. We also lint using `tslint` command. For this as well, we have written node script compile under the `scripts` section.

- **Update the version in task.json files**: Update the version in the `task.json` file. The version needs to be updated every time we would like to release a new version of the task.
- **Update the version in the vss-extension.json**: This is the same, except that you update the version in the `manifest` file. The extension version needs to be incremented each time you would like to release a new version.
- **Copy to dist folder**: Next, we copy all the files required for the marketplace (`icons`, manifest file, `js` file, and `node_modules` folder) to the `dist` folder.
- **Publish artifact**: Finally, we publis

2. h it as build pipeline artifact.

We are using YAML Build, so we have a file named `azure-pipelines.yml` with the preceding build steps. The contents of the `azure-pipelines.yml` is as follows, and is also present in the code bundle under `RCP02-CleanFolder-Extensions` folder:

```
resources:
- repo: self
queue:
  name: Default
  demands: npm

name: 1.0.$(rev:r)

steps:
- task: Npm@1
  displayName: 'install all the dependencies'
  inputs:
    command: custom
    workingDir: 'extensions/clean-folder'
    verbose: false
    customCommand: 'run initdev'

. . . . .
. . . . .

- task: PublishBuildArtifacts@1
  displayName: 'publish contents of dist as artifact'
  inputs:
    PathtoPublish: '$(system.defaultworkingdirectory)/extensions/clean-
folder/dist'
```

Once we've created the build pipeline successfully, we should now have the artifacts required to create an extension:

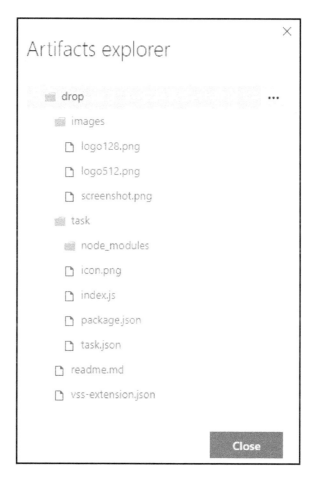

Creating the release pipeline

We now have a build pipeline that produces versioned artifacts for every build. This will ensure we always publish a newer version, as Visual Studio Marketplace expects the version number to be incremented every time we would like to publish the extension:

1. We go to the release hub and create a new release pipeline:

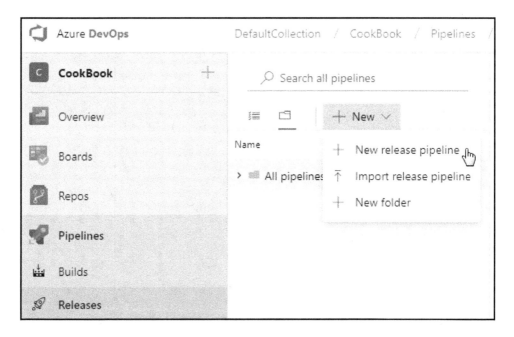

2. We will select the empty job template and rename the stage to `local` to depict our on-premises Azure DevOps Server. Then we add the artifact by selecting the build pipeline:

3. Search for the `Publish Extension` task from the **Azure DevOps Extension Tasks** and add it to the pipeline:

4. To use this task, we first need to create a service connection for our instance of Azure DevOps Server extension gallery. Select **Team Foundation Server** and click **New,** as shown in the following screenshot:

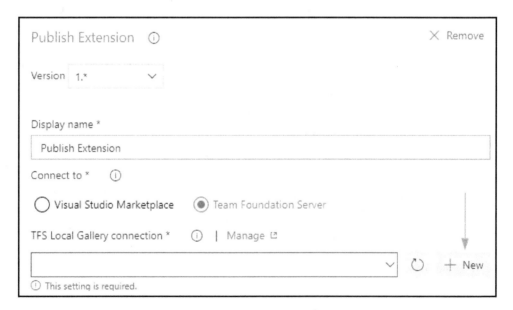

5. A new dialog will open; enter the local Azure DevOps Server URL and personal access token. For more information on creating a personal access token, visit this link: `http://bit.ly/2DZzgL6`:

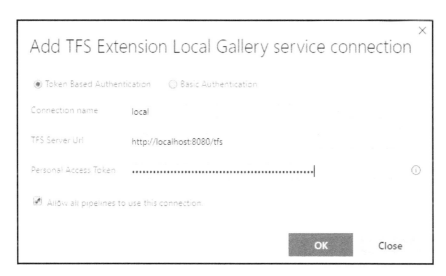

6. Click **OK** and select the service connection from the dropdown:

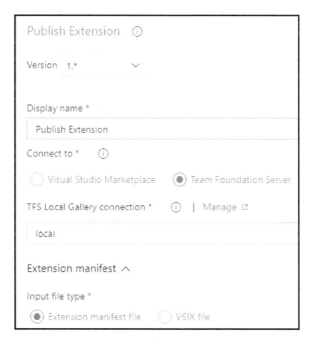

7. Finally, for the root manifest folder field, select the folder path where your `vss-extension.manfiest` file is:

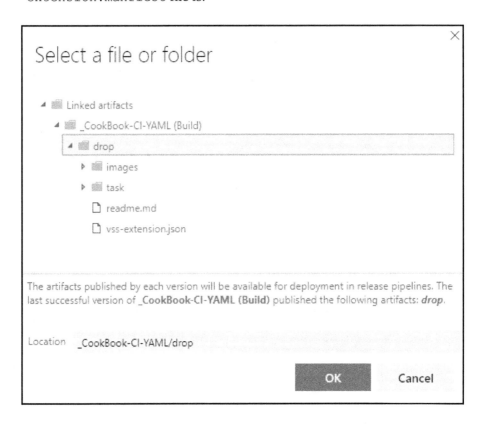

After that, ensure that you set the extension visibility to `Private`. Notice in the following screenshot that I am not overriding any of the fields in the manifest. The task gets the details from the manifest if not specified:

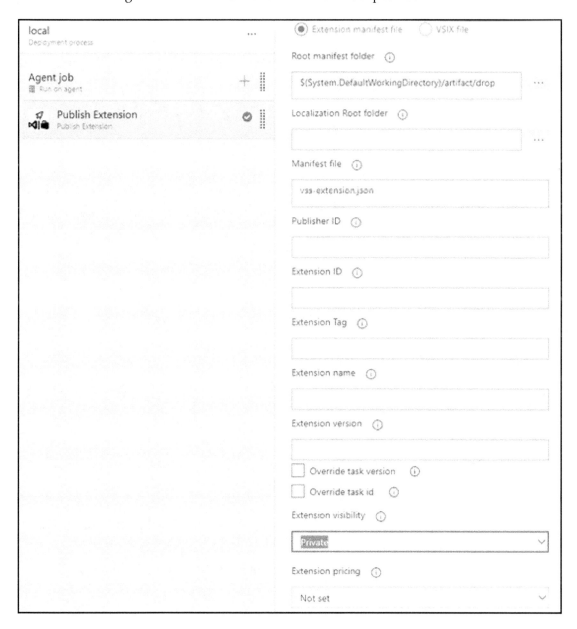

8. That's it; save the pipeline and create a new release. Once the deployment is successful, you should have your extension published to the local Azure DevOps Server gallery: `http://<yourservername>/tfs/_gallery`:

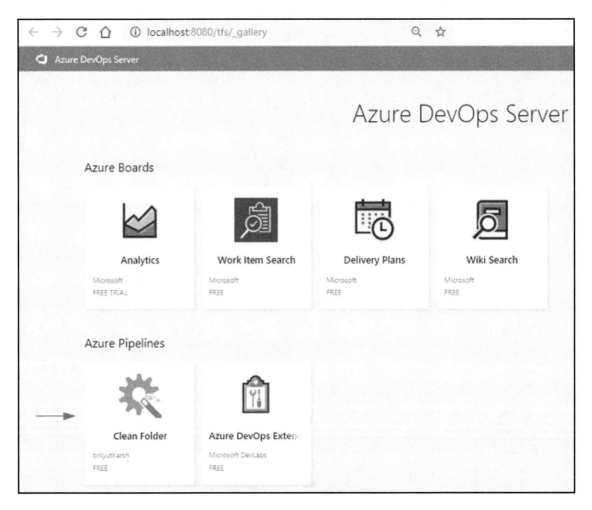

Publishing the extension just makes the extension available for installation from the local Azure DevOps Server gallery. You will need to click on the extension and install it.

This allows us to test our extension on our Azure DevOps Server before publishing to Visual Studio Marketplace.

Publishing to VS Marketplace

Assuming our extension works as expected in our Azure DevOps Server, we can now publish the extension to the Visual Studio Marketplace to make it available to the general public:

1. Let's add a new stage called **marketplace** by cloning our existing stage, which is named **local**. Now our pipeline looks as follows:

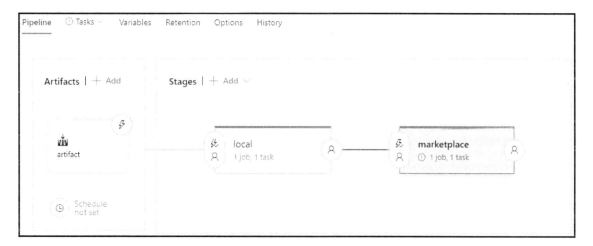

2. Click on the **Publish Extension** task in the marketplace stage, and modify the task input fields so that we can publish our extension to the marketplace. The first thing we change is the service connection.

2. Select the **Visual Studio Marketplace** connection:

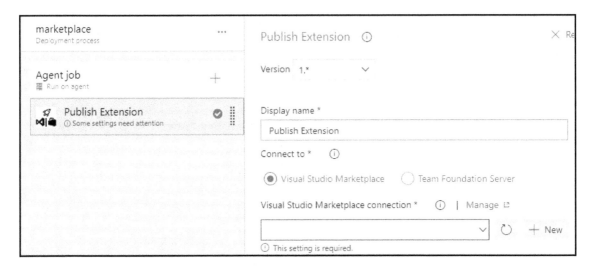

4. Click **New** and create a service connection using your personal access token:

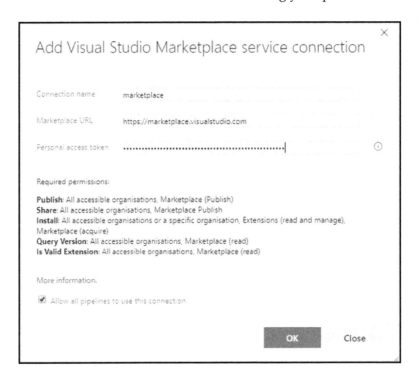

5. Click **OK**. Ensure the service connection you selected is for the marketplace. As in the previous stage, for the root manifest field, we will select our `drop` folder. For this recipe, we will select the extension visibility field as **Private Preview** just to ensure that this extension is not public. Once the publish is successful, our extension will be available in the marketplace:

Our extension is private and you will be able to share it with any accounts or view installed reports by going to the marketplace publisher page:

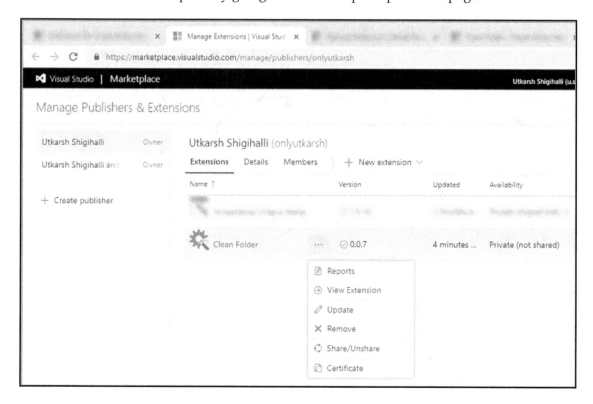

How it works...

In this recipe, we saw how we set up a build and release pipeline for our Azure DevOps extensions. First, we set the build pipeline to transpile our typescript into JavaScript files and lint, and publish all the required files. In the pipeline, we incremented the build number each time the build was triggered. This ensured that we were able to publish the newer version to Visual Studio Marketplace. This is because Visual Studio Marketplace accepts the version number of the extension to change each time we are publishing it.

Next, we set the release pipeline, which publishes the task to the Azure DevOps Server gallery. Later, we added another stage to release the pipeline to publish to the marketplace. The Azure DevOps extension tasks make it really easy to create a service connection and publish your extension to the marketplace in faster release cycles.

We published our extension to the marketplace as a private extension. Any extension that doesn't have visibility set to `public` will not be visible in the marketplace.

There's more...

Azure DevOps Extension Tasks has many tasks, from publishing extensions to the marketplace to sharing extensions to other accounts. The extension is open source on GitHub and also has a task to publish Visual Studio extensions. Check it out on GitHub: `http://bit.ly/2GyFALo`.

Other Books You May Enjoy

If you enjoyed this book, you may be interested in these other books by Packt:

Hands-On Azure for Developers
Kamil Mrzygłód

ISBN: 978-1-78934-062-4

- Implement serverless components such as Azure functions and logic apps
- Integrate applications with available storages and containers
- Understand messaging components, including Azure Event Hubs and Azure Queue Storage
- Gain an understanding of Application Insights and other proper monitoring solutions
- Store your data with services such as Azure SQL and Azure Data Lake Storage
- Develop fast and scalable cloud applications

Learn Microsoft Azure
Mohamed Wali

ISBN: 978-1-78961-758-0

- Understand the cloud services offered by Azure
- Design storage and networks in Azure for your Azure VM
- Work with web apps and Azure SQL databases
- Build your identity management solutions on Azure using Azure AD
- Monitor, protect, and automate your Azure services using Operation Management Suite (OMS)
- Implement OMS for Azure services

Leave a review - let other readers know what you think

Please share your thoughts on this book with others by leaving a review on the site that you bought it from. If you purchased the book from Amazon, please leave us an honest review on this book's Amazon page. This is vital so that other potential readers can see and use your unbiased opinion to make purchasing decisions, we can understand what our customers think about our products, and our authors can see your feedback on the title that they have worked with Packt to create. It will only take a few minutes of your time, but is valuable to other potential customers, our authors, and Packt. Thank you!

Index

build usage data
  analyzing 140, 141, 142

C

Centralized Version-control System (CVCS) 66
code history
  used, for migrating from TFVC to Git 69, 70, 71,
  72
code search
  configuring, as search engine 115, 116, 117
Coded UI testing 205
Coded UI Tests (CUITs) 205
Commit Network extension
  reference 81
Continuous Deployment 243
Continuous Integration 158

D

DACPAC 193
dashboards
  work, planning 61, 62, 63
  work, tracking 61, 62, 63
database project
  build pipeline, setting up for 193, 194, 195, 196
  creating 245, 246
database
  deploying, to Azure SQL 243
  importing 245, 247
Decompose work option 34, 36, 37
delivery plan extension
  reference 57
delivery plan
  about 56
  multiple teams, tracking 57, 58, 59, 60
demands
  building, for special builds 150, 151, 152
deployment groups
  configuring 134, 135, 136, 137, 138
deployment slots
  reference 286
Diagnostics Tasks
  reference 185
Distributed Version Control System (DVCS) 67
dotnet commands
  reference 332

E

Excel
  requisites, importing from 18, 19, 21, 22
extension, publishing to marketplace
  build pipeline, creating 413
  release pipeline, creating 416, 418, 419, 420,
  422
extensions
  about 365
  assets 366
  manifest.json file 366
  pipeline (build/release) task extensions 367
  prerequisites, for publishing to marketplace 411
  publishing, to marketplace 410, 413, 426
  publishing, to VS Marketplace 423, 426
  scripts 366
  structure 366
  UI extensions 367

F

feature flags
  reference 221
  used, for testing in production 216, 217, 218,
  219, 220
feature toggles types
  reference 221
feed 327
Foundation Version Control (TFVC) 66

G

Gherkin 229
Git branching model
  for continuous delivery 105, 106, 107, 108, 109,
  110, 111, 112, 113, 114, 115
Git forks
  using, with upstream PR 119, 120, 122, 123
Git History
  reference 83
Git hooks
  using, with Azure DevOps Server 97, 98, 99
Git Lens
  reference 83
Git LFS
  using 101